About the authors

GIORGIO BLUNDO currently holds a senior position at the École des Hautes Études en Sciences Sociales in Marseilles. He is President of the Euro-African Association for the Anthropology of Social Change and Development (APAD) and a member of the editorial board of *Politique Africaine*. His previous publications include *Monnayer les pouvoirs: espace, mecanismes et representations de la corruption* (Paris: Presses Universitaires de France, 2000).

JEAN-PIERRE OLIVIER DE SARDAN is Professor of Anthropology at the École des Hautes Études en Sciences Sociales in Marseilles and Director of Research at the Centre National de la Recherche Scientifique in Paris.

Everyday Corruption and the State

Citizens and Public Officials in Africa

Giorgio Blundo & Jean-Pierre Olivier de Sardan
with N. Bako Arifari & M. Tidjani Alou

Translated by Susan Cox

DAVID PHILIP
Cape Town

ZED BOOKS
London & New York

Everyday Corruption and the State was published in 2006.

Published in Southern Africa by David Philip
(an imprint of New Africa Books), 99 Garfield Road, Claremont 7700,
PO Box 46962, Glosderry 7702, South Africa

and in the rest of the world by Zed Books Ltd, 7 Cynthia Street,
London N1 9JF, UK,
and Room 400, 175 Fifth Avenue, New York, NY 10010, USA

www.zedbooks.co.uk

Designed and typeset in ITC Bodoni Twelve
by illuminati, Grosmont, www.illuminatibooks.co.uk
Cover designed by Andrew Corbett
Printed in the EU by Biddles Ltd

Distributed in the USA exclusively by Palgrave Macmillan, a division of
St Martin's Press, LLC, 175 Fifth Avenue, New York, NY 10010

A catalogue record for this book is available from the British Library
Library of Congress Cataloging-in-Publication Data available
Library and Archives Canada Cataloguing in Publication Data
available

ISBN 10   1 84277 562 6 Hb
ISBN 10   1 84277 563 4 Pb
ISBN 13   978 1 84277 562 2 Hb
ISBN 13   978 1 84277 563 9 Pb

Contents

PART I

Approach, Method, Summary

I

Why should we study everyday corruption and how should we go about it?

G. Blundo and J.-P. Olivier de Sardan

This book is based on two years of field and documentary studies carried out in Benin, Niger and Senegal from 1999 to 2001. The subject of the research was petty everyday corruption, which is widespread and systemic throughout the public – that is, administrative and political – sphere in all three countries.[1] The research focused on the following specific areas and sectors: transport and customs (in the three countries); the legal system (in the three countries); health (in Benin and Niger); public procurements (in Benin and Senegal); the local tax system (in Senegal); the way corruption is dealt with by the press (in the three countries); development-aid projects (based on the example of the scandal surrounding Italian–Senegalese development cooperation); and the policies adopted to fight corruption in the three countries.

The team consisted of six researchers of six different nationalities;[2] we also availed of the services of fourteen research assistants who were trained by us in the field.[3] The findings of our research were first collated and debated in the three countries concerned and were then presented in a report[4] and a thematic issue of the journal *Politique Africaine*.[5] This book, which is being published simultaneously in French and English,[6] differs considerably from these publications in terms of both its structure and its content and incorporates new analyses and an extended and updated bibliography. It is the first detailed and systematic anthropological study to be carried out in a group of countries on the specific topic of everyday corruption in Africa.

Why study corruption?

The individual members of our research team already had extensive experience in carrying out research on topics involving the anthropology of development and political anthropology – that is, the decentralization of local powers, public health, development projects and the management of local resources – in the three countries involved in the study.[7] The topics of corruption and administrative dysfunction continually arose in conversations and interviews with informants in the course of these studies. Thus, without consciously seeking it out, we were constantly confronted with the issue of corruption in our previous work.

Despite this, we never considered corruption an autonomous field of research, a scientific construct per se. It was never our aim to establish a subdiscipline to be known as the 'anthropology of corruption'; nor was it our objective to hunt down and investigate cases of illicit administrative practices everywhere. From the outset, we viewed corruption as a stepping stone leading to other phenomena, as a particularly useful way of accessing other realities and a way of penetrating further into the daily routine of the public services right to the core of the relations between public services and their users. Thus, productive perspectives emerged in the course of our research that could contribute towards the identification of an anthropology of the state, of professional cultures, of administrative conduits and of the ethics of the public service, or what could be described more generally as a 'socio-anthropology of African public spaces'.[8]

Once we go beyond the organizational charts, legal and regulatory texts and political declarations, we find that the 'real' functioning of the state in these three countries is actually very removed from its 'official' functioning. Without expressing any value judgements, it is valid to refer to a 'generalized informal functioning' of the state here. Indeed, based on the laws and regulations in force, public discourse and the expectations of the users of state services, one could even go so far as describing it as 'generalized dysfunction'. Of course, generally negative perceptions on the part of service users is the lot of all 'interface bureaucracy', even in Europe. Indeed, it is an almost structural characteristic of public services that they give rise to a disproportionate level of demand in relation to the actual supply available and that they show complete indifference to – if not disregard for – their users' time (Lipsky 1980). Nonetheless, the concrete situations observed in the course of our study would suggest that our informants' grievances should not be classified as mere local variants of the characteristic stereotypes of the world of bureaucracy (see Hertzfeld 1992). Of course, this 'generalized informal functioning' of the state does not mean that there is a complete absence of rules and regulations, or that the corrupt practices are merely a matter of the 'law of the market' or simple power relations. On the contrary, everyday corruption is a social activity which is regulated de facto and in accordance with complex rules, and tightly controlled by a series of tacit codes and practical norms. These tacit codes and practical norms differ significantly from public codes and official or legal norms and it was the main objective of our study and this book to identify and describe them – for they are never explicit and are often even unconscious and automatic.

The tacit codes and practical norms at work in the context of corruption largely exceed the scope of the latter and concern the habitual behaviours in the public services, and even the societies, studied. The 'generalized informal functioning' of the state provides fertile ground for the existence of corrupt practices, but does not fully merge with them. For example, it is difficult to identify a clear boundary between 'favouritism', clientelism and 'string-pulling', on the one hand, and 'arrangements' involving monetary compensations, on the other, and similarly between legitimate commission and tips and illegal *pots-de-vin* – bribes – and extortion. In order to take into account this overlap between corrupt practices and all of the 'real' everyday practices of state services,[9] we adopted the broadest possible acceptation of the 'complex of corruption'[10] and one which is far removed from strictly legal definitions: that is, all practices involving the use of public office that are improper – in other words, illegal and/or illegitimate from the perspective of the regulations in force or from that of users - and give rise to undue personal gain.[11] *Moreover, we were extremely wary of defining a clear distinction between what constituted corruption and what did not.* This helped us understand the links between the apparently corrupt practices and apparently non-corrupt practices closely associated with them.[12] In ranging between the dimensions of exchange and extortion, as we shall see, these practices give rise to processes involving the informal redistribution of public resources and of forms of power and authority. However, they also generate mechanisms of inequality and exclusion in terms of the access to these resources. Thus, the study of corruption enables us to penetrate to the actual heart of modern African states, their administrations and their public services, and a phenomenon that is apparently peripheral in nature provides the key to the very centre of things.

This issue of knowledge is also a social and political issue. The topic of the war against corruption and the promotion of 'good governance' recurs like a leitmotif in the debates surrounding the reform of African states and the definition of new policies. Efficiency, accountability, transparency and the rule of law have become the keywords of this new form of aid conditionality which is inspired in particular by the neoliberal movement. The limits, ideological perspectives and paradoxes of these anti-corruption reforms and reforms for the establishment of 'good' governance have already been highlighted elsewhere and include: a normative and teleological approach that emphasizes 'neutral' technical solutions to problems stripped in advance of their ideological and political valence (Ferguson 1990; Polzer 2001); a barely dissimulated universalist claim; the uncritical and naive exaltation of a 'civil society' erected as a counter-power to a state that is permanently under suspicion of various downward spirals (Szeftel 1998); and a serious ignorance of the situations that they claim to be reforming. However, the criticism of 'good governance' mainly comes from post-structuralist authors or development deconstructionists (see Escobar 1991, 1995, 1997) who confine themselves to an analysis of discourses and, as a result, neglect actual practices and the processes of sidetracking and disarticulation of international campaigns for public integrity by local actors. It should be noted that doublespeak reigns supreme in contemporary Africa. In other words the political elites are past masters in terms of their capacity to produce an official discourse that fulfils the expectations and conditions of their donors and is extremely far removed from the realities that remain largely inaccessible to the donors[13] – that is, the very people who wish to inspire or impose the 'war against corruption' as a condition for the granting of their support. On the other hand, the discourses surrounding the war against corruption among the power elites also constitute a response to 'internal' political issues (i.e. elimination of political competitors, the elimination of political groups that were defeated in the polls, the creation of scapegoats to satisfy public expectations etc.) involving the settling of old scores and not the real improvement of governance.

Corruption is also condemned, albeit in a different register, by the users of public services, by certain 'reforming' national officials and, more generally, by the African public, who are sickened by the decline of the states and the rapaciousness of the political classes. In other words, the debate surrounding 'governance, the state and corruption' is not limited to management contexts and neoliberal ideologies. It is our aim to participate in this wider debate through this book, however on the basis of our research. We believe that researchers can only make a positive contribution to the necessary reforms by producing well-documented, realistic and incontestable data that are as free as possible from normative judgements and ideological side-taking, in other words far removed from the hackneyed official formulations that dominate in the development, administrative and political sectors. For example, in this book we show that the war against corruption may not be divorced from a more general reform of bureaucratic and administrative practices and that the top-down creation of anti-corruption institutions on the instigation of external partners does nothing to halt corrupt transactions in the current context. Naturally, as researchers we are not in a position to be able to formulate 'recommendations' and direct activities, but we can at least make a modest contribution to informing the actors concerned – both 'high up' and 'low down' – about a reality that must first be known about before it can be reformed.

Nonetheless, it is only through the quality of the data produced and the interpretations made on their basis that we can make a worthwhile contribution to both the academic and the public debate concerning the state and everyday corruption. All social actors, both eminent and humble, all citizens and all decision-makers have their views on corruption and the state. The only comparative advantage enjoyed by the social science researcher is the possession of a documented point of view based on knowledge acquired through research. Therefore we should now explain how we carried out our research, in terms of both the research posture adopted and the methodological approach used.

A comprehensive research posture

Our initial and primary objective was to try to describe the habits, procedures and justifications involved in corruption and, furthermore, to *understand* how public services work 'in reality'[14] and how their users participate in or adapt to this mode of operation. For various reasons, which mostly concern the specific characteristics of corruption, the main studies carried out hitherto on the subject are based paradoxically on extensive quantitative surveys, which are not very suited to providing an explanation of the phenomenon. The most obvious of these characteristics is the fact that corruption is illegal everywhere and in most cases also illegitimate. Even if it is de facto tolerated or widespread (in the form of 'white' or 'grey' corruption as defined by Heidenheimer 1990), it is still at odds with the legislative and regulatory system, which is generally a Western artefact, and is condemned by numerous social and political actors. Thus all research on corruption concerns largely clandestine or concealed practices and highly normative representations. As a result, it encounters the problems faced by sociological research on petty and serious crime, on parallel distribution networks and the drugs economy. Therefore we face one difficulty and one risk here: on the one hand, we are dealing with an area that is not very accessible to the uninitiated, and, on the other hand, we could be tempted to 'criminalize corruption' excessively, in other words to divorce it from ordinary forms of sociability while in reality it is often embedded in them (Olivier de Sardan 1996a). Corruption has two faces: the first overtly illegal one is broadly condemned and the second, which is legitimized by social practices, is tolerated and sometimes even encouraged – albeit 'unofficially'. Moreover, for the most part, the 'facts' of corruption are not established, substantiated and visible. Indeed, it is one of the characteristics of corruption that it is constantly condemned without major proof. Therefore in studying corruption we are essentially dealing with allegations, accusations, suspicions that are aired either in the press[15] or in private conversations. In this regard, we are approaching a sociology of rumour (Blundo 1998) and face the risk of reducing corruption to what is said about it.

Finally, it is not possible to engage with the world of corruption and its practices without posing questions of an ethical and deontological nature. The first – and most obvious – concerns the distance that must be taken from such a research object. Even if we condemned corruption *as citizens*, it was important that, *as researchers*, we refrained as far as possible from all moral condemnation and normative judgement throughout the duration of the study. It would be simply impossible to carry out effective research on a phenomenon as widespread as petty corruption in Africa if we were to consider every customs official or every police officer we encountered a criminal or offender. Moreover, in the course of our fieldwork we frequently encountered clandestine practices, the disclosure of which could have had negative repercussions for the actors involved, with whom we had built up relations of trust. Thus, our study was driven by the constant preoccupation that our analyses be based on reliable data, which had been rigorously examined and verified, without, however, moving in the direction of a police-type inquiry or involving strategies that were incompatible with our professional ethics – that is, seeking out confessions, concealing our research objectives, revealing identities and so on. Indeed, the dearth of field research on the subject of corruption can be explained by the specific nature of the phenomenon while the literature on the subject abounds in essays containing definitions and hypothetical-deductive models divorced from any empirical data (Robinson 1998: 12; Williams 1999: 504). Although changes are definitely afoot in this regard, as demonstrated by a recent study (Doig and Mclvor

1999: 660), the research currently being carried out on corruption basically involves comparative macroeconomic analyses of its causes and effects which are based on 'survey' type quantitative data on perceptions of corruption (Lambsdorff 1998; Mauro 1996; for a presentation of these processes, see Cartier-Bresson 1998; Ades and Di Tella 1996).

The first of these survey types features sources based on the ubiquitous Corruption Perception Index which is compiled by the German economist Johann Graf Lambsdorff on behalf of Transparency International (TI). The 2005 edition of this regularly updated index classifies 158 countries on a scale from 0 to 10 – that is, ranging from the country in which 'under the counter' activities are perceived as most widespread to that evaluated as the least corrupt. The TI index presents itself as the 'survey of surveys' and is compiled on the basis of sixteen different sources.[16] While some of the bias of which this index has been accused, in particular the fact of focusing on the perspective of the business community and international experts, has been eliminated over the years, its weakness lies elsewhere: even if Lambsdorff is convinced that the sources he consults quantify the same phenomenon (1999: 7), the surveys on which his index is based do not all ask the same question or start from the same definition of corruption. Furthermore, there is nothing to indicate that such different informants quantify corruption using the same ethical and moral yardstick. In other words, the question arises as to whether it is possible to compare surveys carried out among elites with those carried out among the general public, or the perceptions of expatriates with those of economic operators and national civil servants. While acknowledging the relevance of these problems, the author of the TI index deems them of little significance and, based on the high level of correlation between the different surveys, insists that they do not impair the validity of the index.

The TI index, which is widely used on account of the 'false precision of its figures' (Médard 2001: 83), is primarily an instrument of political pressure and should be evaluated as such.[17] However, it would also like to engage in dialogue with social scientific and economic research. In our view, the Corruption Perception Index can at best provide an initial instrument in the context of an extended

comparative approach based on the traditional methods of the political sciences (see Heidenheimer 1996), but under no circumstances
can it satisfy the anthropologist who prefers research on local and
contextualized *representations* of corrupt practices to comparisons
of decontextualized *perceptions* at global level.

The other main type of quantitative research on corruption consists of surveys and studies based on questionnaires carried out at
national level and often constitutes the core of such research.[18] The
use of extensive surveys based on highly standardized questionnaires
poses a number of problems, the first of which is the representativity
of the sample used. For example, the CLARION (1994) study, which
aimed to provide an accurate image of the spread of corruption in
Kenya, used a sample composed of an urban and educated population
and was based on the assumption that corruption is a phenomenon
most widespread among urban elites. Second, questionnaire-based
studies approach the topic of corruption directly and without taking
any detours. Thus informants are requested to estimate the extent
of corrupt practices in a given service, to specify the sums involved,
and to select between different options in the context of one typical
situation. In our view, the adoption of such a direct approach to
illicit or socially condemned practices using an interview technique
– i.e. the questionnaire – that could be perceived as resembling
police interrogation would immediately prejudice the results. If
they do not withdraw into an embarrassed silence, the informants
would be forced to adopt the role of the victim or to provide a
normative discourse condemning corrupt acts. Moreover, unlike the
semi-structured or open-ended interview which may be more easily
structured around other topics – for example, the perception of
public services, the career paths within the administration, personal
biographies and so on – it is impossible to record the process through
which the informant spontaneously links the topic of corruption
with other topics.

For this reason it is our belief that 'qualitative' studies are necessary because they are the only approach that make it possible to
demonstrate the *action logics* of the actors involved, the description
of corrupt *processes* and the associated techniques, the analysis of
the popular *representations* and forms of *justification* and condem-

nation associated with corruption. Anthropology provides suitable research methods that can meet the requirements of a 'comprehensive' research objective aimed at producing data that reflect with maximum accuracy practices which are difficult to observe as they are either concealed or so widespread that they are easily confused with other practices and are more likely to originate from rumour than from official channels (press, legal information). Furthermore, it is not possible to dissociate corruption analytically from a regime of 'favours', 'preferential treatment', 'recommendations', 'string-pulling', nepotism and the various and myriad advantages bestowed in the name of family, neighbourly relations, friendship, school, university and professional relationships and professional protectionism, all topics that have long been examined by anthropology. Thus any study of corruption that understands it as a transaction between power and money (see Scott 1969: 321) must also take transactions between power and influence, power and networks, into account. Any study on corruption is also a study of practices which exist beyond corruption, but are functionally, structurally or culturally closely related to it. The corrupt exchange is not separable from other similar or closely related forms of exchange involving social capital as opposed to economic capital.

A qualitative methodology

Therefore the method we used in this study involved various standard anthropological tools, in other words: (a) the research and analysis of existing documentary sources, on the one hand; (b) the production and analysis of 'fresh' data, on the other.[19] This second category of tool or *fieldwork*, strictly speaking, which is particularly costly regarding the investment required in terms of both personnel and time, is obviously indispensable. Thus in our view the originality of this study lies in the fact that it presents for the first time a corpus of first-hand qualitative data on corruption in Africa, which was collected in no less than three countries using carefully designed and exacting procedures. This corpus comprises four main categories of data: interviews, observation, case studies and intensive survey procedures.[20]

All of these methods used in anthropological fieldwork usually involve the expertise of the experienced and isolated researcher working on a single site. It was our ambition, however, to put them to use in the context of a comparative programme that involves several countries and several types of public services simultaneously, and derives its structure from a truly generalized and collective research problematic.[21] Thus we needed to adopt an original methodological approach that makes use of certain recent innovations or would develop new tools for our project. As it happens, these innovations involved five different levels:

- the systematic use of a collective study phase on each topic and in each country;[22]
- the close coordination of individual studies carried out by qualified researchers trained by us;
- the exhaustive nature of the review of the press and legal archives in each country;
- the organization in each country of a seminar on the findings of all of the team members ('synthesis and feed-back seminar');
- the staging of an annual seminar (for three years) and symposium at the end of the research at which the results of the research are compared with the work of researchers working on corruption using other methodological approaches and in the context of other cultural milieus, other continents and other periods.

Conclusion

Given its location somewhere between an anthropology of criminal practices and an anthropology of everyday activities, empirical fieldwork on corruption provides access to a new area of research – that of the relations between public servants and 'civil society', between administrations and the subjects of administration and between public services and their users. These areas, which have mainly been explored by the sociology of work and the sociology of organizations in Northern countries, have received little or no attention from anthropologists, in particular those working in Africa. Thus their analysis is undoubtedly crucial to the understanding of the modalities of the construction of states in Africa and, conversely, their current decline. The popular semiology and ethics of corruption should be related inter alia to a popular semiology and ethics of administration and of the public service. Similarly, corrupt practices cannot be isolated from clientelist practices, the widespread exchange of favours, or from the culture of impunity within administrations and public services. Thus, this point of access via corruption has become an important element of a far wider and far from complete work-in-progress around *public spaces in Africa*, in other words around all of the forms involving the supply, management and use of public or collective goods and services.[23] Moreover, unlike certain futile 'new objects' sometimes addressed by contemporary anthropology in Northern countries, these 'new objects' constitute important societal issues that play a central role in both current and future debates on both good and bad 'governance' in Africa, its concrete forms, its daily manifestations, its contradictions, downward spirals and obstacles.

Understanding corruption represents an initial step towards a better understanding of the state, at both central and local levels, a better understanding of administrations, of municipalities, development projects and even civil society and the associative movement. This, in short, is the central scientific objective of this book. To this objective is added a subsidiary and socially aware objective which is closely dependent on the first: that is, reaching a better understanding of the everyday functioning of the state, administration, municipalities, development projects and associations as an essential prerequisite for their reform. Thus, by availing ourselves of all of the resources offered by anthropological methods in terms of their variety, combination and untiring quest for detail, we hope to have contributed to these objectives and that this book will succeed in attesting to this.

2

Corruption in Africa and the social sciences: a review of the literature

Giorgio Blundo

With just a few clicks of a mouse even the novice Internet user can access a new kind of world map representing the global distribution of perceptions of corruption.[1] With its spectrum ranging from vermilion to dark red, Africa is one of the regions that stand out most clearly in this world of white, pink and red tones. Thus one could be tempted to draw the conclusion that *hic sunt corruptos...* Based on the apparently scientific nature of its data, the index associated with this map corroborates the reputation for corruption attributed to the African continent by the academic literature (Médard 1997; Heidenheimer and Johnston 2002): of the 37 sub-Saharan African countries included in the Corruption Perceptions Index in 2005, 32 are located between 70th and 158th place and the bottom position is occupied by Chad. However, this influential instrument for blacklisting countries with a reputation for a lack of integrity remains silent – and justifiably so – on the forms taken by the corruption in a given context, on its actors and their strategies, on the factors that contribute to its reproduction or decline and on its long-term evolution. Furthermore, once one strays beyond the reassuring accuracy beloved of decision-makers and reformers to explore the contribution of the social sciences to the study of African societies, one is faced with uneven, sporadic and sometimes redundant contributions which are almost always weak in terms of their empirical basis.

In this book, which is based resolutely on empirical and comparative research, we considered it important to compare our data and interpretations with the specialist literature that has been more or less grappling with the topic of political and administrative corruption in Africa since the early 1960s. Certain observations must be made from the outset. The first and most obvious is that the differences between one country and another are just as important as the similarities, and they are not limited to the scale of the corruption, but concern the nature of the relationships it maintains with the economic and political arenas, the public debates it has triggered, the measures taken to combat it and the links with the international dimension (see also Williams 1987: 103). Second, despite or, rather, due to this diversity, no truly successful summary of the situation has yet been compiled. With the exception of Médard's work on neo-patrimonialism in anglophone and francophone Africa (Médard 1986, 1990, 1998, 2002) and on the international clientelist relationships that the old African colonies maintain with their former colonialist powers (Médard 1997), most of the studies consulted limit themselves to a comparative approach confined by linguistic barriers: for example, Williams (1987) juxtaposes the cases of Kenya, Zambia and Nigeria, and Mbaku (2000a) bases his arguments on Cameroon, Ghana, South Africa and Nigeria. However, both authors claim that their generalizations apply to the entire continent. Attempts to compare African experiences with those of other cultural regions are rare and essentially limited to French authors: they include comparisons of Africa and Southeast Asia, either global comparisons (Sindzingre 1997) or a comparison of two countries (Daloz and Heo 1997), and an unsuccessful outline in which a comparison between Mali and eastern European countries fails to deliver on the promise of its title (Amselle 1992).

The somewhat more modest aim of this chapter is to explore from a historical perspective some of the major debates on corruption in Africa engaged in by the social sciences. The corpus analysed for this purpose was limited to the social sciences, history, sociology, anthropology and political science (or political sociology). While a few select texts by lawyers and experts in administrative science were also included, we did not incorporate the extensive body of literature produced in the fields of economics and, in particular, econometrics. We also excluded journalistic texts and pamphlets from the analysis and all grey literature, which is relatively plentiful from the late 1990s and, given that it is generally produced by institutions for bilateral or multilateral cooperation involved in the promotion of 'good governance', determinedly 'policy oriented'. The 150 works analysed are exclusively academic – that is, articles, chapters from books and entire books. They can be divided into three categories: essays of a general nature whose objective is interpretative, historical studies of individual countries, and studies of a specific sector in a given country.

In terms of the disciplines represented, our corpus is dominated by publications from the field of political science. Anthropology, which for a long time showed no interest in the phenomenon of corruption, has been producing original contributions on the topic since the mid-1990s. However, it is difficult to establish a clear boundary between these two disciplines as they have tended to feed into each other since they are dealing with a common topic: the state and its (dys)functionality. In terms of the distribution of the studies by country, attention has tended to focus mainly on anglophone Africa. Nigeria, Ghana, South Africa, Botswana and Cameroon account for over half of the texts consulted.

Following a discussion of the contribution of anthropology in terms of the principal paradigms on which the main interpretative frameworks for the phenomenon of corruption in Africa are based, we shall address three issues that appeared central to us in the context of the corpus studied: the culturalist controversy, the weight of the colonial experience, and the varying trajectories of the post-colonial state. By way of conclusion, we will suggest some research areas that will merit further exploration in the years to come.

'Africanist' anthropology and corruption

Despite being the first academic discipline to have set foot on African soil, anthropology is the one which has devoted least attention to the subject of corruption there. This statement is not uniquely applicable to Africanist anthropology: as far back as 1971, Caplan (1971: 266)[2] raised the question of the remarkable silence of anthropologists regarding a phenomenon that is extremely widespread in the majority of the states in which they carry out their research. Leaving aside a few exceptions, this question is also topical in the context of Africa and any attempt to answer it would require a study of its own. However, it is possible to formulate some explanatory hypotheses concerning certain methodological, ethical and epistemological dimensions.

The first two have already been referred to elsewhere (Blundo and Olivier de Sardan 2000; Werner 2000; Blundo 2003; Shore and Haller 2005). It is sufficient to recall here that the phenomenon of corrupt practices does not lend itself well to the participant observation method, given that it involves behaviours that actors tend to keep secret and entails risks associated with the disclosure of 'sensitive' information, ranging from retaliation of a criminal or social nature, to which the researcher's informants may be subjected, to the blocking of access to the field of study. However, these problems are not limited to the research of corruption and are not sufficient to explain the silence or blindness of anthropologists in relation to this subject. Thus the focus must instead be placed on the epistemological dimension.

In this context, we can refer first and foremost to the influence exerted for a long time by a research tradition inspired by Radcliffe-Brown's functionalism, which emphasized the study of the institutions and norms that contribute to the stability and reproduction of social systems at the cost of socially deviant phenomena. However, Mertonian functionalism inspired studies on corruption in sociology and in political science that tried 'to demonstrate [its] "social utility" ..., i.e. its integration into legitimate social functions' (Lascoumes 2000: 56). This so-called 'revisionist' trend found ideal ground for the testing of its hypothesis in developing countries. Thus, in the words of one of its most widely quoted authors, corruption acts as an 'emollient, softening conflict and reducing friction' (McMullan 1961: 196): it facilitates foreign investment blocked by national protectionism; it makes it possible to circumvent the administrative obstacles that sap entrepreneurial spirit; it promotes national integration and increases citizen participation in public affairs (Gould 1980: 3–4). Considered from a contemporary perspective, these publications seem very outdated. They have been undermined by an unprecedented stigmatization of corruption and stand accused of 'empirical irrelevance' and 'myopic selectivity' (Price 1975: 142). Moreover, their authors did not engage in dialogue with their contemporaries, in particular the anthropologists of the Manchester School who devoted themselves to the study of social change, processes of urbanization and political phenomena previously considered deviant, such as factionalism. To our knowledge, the first anthropologists – and the only ones up to the late 1960s – who carried out research on the topic of corruption in Africa were S. Ottenberg and M.G. Smith. Ottenberg studied the phenomenon in the local governments of southern Nigeria. According to him, corruption goes hand in hand with societies undergoing rapid change, in which the coexistence of different styles of political action exacerbate the gap between legal norms and pragmatic political behaviour. He also observed that by borrowing from forms of gift exchange and reciprocity current in the sphere of family relationships, the corrupt exchange makes it possible to secure and regulate relations between unrelated partners (Ottenberg 1967). The anthropologist M.G. Smith, who combined ethnographical fieldwork and historical research on northern Nigeria in the period 1949–51, described the evolution of corruption in the Hausa milieu between the jihad of Dan Fodio in 1804 and the decade prior to independence. He also instigated the first systematic observations of the phenomenon of corruption: in order to test the veracity of the local allegations concerning the practices of the 'cotton mallams' who were responsible for the purchase of cotton on behalf of the Native Administration, he organized experimental sales of cotton at several markets using different local agents who were required to swear to the accuracy of their reports on the Koran (Smith 1964: 187).

A second factor that could explain the lack of interest shown by anthropologists in corrupt practices could be sought in their miserabilist or populist tendencies.[3] On the one hand, as Shore and Haller (2005: 15) admit, the 'people under study are often poor and marginalized anyway, and ... anthropologists do not want to add to the problems of "their" people. Our research on corruption can put them in serious jeopardy', while, on the other, Africanist ethnology – in particular French Africanist ethnology – has tended to take refuge in a numbing 'indigenophilia' (Dozon 2003). With their focus on rural communities, many studies have tended to exalt local knowledge, in some cases, and, in others, the popular capacities for resistance to a state considered as a predator, while remaining firmly outside of the field of observation: 'we may see corruption among our informants as a subversive form of revenge and empowerment' (Shore and Haller 2005: 15). While the adoption of such a stance distanced anthropology from the moralizing trend that was in vogue up to the late 1950s and viewed corruption as a matter involving individuals lacking in education and moral principles,[4] its confinement in the dialectic of domination and resistance and exclusive focus on the dominated pole, while favouring the study of closed communities examined in spatially defined contexts, prevented the emergence of a detailed ethnography of corrupt practices. Because the latter consist in informal transactions involving complicity and complex interactions between actors 'at the top' and those 'at the bottom', 'the corrupters (and corruption) largely escaped – as is normal – the scrutiny of localized anthropology because the phenomenon is created and reproduced in the establishment of a connection between actors evolving on a universal scale from different "incommensurable" life worlds' (Jacob 2001: 12). The current focus on 'multi-sited' anthropology will undoubtedly enable the extension of the field of observation while shifting the emphasis to translocal and transnational networks and connections (Gupta 1995).

The third factor concerns the disciplinary division of research objects whereby the study of bureaucratic organizations and the contemporary state became the task of political science and sociology. While Europeanist anthropology progressively embarked on empirical studies of political and state institutions in northern countries (Abélès 1988, 1990), the study of African politics was only approached from a 'top-down' perspective, by way of analogy with the formation of the Western state[5] and from an essentially political-science or legal perspective. Thus, over the past two decades, neo-patrimonialism and the 'politics of the belly' have been the main concepts around which the debates on the nature of the state in Africa have been structured. Inspired by the theoretical work of Eisenstadt (1973), Jean-François Médard used the concept of neo-patrimonialism, which is 'less normative than that of corruption and more comparative than that of "politics of the belly"' (Médard 1990: 29), to characterize the contradictory nature of African states, in which the process of bureaucratization coexisted with the patrimonial management of public resources. In other words, while the constitutions of the African states acknowledge the formal differentiation between the public and private sectors, this distinction is not respected or is ignored in the concrete political practices of their leaders (Médard 1982, 1990, 1998; Médard 2002). According to Médard, the idea of neo-patrimonialism makes it possible to analyse under one heading phenomena such as corruption, clientelism, patrimonialism, prebendalism, nepotism and tribalism, which are generally dealt with in isolation. While distancing itself from what he recently defined as 'a neo-Weberian taxonomy of Parsonian inspiration' (Bayart 2004: 94), the historical sociology of politics, which Bayart lays claim to, in turn highlights the hybridization of rather than incompatibility between native and non-native logics in the construction of the contemporary African state. According to this reading, corruption is one of the – all things considered – banal manifestations of the 'politics of the belly' which reflects the straddling of positions of power and accumulation that is systematic at all levels of authority (Bayart 1989: 288). In Bayart's view, it is under this form of widespread predation and greed that the social struggles surrounding the hegemonic quest for and production of the state in Africa are expressed. In keeping with a *rentier* conception of the economy in Africa 'this field of corruption is one indicator among others of the reappropriation or appropriation of the western model and politics by African societies' (Bayart 1990: 39). While these two approaches are ultimately less contrary than they claim,[6] they differ with respect to the conception of the state on which they are based: while for Médard neo-patrimonialism demonstrates the failure of the institutionalization of the state in Africa (Médard 2003), for Bayard the rot and inanity of formal state structures mask the vitality of the rhizome state, which is pervaded

by battles for position and factional conflicts. This theory was explored empirically by W. Reno (1995), who demonstrated the role
of informal markets in Sierra Leone in the construction of parallel
forms of political authority which develop in a context of the decline
of formal state institutions: political authority is exercised de facto
by businessmen and politicians who control the resources produced
by the illegal diamond industry. In this context, the state is both
'shadow' and real: it does not constitute a pale copy or distortion
of the Weberian state, but represents something radically different.
Common to all of this generalizing political science output, which
can be associated with studies on the 'predatory' (Darbon 1990;
Fatton 1992), 'kleptocratic' (Coolidge and Rose-Ackerman 2000)
and 'prebendal' (Joseph 1987) state, is that it excels in the exercise
of labelling the African state without, however, empirically exploring
its daily functioning and the changes under way in its bureaucratic
system (see Olivier de Sardan 2004).

However, anthropologists also distanced themselves from the
study of corruption for another reason: the fact of being confronted
with a concept that flirted dangerously with enthnocentrism. The
critique of normative approaches that associate corruption with the
dysfunctionality and crisis of the African state led to the re-exami-
nation of the importance of corruption as a topic for research. For
Emmanuel Terray, the recourse to terms such as 'corruption' and
'nepotism' is based on an ethnocentric judgement as, 'when practised
in a "well-tempered" manner, they can become stable modes of
domination and exploitation' (Terray 1987: 19); these phenomena
only trigger a crisis when they produce an unequal distribution of
jobs and wealth.

Other authors have expressed reservations about the interest of
studies concerning corruption in that they tend to adopt externalist
(developmentalist or dependentist) interpretations of the evolution of
politics and the state in Africa. Thus, Mamadou Diouf explores the
heuristic virtues of the concept of corruption, the use of which incorporates the risk of 'very unsuccessfully imitating and reproducing'
(Diouf 2002: 37) the paradigms of the Bretton Woods institutions.
This position is also adopted by Copans, who, having declared that
there is nothing new or exceptional about corruption, reveals to us

that corruption is merely a specific form of 'the general movement of social mobility which invents and is invented by African societies' (Copans 2001: 23). Having become aware, perhaps, that such plays on words do not always produce relevant interpretations, he would soon change his perspective. Thus, two years later, in the words of the same author, corruption becomes 'a new object which combines public and private, economics and politics, clientelism and social categories'. It enables the study of 'the public system from below' and therefore constitutes 'a subtle means of revisiting the formation of political actors from below' (Copans 2003: 74).

However, for around twenty years now, a number of researchers working independently have been trying to show that the anthropological method based on participant observation and a holistic perspective is the approach most capable of dealing with the complex phenomenon of corruption by setting it in a wider social context (Van der Geest 1984: 88). In the francophone milieu, the first studies of an ethnographic nature on corruption were produced in the 1980s by Morice, who became interested in the phenomenon while studying the parallel economy in Angola (Morice 1985) and in post-Sékou Touré Guinea (Morice 1987). Also worth mentioning here is the rather unsuccessful attempt by Amselle to carry out a comparative analysis of corruption and clientelism in Mali and eastern Europe. Apart from the fact that the analysis basically concerns Mali, the 'anthropology of corruption and of clientelism' he claims to create is limited to the evocation of the 'mechanisms of service, predation/redistribution that surround large sectors of the economy' (Amselle 1992: 635), for which little empirical data is presented. As opposed to this, the analyses by Fay (1995) and Bouju (2000), which are also based on Mali, are backed up by long-term empirical research which enables these authors to go beyond the level of mere anecdote. The former analyses the links between the democratic opening and the crisis in the redistributive clientelist system. Boujou focuses his attention on the study of clientelism and corruption within local political arenas, showing that these exchanges enabled the expression of different local, historically cumulated, powers under the protection of the state. Other authors also 'discovered' the importance of illicit practices while doing fieldwork. They report on them in articles located on the periphery of their main work which focuses on other research interests, as, for example, the studies by Laurent (2000), who explores the 'popular semantics of embezzlement' in the Mossi milieu, and Arditi (2000), who provides a historical outline of the phenomenon of corruption in Chad. However, for several years now, one area of anthropological output, both francophone and anglophone, has been consistently involved in the study of corruption as a complete social fact and has been carrying out systematic empirical research on the topic.

For example, Blundo (1998, 2001b) has carried out detailed analyses of corruption and embezzlement in various local Senegalese political configurations that are dominated by factionalism. On the anglophone side, D.J. Smith's (2001, 2003, 2005) research on Nigeria attempts to understand how ordinary people participate in the social reproduction of corruption despite being its main victims. These studies are based on a detailed and documented ethnography using case studies that are representative of a broad spectrum of contexts and situations. Anders (2005) devotes a chapter of his book on the social life of civil servants in Malawi to the topic of corruption. He expresses the view that although the study of corruption teaches us a lot about the functioning of the state and the way it is perceived (which is also one of the theories behind our research for this book), it should not be adopted as the sole point of access because these practices are secret and confidential and therefore difficult to observe. On the contrary, the detailed study of the social lives of public-sector workers makes it possible to understand both the state and corruption (Anders 2005: 192). Also relevant in this context are Hasty's (2005) recent study on the idioms and popular representations of corruption in Ghana and Bähre's work (2005) on the way in which corruption is denied and concealed in the context of development programmes, as illustrated by a case study carried out in South Africa.

Certain constants emerged from this overview of the literature: the majority of studies that deal directly with the phenomenon of corruption are the work of political scientists who are interested in grand corruption – that is, the kind that causes scandals, which they tend to depict with very broad brushstrokes. As opposed to this, the anthropological research on the topic, which is still in its infancy, examines petty corruption, but is mainly interested in the discursive and representational dimensions of the phenomenon. Up to now, no studies have been carried out which approach the phenomenon systematically and from a comparative perspective while also examining several dimensions simultaneously – that is, the representations and mechanisms of corruption and the locations and sectors in which it is found. This was the objective of our research.

Culture and corruption

Although Africa may not be the only area of confrontation for the 'culturalist controversy' (Dartigues and de Lescure 2000: 335), it clearly occupies an important place in this regard. Three points should be noted from the outset:

1. Despite certain condemnations issued rather hastily by researchers keen to engage in polemics, none of the documents in the corpus analysed as part of our research went as far as confirming that corruption is an exclusively African pathology and that the ultimate cause of this pathology should be sought in an improbable 'culture' specific to the continent.

2. Of course, expressions such as 'culture of corruption' (Le Vine 1975b; Good 1992; Kpundeh 1994; Médard 2002), 'culture of embezzlement' (Sindzingre 1997) and *'culture des pots-de-vin* (i.e. 'culture of bribes')' (Collectif 2003) are frequently encountered in the literature. The extensive use of this concept does not, however, translate into the conviction that corruption in Africa is the product or expression of a specific culture. Instead, it merely acts as a formula for the characterization of situations, in which corruption is systematic, generalized and widespread to the point of becoming a real 'way of life' for the populations in question.

3. Nonetheless, like the actual acceptance and content of the concept of culture, the weight and role accorded to social and cultural logics vary perceptibly from one approach to the other. In other words, apart from a few exceptions, the documents examined all contained analytical elements which associate corruption (ranging from the simple analogy to a direct causal relation) with social practices and behaviours, socially shared values or

norms and characteristics associated with political cultures: the
norms of solidarity within social networks, the dialectic between
strategies for the accumulation of and the duty to redistribute
wealth, the exchange of gifts, the different declensions of the
clientelist relation, the cult of munificence and ostentation, and
so on. However, these different 'ingredients' are not referred to
in one and the same analysis. One tends to be highlighted at the
expense of the other and, furthermore, the causal relations are
more or less pronounced and take varying directions.

Continuity or rupture?

The question that now arises is how the culturalist argument has
been used to explain the phenomenon of corruption in Africa. It is
common practice (Chabal and Daloz 1999) broadly to oppose the
supporters of a continuist approach, who research the genealogy
of corrupt practices, and those who consider the emergence of corruption in African traditions and ancestral values as the result of
a clear historic rupture that coincides with the importation of the
colonial state into Africa. While the 'continuists' claim that corrupt
behaviours are endogenous in nature, the 'rupturists' confirm the
exteriority or foreignness of these practices, which they identify as
definitively modern. In reality, even a very careful examination of
the literature does not enable the unequivocal identification of those
publications that would be representative of what should be considered more as general trends than rigid interpretative positions.

A first circle tends to consider contemporary corruption as the
manifestation of the survival of traditional social practices and logics
in a modern political context. Within the orthodoxy of the theories
of modernization, McMullan identified the cause of the emergence
of corrupt practices in Africa in 'the clash of old customs, attitudes,
etc., with the new forms of government' (McMullan 1961: 186). In
the same vein, Werlin (1972) enumerated among the causes of corruption in Ghana the persistence of traditional values in collision
with a modern way of life: for example, the expectations of the family
towards the public servant or politician, the social appreciation of
generosity, the prestige associated with the fact of having depend-

ants, the system of gift exchange, the preference for personal contacts in the administration, the respect for the elderly, and so on. This radically ahistorical reading, which struggles to isolate the factors or 'cultural' variables that would explain the failure of the grafting of an exogenous conception of the state in Africa (Anders 2005: 187), has re-emerged with some variations in the more recent work of political scientists and experts in public administration (Thompson and Potter 1997). Indeed, the reader could object that even this book assigns a significant role to the logics of everyday sociability and their relationships with corrupt practices. However, we never suggest that the cultural logics that promote corruption are legacies of the past and are rooted in ancestral habits, and we refrain from making any value judgement about them. As opposed to this, continuism, which is the heir to theories of modernization, is underpinned by a teleological evolutionism that considers these logics a – negative – legacy of the past which modernity will hasten to eliminate: for example, Mbaku refers to 'defective cultural norms' (Mbaku 2000a: 50), Nembot castigates the 'pressures of tradition' which render the actor a 'victim of the ethnic group' (Nembot 2000: 314, 316), Hope deplores the social norms that legitimize personalism and favouritism within the administration and lead 'to a development of a corrupt culture' (Hope 2000: 23) and, finally, Sarassoro stigmatizes the 'weight' of traditional social structures, conveying a conception of the family based on parasitism and tribalism and a socio-cultural concept that is immersed in 'superstitions' and 'beliefs' and encourages extravagant spending habits (Sarassoro 1979: 22).

The converse theory of the modern origin of corruption – in the aftermath of the colonial period – also had its ideological offshoots. The 'hardened' versions of this theory exonerate traditional societies, which apparently never experienced corruption, and infer from the absence of a term equivalent to the Western term 'corruption' in local African languages the absence of the practices associated with it.[7] Thus, if traditional African societies were unfamiliar with the concept of corruption, it was because they were fundamentally honest. Some publications try to defend this position. Therefore, contrary to the idea that the pressures of kinship encourage corruption, Osei-Hwedie and Osei-Hwedie assert that 'no traditional society encourages and condones corruption and other immoral conduct as a means to help a member' (2000: 46). Gould (1980), who studied corruption in Zaire under Mobutu, praises the functional efficacy of the pre-colonial empires and kingdoms. However, it is difficult if not impossible to follow some of the rather laconic conclusions, such as that proposed by Sanou on the basis of an – albeit very well documented – analysis of local conceptions of corruption in traditional society in Burkina Faso:

> in principle, the social organization of Bobo society excludes the long-term practice of corruption. In the interest of social stability, it is necessary to restore the order of creation and to ensure at all times that society does not distance itself from its traditional values. Corruption as we now know it is unknown to the Bobo. (Sanou 2001: 35)

In a pertinent intervention in this debate, Le Vine referred to the existence of a system of sanction and controls in traditional political contexts in Ghana, whose objective was to deter chiefs from abusing their functions or obtaining material gain from them, and numerous cases in which traditional chiefs were punished or deposed for embezzlement, the abuse of their prerogatives and violation of the political regulations. Thus the image of the honest traditional chiefs who were corrupted by colonization is an idealized one and untenable from a historical point of view (Le Vine 1975b: 49, 50).

Moreover, once they are stripped of ideological baggage, mythology and legend can demonstrate the interest that traditional African societies had in limiting the abuse of power, even in contexts in which there was little institutional differentiation within the political system. In reference to a story shared by the Mossi and the Samo of Burkina Faso concerning an attempt to purchase the verdict of a chief – who must choose between an ox and a *canari* full of millet or millet beer (*dolo*), depending on the version – Jacob observes that it is largely stereotypical and widely used and should, therefore, belong to a non-contemporary narrative register (Jacob 2001: 9). His conclusion is one with which we can concur: 'the example of traditional societies may not be used to provide either reassurance or a lesson to modern society without falling into anachronism or over-interpretation. They are neither corrupt societies nor societies against corruption' (Jacob 2001: 22).

In reality, these two apparently opposing theories suffer from the same distortion: an essentialist conception of culture, a confusion of culture and tradition, an absence of historical memory and a moralizing and normative conception of corruption. Thus, in this debate, culture is either the ultimate cause of the phenomenon of corruption or it is the victim of an external actor who has perverted or obliterated it. In other words, either the modern state is corrupted by traditional culture, or traditional culture is corrupted by the advent of the modern state. Trapped in an unproductive dichotomy between endogeneity and exogeneity, this controversy loses sight of the fact that culture is itself a social construct and that it can be used at any point in history to legitimize predatory regimes and mask the social inequalities they give rise to. In Ghana, Nkrumah succeeded in establishing and justifying his authoritarianism and the clientelist redistribution of state resources through a syncretic vision combining modernism and pan-African ideology. For that reason, 'the practices of corruption ... were politically constructed as indigenous forms of 'African' resistance to the abstract formalism of the state' (Hasty 2005: 295 n4). Another example of this can be found in Nigeria, which organized the Second World Black and African Festival of Arts and Culture (FESTAC) in 1977. An exercise in the manipulation of native cultural signs and symbols for the construction of a national identity – and financed using petrol resources – FESTAC was the scene of serious misappropriations to the point of being renamed 'festival of arts and contracts'. As a result it represents the archetype of a more general process: the official valorization of local culture as the bearer of development and democracy for the purpose of concealing a context dominated by subterfuge, fraud and corruption (Apter 2005; Smith 2005).

Thus, one can only agree with Sindzingre, for whom culture is an 'easy explanatory trap' (Sindzingre 1997: 396). Nonetheless, we must also ask ourselves if we can be satisfied with Médard's suspensive formula to the effect that 'even if you do not explain anything using culture, you will not understand anything without it' (1998: 56). In reality, the majority of the authors of the works in our corpus choose the midway path which attempts to reconcile the theory of rupture with that of continuity (Jacob 2001) through a historical reading of

the reproduction in Africa of the discourses and practices associated with corruption in a political context undergoing fundamental
change, in which the individual and collective relations to power and
the institutions are all changing. This option was already explored
by Bayart, for whom the 'governmentality of the belly' in Africa is
the result of a complex process of hybridization of the colonial state
and then independent state with native cultural registers. However,
it was Olivier de Sardan who clearly marked out the research that
that was adopted and empirically developed in this book: the 'moral
economy of corruption' in Africa

> is 'post-colonial' and fundamentally syncretic. In no way does it reflect
> a 'traditional' or pre-colonial culture even if ancient cultural elements,
> transformed and recomposed, have been incontestably amalgamated
> with elements inherited from the colonial period and with those pro-
> duced by the period of independence. (Olivier de Sardan 1996a: 99)

If the sterile debate on the origins of corruption can be circum-
vented in this way, another pitfall awaits any study alert to the
cultural or social dimension of corruption: in effect there is a serious
risk of drifting towards all-out relativism, which, at its most extreme,
would conclusively prevent any comparative process. Based on a
suggestion made by Olivier de Sardan (1999: 35–6), it is possible to
identify three main postures in the literature examined here. The
first involves the description of the emic conceptions of corruption
and the worlds of legitimation or stigmatization of illicit practices;
the second involves the attempt to undertake a longitudinal analysis
of the transformations undergone by the official practical norms that
regulate public life; and the third focuses on identifying the social
practices and logics 'dialoguing' with the phenomenon of corruption
without, however, merging with it. Needless to say, these approaches
are in no way mutually exclusive.

Emic conceptions of corruption

The exploration of the semantic field and ideological configurations
of corruption is still in its early stages. The analyses provided in this
book (see Chapter 4) constitute the first systematic attempt in this

regard. In the past, the language and semiology of corruption were not acknowledged in the political scientific analysis of the subject. When a researcher was struck by the richness and variety of the popular terminology associated with corruption, as occurred with Gould in Zaire in the 1970s, the resulting corpus was relegated to the annex of the relevant study (1980: 123–4) and its analysis limited to a comparison with the multiple terms for snow in the language of the Inuit. Ethnolinguistic research is also rare; we can only refer to one study on the longitudinal evolution of the terminology of corruption in Cameroon (Métangmo-Tatou 2000). Contrary to our observations in West Africa, the author of this study states that the language associated with corruption is not important in the languages of Cameroon, despite the fact that it features prominently in the French spoken in Cameroon.

However, strictly ethnolinguistic analyses do not provide access to the local worlds of legitimation as they are not interested in the context in which the language is used and the practices described by the expressions and turns of phrase. Studies carried out in Malawi and Burkina Faso take this course while stressing the differences between the Western and local conceptions of corruption. While the English word 'corruption' is used to express disapproval in Malawi, the terminology in Chichewa covers a range of diverse and dependent practices with more ambiguous representations: for example, the word *katangale* signifies illicit or concealed work practices, nepotism and patronage, and, when spoken in a tone ranging between disapproval and fatalism tinged with irony, it can even describe the actual way that the public administration operates. *Katangale* suggests the idea of redistribution and is tolerated if others benefit from it (Anders 2005: 191). Moreover, two recent studies carried out in Burkina Faso emphasize the incompatibility between the logics of Mossi peasants and those of the state or 'developers'. The first suggests that traditional Burkina Faso societies favour a moral or ethical conception of corruption over a political one: Moore speakers associate the idea of corruption with the word *wegboé*, which means 'to engage in an exchange or unequal sharing that is disadvantageous to someone else'. The term *ni yoogo* or *ni yaalga*, which means 'man of little value', is used to refer to the corrupt individual. Thus the negative moral evaluation applies to individual behaviours which are deemed shameful because they are motivated by material gain (Collectif 2003: 110). P.-J. Laurent, the author of the second study, tries to show that Western concepts of embezzlement and corruption make no sense to the Mossi peasants. In Moore, the former refers to two notions: obligation and pity. The misappropriations deplored by the 'developers' correspond locally to the idea of 'taking money to help one's lineage'. As opposed to this, the idea of corruption is more directly associated with the expressions *rimé ligdi*, to eat the money; *sudungu*, to keep for oneself; and *zuubu wagdem*, to steal, and translates the act of individual monopolization of collective or community resources (Laurent 2000: 222). In this context, the divergence with respect to the norms of good management conveyed by the projects is so clear that the 'good manager' is one who 'allows everyone to gain something from the project' (Laurent 2000: 234), even though he is accused of theft by donors. However, these analyses fail to consider the local incorporation of the rules of 'good governance' into a society which would henceforth experience multiple state and cooperation intervention.

The evolution of public norms and transformation of practices: the example of gifts to the authorities

Before it became a topic for academic debate and analysis, the practice of giving gifts to the authorities was a political and administrative matter. Dan Fodio equated the gifts (*gaisuwa*) demanded by the Hausa chiefs of northern Nigeria with an abuse of power and used this as one of the justifications for launching his jihad in 1804. However, a century later when Lord Lugard amalgamated the different tributes to the chiefs into a single tax (1906) and then granted a salary to the traditional chiefs (1911), he did not abolish the practice of the *gaisuwa* (Smith 1964). In pre-colonial Africa, the gift was part of the traditional diplomatic customs. In central Sudan in the nineteenth century, these gifts sealed the relations between the Muslim kingdoms and the foreign traders in the capitals who offered them in exchange for the protection of their caravans against looting and plunder (Arditi 2000: 254–5). In the pre-colonial states of the Chad basin they fulfilled a range of functions: for example, the sealing of an allegiance, the reinforcement of friendships between equals, and the 'purchasing' of peace (Issa 2004).

Throughout the colonial period, the English were plagued by the question of the legitimacy of traditional gifts, which were prohibited by the rules of the British administration. Thus the constitution of Governor Richards in 1946, which included the formal delegation of powers to local chiefs, assented to the practice of offerings to the Obas, despite the fact that it constituted a violation of modern administrative norms (Brownsberger 1983: 222). The 'Report on the Exchange of Customary Presents in the Northern Region of Nigeria', which was published in Nigeria in 1954, summarized various views on this topic: for example, the peasants viewed the gifts offered to traditional chiefs or in response to a positive judgement by the Native Courts as legitimate, while the 'educated' clearly considered them as acts of corruption. However, according to the report, the general trend involved the progressive delegitimization of gifts, which had become so widespread and so widely claimed for reasons of ostentation that they represented an abuse of tradition and a burden on the community (Wraith and Simpkins 1970: 335).

In reality, according to Issa (2004), the contact with the colonial system prompted the chiefs to consider the gift as a 'preliminary to every transaction'. Moreover, the political delegitimization of the traditional chiefs during colonization reinforced them in their quest for parallel means of accumulating wealth: 'from then on the gifts of allegiance offered by the villages, the territories and the vassal chiefs had an irrefutable economic value'. The occasions on which they could be solicited also multiplied: some *cola* was offered for the reduction of the number of heads of cattle required by the administration, to save children from the white school and when availing of traditional justice (Olivier de Sardan 1984: 207–24). The case of the 'dash' in Ghana and in English-speaking West Africa constitutes another interesting example of the transformation of a local institution. A preliminary to the establishment of all commercial relations at the time of the initial contact between Europeans and Africans on the Gulf coasts of Guinea (Price 1975: 121), in contemporary Ghana, the 'dash' has become 'the transfer of a material gratuity

... between client and civil servant' (Price 1975: 116) and is given in the guise of a tip offered prior to seeking a service, to which the public is legally entitled. According to Price, the 'dash' draws its meaning from traditional social practices, according to which the transfer of material objects, and in particular food and drink, serves in sealing agreements and in marking relations and social events. In the bureaucratic universe, it fulfils two simultaneous functions: first, it acts as an insitutionalized mechanism for establishing a personal link between the client and the bureaucrat if they are unknown to each other; and, second, giving the 'dash' is an act of deference constituting the symbolic affirmation of the unequal status of the two partners (1975: 118).

The culturalisms

In an article published in 2002, Dahou launched an attack on the culturalist interpretations of corruption – paradoxically adopting the fundamentally non-culturalist work of the authors of this book as his main target – which he sees as inherent to the fact of adopting corruption as an object of inquiry: 'do not the studies that attempt to make corruption into an entirely separate anthropological issue contribute to the confusion of the discourses on the relations between culture and corruption?' He questions 'the relevance of focusing research on the "embeddedness" of corrupt practices in a cultural register', an approach he condemns because it leads to a relativism which would serve 'the discourses that try to explain the massive nature of corruption in Africa through the culture' (Dahou 2002: 292). However, although this author starts from an interesting prem-iss, which we ourselves adopted some time ago, namely the rejection of culturalist explanations that tend to identify corruption as an essentially African problem and avoid any reference to history, his argumentation, which is particularly polemical and based on crude amalgams, targets the wrong enemy and lays him open to a series of criticisms on the level of both methodology and the analysis of the empirical data presented.

According to Dahou, the 'developmentist' approaches (he attacks the anthropology of development, which he incorrectly confuses with the vision of the international cooperation institutions, and refers to it in a caricature-like tone without quoting any precise sources in support of his criticism) overestimate the cultural explanation, highlighting the multiplicity of the norms which shape the behaviour of the administrations, and ignore the weight of the development apparatus in the reproduction of corruption. He suggests that this reading masks 'a number of rent systems that exist within the actual development "machines"' (2002: 290). And because the approaches that propose studying the embeddedness of corruption in local cultural logics lead 'unwittingly [*sic*] to feeding into the culturalist theories of the development world' (2002: 291), in Dahou's view, doubt should be heaped on the scientific interest in the study of corruption as an anthropological object! It is his belief that focusing on the redistributive quality of community structures would result in the elimination of any political explanation. The author appears to forget here that the logics of redistribution are a common mode of management and political regulation, and, indeed, he is forced to admit this elsewhere when he tackles the subject of redistribution within Senegalese factions. Following an attempt 'to historicize' corruption in Africa, adopted directly from the work of A. Mbembe and M. Diouf (whom he does not, however, quote), he presents the case of the misappropriations in the delta of the Senegal river. Surprisingly, he reveals to us here that the generalization and impunity from which these practices benefit are closely related to the logic of honour in contemporary Waalo. It would be helpful to know in what respect this reading is not culturalist, especially because, according to Dahou, this constitutes the only truly explanatory factor, the only logic worthy of analysis and one that he uses to present a summary comparison with ... Corsica! While wishing to 'deculturalize corruption', Dahou actually reculturalizes it and, moreover, falls head first into the main trap of culturalism: the isolation of a single cultural 'factor' from many others, which then becomes the only explanatory key.

A thorough examination of the literature would have enabled this author to identify other pitfalls of the culturalist explanation. What we have in mind here primarily are references to vague general notions based on 'cultural registers' and native 'idioms' divorced from empirical data. The most important example of this is Bayart's (1992) 'politics of the belly', which, according to the author, refers to two African cultural registers, munificence and the world of the invisible. Bayart summarizes the world of political predation exclusively in terms of the metaphor of manducation (see our critical analysis in Chapter 4). This is also the case with Hasty, who states that in popular culture in Ghana corruption is less of a question of 'rational' personal interest than one of physicality and affects (2005: 274). Two local idioms related to these practices express the central notion of the vital flows that run through the political body: the idiom of consumption (or 'chopping') and the idiom of blood flow, which is in turn associated with the circulation of money. Corruption in Ghana is perceived by this author as 'a problem of hyperengagement in vital socio-political flows of desire and affect as well as materiality' (2005: 284). The problem with these interpretations is that they constantly flirt with overinterpretation through the academic formalization of common-sense elements without sifting them through the screen of empirical study.

A second and relatively common bias resides in the confusion of a social practice with an act of corruption. This is the case with Brownsberger (1983), who equates the gift with 'polite corruption', and Ekpo (1979), who confuses the exchange of gifts within client–patron relationships with corruption.

More widespread and misleading is culturalist determinism that attributes to social logics a capacity to determine and condition the behaviours of individuals and claims to use cultural variables to explain, but not understand, the phenomenon of corruption. Our research shows that, on the contrary, far from being prisoners of social obligations, social actors retain a certain margin of manoeuvre and use this argument to justify their illicit practices. We agree with Anders, who, while recognizing the role of traditional or informal networks, reminds us that corrupt practices are not always motivated by the logic of solidarity within a kinship network. What is often involved here are arguments justifying practices which conceal egoistic or antisocial objectives (2005: 213). Moreover, 'instead of speaking of rights and duties it seems more appropriate to speak of expectations and feelings of obligation arising from multiplex social relationships' (2005: 214). Furthermore, in a study concerning the distribution of gifts during electoral campaigns in Cameroon, Socpa (2000) demonstrates that the logic of indebtedness, which incorporates an obligation of reciprocity, no longer works in certain circumstances. Thus the rural electorate of Cameroon is increasingly opting to accept material or financial gifts from all of the politicians who come to their villages without voting for them when the time comes.

Corruption and colonialism

Although the historical data available on corruption during the pre-colonial period are scarce and largely unsystematic, several studies nonetheless establish a clear link between the experience of colonial domination and the institutionalization of corruption in Africa. In effect, the 'colonial situation'[8] engenders a particular perception of the public sphere and crystallizes a series of behaviours and power relations which re-create fertile ground for widespread corruption in the modern sense of the term.

There are two extreme positions in this debate which should be mentioned here. On the one hand, we have the studies which suggest that the colonial administration was free of corruption and that the phenomenon emerges essentially from incompatibility between a bureaucratic Weberian-type model and the pre-colonial modes of political management (McMullan 1961: 186). Some authors, like Andreski, go as far as stating that the colonial administrators' only flaw was that they opted for a 'hasty departure' instead of progressively 'Africanizing' the public service and the army and thus patiently instilling probity in their successors (Andreski 1970: 353). On the other hand, we have studies that are based on an idealized vision of pre-colonial political societies whose principles and values of solidarity, integrity and democracy were perverted by colonial domination. Hence, as these studies see it, the corruption in the public sphere was caused by the corruption of ancestral values and customs (Collectif 2003; Njoku 2005). It should be noted, however, that other more in-depth analyses carried out by historians and anthropologists offer a more detailed picture as compared with these diametrically opposed arguments whose ideological scope can easily be identified.

The characteristics of the system of colonial domination

First, the theory dear to the hearts of the theorists of political modernization, which postulates the incompatibility between a legal–rational bureaucracy exported by the colonist and the local modes of governance, does not stand up to historical analysis: it is clearly useful to recall that the colonial bureaucratic model – both French and English, to stay with these two examples – has characteristics which distance it considerably from the bureaucratic model of the motherlands.

The colonial administration is first and foremost an incomplete and 'truncated object' (Darbon 1985): the administration was mainly implanted in the urban centres while the rest of the territory was administered by a lax bureaucratic structure, in which a limited number of officials[9] were in office for short periods and subcontracted authority to a range of local auxiliaries. It is also a hybrid model which combined, at least in the case of the French model, the properties of the bureaucracy of the *Ancien Régime* with ambitions that presented it as a progressive and avant-garde administration as compared with the motherland administration (Sibeud 2002). However, it was primarily based on a regime of exception 'whose particularity was to depart from the supposed common law' (Mbembe 2000: 48). This regime created a double differentiation in terms of statutes and rights, which Mamdani (1996) describes using the term 'bifurcated state'. This differentiation existed, on the one hand, between the colonial officials (one need only think of the *commandants de cercle*, i.e. district commanders, who were invested with exceptional powers as compared with the motherland administration) and the subjects ruled by the *indigénat* regime; and between the 'kings of the bush' (Brunschwig 1983) (i.e. the canton chiefs, warrant chiefs, interpreters, marabouts, major native traders who benefited from significant powers and a system that exonerated worthy subjects from the impositions of the *indigénat* regime) and the rest of the population, on the other.

According to Mbembe, this regime of exception was coupled with a regime of favours (the right to collect taxes and rent and to maintain troops; laws created for the benefit of the colonies, etc.), privileges – 'an advantage which was always enjoyed at the cost of others' (Mbembe 2000: 50) – and immunities. Government, command and civilization were confounded under colonization. As a result, the colonial subjects were integrated into the structures of production by means of coercion, violence and corruption (2000: 51). Finally, the institutions, procedures and technologies imported by the colonial state did not serve the public good, but attended to absolute submission, which Mbembe refers to as 'circular sovereignty' (2000: 53). Similarly, Olivier de Sardan (2004) analyses the construction of the colonial bureaucracy both as breaking with pre-colonial forms of power and as exception with respect to modern European bureaucracy (which is associated with the emergency of citizenship): thus the colonial bureaucracy contained the seeds of the majority of the characteristics of contemporary African states, including their corruptibility.

The question that arises at this point concerns the actual forms of corruption that emerged in the colonial era and the sectors and levels of the administration that were mainly affected by it. Based on the information currently available, it would appear that the corruption involved here mainly took the form of racketeering, the payment of tributes, embezzlement and hoarding. It primarily occurred on the level of the local administrative districts and involved the administrative and traditional chiefs and the auxiliaries of the colonial administration. The courts of law, the tax system and conscription for the colonial military services were the main sectors in which the intermediaries between the command structures and the colonies' subjects were able to cash in on their power and accumulate wealth. Under colonization, the local chiefs – of whom some originated from traditional aristocracies and others were the complete creations of the colonists in regions in which they found no centralized political system – quickly became notorious for their authoritarian and arbitrary style of rule, which also enabled their rapid accumulation of wealth.

So diverse are the origins of the chiefs, the conditions of their appointment, the relations they entered into with the colonial subjects and officials and, again, the attitudes of the colonial authorities with respect to their styles of rule, that it would be impossible for this study to provide an exhaustive synthesis of the fraud perpetrated at the local levels of the colonial administration. The English considered that their system was better at giving the native chiefs responsibility for the new tasks of command and management, in particular by entrusting them with the task of managing local taxes.[10] However, in general, abuses were documented in both the territories under direct administration and those subject to indirect rule.

However, it would appear that the exactions were particularly acute when the local authorities did not benefit from any traditional legitimacy. In the case of French West Africa, we can refer here to the case of the Senegalese territories to the north of the Gambian enclave under British protectorate, corresponding to the district of the Rip-Niani. From 1887 to 1914, the French imposed Muslim chiefs of Wolof and Toukouleur origin in this area with its animist Mandingo majority. Ill tolerated by a population who saw them as the descendants of the initiators of a holy war, which had devastated the traditional country of western Saloum between 1861 and 1887, these chiefs engaged in all kinds of abuses, ranging from the abusive sale of slaves and the embezzlement of the colonial taxes to the requisition of village residents for forced labour from which the chiefs themselves benefited (see Blundo 1998: 46–8).

This trend can also be observed in the regions in which the English were confronted with the administration of so-called acephalous societies. To establish control on the Kikuyu, Ibo, Masai and Kamba societies, which were traditionally managed by councils of elders and did not have dominant dynasties, the English created chiefs who had extended powers up to the late 1930s (Tignor 1971). Despite having shown remarkable stability and continuity, these indigenous local administrative chiefs did not receive substantial budgets from the colonial administration: badly paid and equipped with only a few assistants, these new leaders had to create their own para-administrative and military corps to satisfy the requirements of the colonial power, in particular with respect to the collection of taxes and recruitment of the workforce. This first factor was the direct cause of corruption. The chiefs engaged in all kinds of abuses of power, demanding gifts for the regulation of disputes and bribes for exempting subjects from their colonial obligations (collective work, taxes, etc.). Both the Europeans and the Africans of the period deplored the corruption of the Ibo and Kikuyu chiefs, who 'were enormously well-to-do and lived beyond their official means'. In effect, corruption 'was a necessary ingredient of local administration and the fuel of the local administrative engine' (Tignor 1971: 350). These local systems had to be financed and the chiefs had to obtain payments from the population, which the colonial authorities henceforth considered as illegal tributes.[11] In Kenya, some district commissioners denounced the complicity of the colonial government with these practices, which were expected to persist as long as the chiefs' salaries were not increased.

However, as demonstrated by the research carried out in the 1950s in the Emirate of Zaria in northern Nigeria (Smith 1964), the same behaviours were also adopted by local authorities that benefited from a degree of political legitimacy. In northern Nigeria, the district heads underpaid the producers for their cotton or sold the quotas of rice that were supposed to be distributed free of charge to the villagers and demanded gifts from the village chiefs under various pretexts (repair of the conference room, travel to the capital, reception of a British officer and the nomination of a prison guard or village chief). The village chiefs themselves under-declared the taxable contributors in the villages so as to embezzle part of the taxes they collected. They also extorted illicit payments from the villagers under the pretext of accusing villagers of harbouring diseases in their houses and for authorizing them to sell agricultural products and animal hides. Apparent excesses in the recovery of local taxes were documented in a study concerning the Caliphate of Sokoto and in Borno in northern Nigeria (Adebayo 1995). The system of colonial taxation set up by Lord Lugard to reduce the fiscal pressure on the emirs was also characterized by abuses and irregularities, which did not spare certain British officers, indeed far from it (Awal 1987).

The custom of offering presents to the authorities changed in this new context. Tolerated within certain limits among renowned leaders as enabling them to represent the community with dignity, it became particularly unacceptable to the populations when practised by illegitimate authorities because they were imposed from above and exercised their authority through coercion (Tignor 1971: 352). Moreover, these local potentates did not assume the function of 'political machines' and engage in a certain degree of redistribution. The fruit of their abuses of power was used almost entirely for the maintenance of their courts and their para-administrative entourages.

The cadis and chiefs also became auxiliaries in the administration of justice. The French realized that it was necessary to maintain the local legal institutions in French West Africa. Thus, although they experienced a reduction in their traditional prerogatives in relation to the law – a decree of 1892 assigned jurisdiction for events qualified as crimes to the district commanders, confining the chiefs to the regulation of minor infractions – the local chiefs compensated this loss through the application 'without judgement of heavy fines ... The vast majority of cadis were obsessed with becoming rich at the expense of litigants. They handed out fines with excessive zeal, from which they received sums for themselves and for the local administrative chief on whom they were dependent' (Gueye 1997: 155). Another consequence of this kind of system was that the 'cadis like the indigenous chiefs only pursued the perpetrators of crimes whose sanctions brought them monetary or material rewards' (Gueye 1997: 156). Similar situations are documented for the territories that were colonized by the British: in Nigeria (in particular after 1914 when the English officers no longer presided over the Native Courts), the court clerks used their position as legal experts and interpreters of the law to sell their expertise. They also exploited the labour of prisoners and made a name for themselves as usurers (Njoku 2005: 106).

Several studies highlight the ambiguous role of colonial interpreters: an indispensable cog in the colonial administrative machine, they were among the best-paid auxiliaries and their salaries could be as high as those of French administrators in Europe (Brunschwig 1983: 111). Despite this privileged situation, 'even the most honest ... substantially increased their salaries by taking advantage of their situation, gifts from the natives to whom they provided a service, facilities for obtaining European goods etc.' (Brunschwig 1983: 109). Thus they were often accused by the population of corruption, of peddling influence and of various other abuses, in particular when they did not originate from local society (Mopoho 2001). Another group that profited from the multiplicity of rules and regulations during the colonial period was the surveyors. Alternating between the traditional and official systems, they were able to obtain the best plots of land, such as those close to the market of Mont-Bouët in Libreville (Piermay 1986).

It should also be noted that the colonial administration was not spared from corrupt behaviours and irregularities: the official journals and inspection reports are overflowing with notes concerning the abuses perpetrated by colonial officials in French West Africa. For example, in 1984, Merlin, the director of public affairs, harshly criticized the exercise of absolute power in Senegal, and, in 1906, the governor of Guinea condemned the acceptance of gifts from natives and purchases of various types of goods 'at extremely low prices'. However, impunity was an inherent characteristic of this group: 'the sanctioning of white officers in the colonies is rare' (Brunschwig 1983: 21, 24, 26). The same impunity applied to the interpreters as there was a reluctance to condemn them in view of how difficult it was to replace them.

The English administration appears to have been more honest than the French, at least on the level of its upper echelons (Tignor 1993: 178) (Le Vine 1975b; Médard 2002). For example, the Customary Presents Order was promulgated in 1954 to eradicate the practice of offering gifts to public officials (Tignor 1993: 198). While it is difficult to identify the precise level of corruption during the colonial period, the fact remains that public and political probity became a very important topic and was undoubtedly the most important subject for debate after that of independence: 'Britain's last legacy to Nigeria was to open up the discussion concerning governmental malfeasance and to make it a prominent issue' (Tignor 1993: 177).

Reactions to corruption during the colonial era

It is very difficult to speak of the existence of any real policies for combating corruption during the colonial era. The administration was regularly confronted with complaints from the populations

regarding the abuse of power by the chiefs and auxiliaries. On occasion these grievances actually escalated into revolt: for example,
the protest that erupted in Aba in eastern Nigeria in 1929, which
is known as the 'Women's war' (Njoku 2005: 105).[12] The colonial
administration appears to have adopted an essentially pragmatic
attitude to the phenomenon of corruption: very shady leaders were
deposed, but the colonial authorities tried to close their eyes to
hoarding activities so long as they did not affect the administration
and its image. The colonial administration in the south-west of
Tanzania provides a good example of this opportunistic approach:
having adopted a benevolent and condescending attitude to the
services of the *wakulungwa*, the local chiefs with responsibility for
the administration of the villages, from 1936 the district officers
described these political intermediaries as corrupt and incompetent.
Becker (2006) shows that this change in attitude was intended
to conceal from or justify to central government the poor results
achieved by the colonial agents and their collaborators in the collection of taxes. Moreover, the official condemnation of the corrupt
practices was selective: as long as they remained in the good books of
the colonial officers, certain *wakulungwa* could continue to benefit
from the advantages associated with their position without concern.
More generally, throughout the colonial period, the accusations
of corruption became an instrument used by the English colonial
administrators to explain the constant difference between the formal
ideal of the functioning of local political institutions and the way
they functioned in reality.

In the decade prior to Nigerian independence, the English colonial
administration encouraged a public debate on corruption through
the institution of commissions of inquiry[13] and the dismissal of
certain shady politicians and administrators. This undertaking was
motivated by entirely political ends, however. The bad administration
and corrupt practices observed on the level of local government were
used as an argument by the British to justify their reluctance in the
matter of granting independence and represented an overt criticism
of nationalist claims. The inquiries actually involved the regions
in which the opposition to the colonial regime was strongest and
targeted the leaders of African trade unions and nationalist parties,

in particular the National Council of Nigeria and the Cameroons (NCNC). As opposed to this, the north of the country was almost entirely spared these commissions of inquiry. As supporters of the Northern People's Congress (NPC), a party with a Fulani majority, the English preferred not to promote public inquiries there, which could have proven disastrous in terms of the reputations of local politicians, and instead promoted reform 'from behind the scenes' (Tignor 1993: 197).

The effects of the colonial experience on political practices and representations

'When Africa became independent around 1960, all of the tools for the intensive practice of corruption were already in place' (Bayart 1990: 37). This rather laconic observation merits exploration. In other words, we need to examine how the colonial legacy created a favourable climate for the emergence of corrupt practices at political, institutional and representational levels.

The colonial experience contributed first to the emergence of a new idea of authority and the public service: authority no longer derived from the people, but came from above, was often illegitimate and exercised with brutality, and the public service offered significant opportunities for rapidly accessing material wealth and prestige (Njoku 2005: 107; Tignor 1971: 353). The overlapping of positions of power and accumulation of wealth, already documented for the pre-colonial period, intensified during the colonial period, in particular among the native collaborators (Bayart 1992). The fact that the imposition of state control over colonized society was based on local patronage networks will have 'paved the way ... to an unprecedented privatization of public privileges' and the 'socialization of the arbitrary' (Mbembe 2000: 52).

Second, the colonial system promoted the development of 'zero-sum politics'. The chiefs only protected their supporters and those who could corrupt them. The only real reward to be gained from this kind of local bureaucracy was the avoidance of certain abuses. Those who remained outside the system paid for the others and were subject to the corvées imposed by the colonial power (Tignor 1971).

Third, a colonial bureaucracy of foreign origin which was controlled from a distant homeland and managed by officials whose pressures and objectives do not concern the local population (McMullan 1961) and which did not create spaces of civic identification outside of the community spaces (Bouju 2000) promoted the emergence of a culture in which there is a lack of commitment for the common good: in this new context public affairs were synonymous with 'nobody's affairs' or at most 'the white man's work' (Njoku 2005: 104, 110).

Fourth, to the extent that the colonial government was considered illegitimate, the traditional norms sanctioning the theft of collective property and the abuse of authority were no longer implemented (Le Vine 1975b). In other words, if we adopt Ekeh's hypothesis, the regulation of behaviour in the public sphere continued to be applied exclusively among the 'primordial public' which 'is moral and operates on the same moral imperatives as the private realm' (Ekeh 1975: 92). The 'civic public', as embodied by the colonial state, 'is amoral and lacks the generalized moral imperatives operative in the private realm and in the primordial public' (92). Thus, it became 'legitimate to rob the civil public in order to strengthen the primordial public' (108). A closely related argument suggests a link between corruption and the opposition of the nationalist movements to colonization. According to Werlin (1972: 255), corruption became a form of sabotage of the colonial government. This suggestion is echoed by Osei-Hwedie and Osei-Hwedie (2000: 45), for whom 'cheating the government became a patriotic gesture'. However, more generally, it is the actual relationship with the rules that changed: most of the time the laws and regulations imposed by the colonial system, which at the same time maintained or tolerated elements of the native normative systems, were simply inapplicable and this promoted the circumventing of the rules and granted vast discretionary powers to the officials (McMullan 1961).

Fifth, through its distinctions, honorary titles and the privileges granted to its officials, colonial bureaucracy engendered among the native officialdom the desire to emulate and imitate the former European leaders (Price 1975) so as to overcome the frustrations endured under domination and to taste the formerly forbidden fruits of power (Tangri 1982). This involved the adoption of a European lifestyle through the consumption of luxury goods, the majority of which were imported and unattainable on salaries which were not maintained at the level of those of the colonial officials (Sarassoro 1979).

Corruption and the construction of the post-colonial state

Corruption and political regimes

All political change in Africa raises the topic of the war against corruption – that is, the popular disapproval of illicit gain by the deposed rulers is mobilized and acts as a means of legitimation of the new political classes. However, the latter quickly forget their promises and devote themselves to selective political campaigns essentially aimed at excluding rival factions from access to the financial resources necessary to engage in democratic politics (Harsch 1993: 32–3). Hence, commissions of inquiry are a common by-product of regime change.

In Niger, the military coup that brought an end to the Hamani Diori regime and installed Seyni Kountché in power was followed by the immediate establishment of a commission of control and inquiry which enabled the seizure of the properties of three members of the previous civil regime and the arrest of over fifty officials on charges of corruption in 1976. However, the commission was subsequently dissolved due to the 'corrupt procedures' of its president, Captain Gabriel Cyrille (Amuwo 1986).

In Sierra Leone, the seizure of power in 1992 by Valentine Stasser gave rise to the creation of three commissions of inquiry into corruption, whose purpose was to examine the origins of the assets of the presidents, vice-presidents and ministers in office from 1986 to 1992, and to evaluate the level of corruption in the ministerial departments, the parastate companies, the armed forces and the police. The three reports produced by these commissions brought to light the waste, embezzlement and illicit accumulation of enormous sums and gave rise to the imposition of sanctions and restitution or confiscation of the money and goods embezzled for ministers, secretaries of the president, high-level officials, businessmen and presidents Stevens and Momoh (Kpundeh 1994: 146; Thompson and Potter 1997).

From his accession to the presidency of the Tanzanian state in November 1995, Benjamin Mkapa hastened to establish the 'Presidential Commission of Inquiry against Corruption', which submitted a detailed report in 1996, referred to as the 'Warioba Report' (Tanzania 1996). The Commission was behind several initiatives aiming to improve the legal system, police services, tax system and lands services. Twenty thousand 'ghost' civil servants were also removed from the administration's payroll (Langseth and Michael 1998). In South Africa, the final decade of apartheid government was punctuated by several commissions of inquiry (Lodge 2002), and the deposition of Nkrumah in Ghana in 1966 was followed by the establishment of over forty commissions for the investigation of corruption during his period in power (Werlin 1972: 251–2).

Nonetheless, the main conclusion that may be drawn from historical analyses of African politics is that, even if the visibility and forms taken by corruption tend to depend on the specific nature of different types of political regime, no single type, be it authoritarian or pluralist, military or civil, is more likely than the others to engender corruption. Thus, it is plausible to follow Médard's lead and establish a correlation between the stability of a regime and the forms of corruption that occur under it.

Authoritarianism and corruption: single-party government and military regimes

The legislative machinery created after independence was generally more repressive and severe than that which existed during the colonial era. While the colonial texts respected the legal principles that protect those accused of crimes, when they did not simply consign powers of repression to the military courts, as was the case in Zaire (1965–67) and Ghana (1972–77), the new African states did away with reprieves, suspended sentences, attenuating circumstances and rehabilitation, and restricted the principle of the presumption of innocence (Sarassoro 1990). In the newly independent African countries that were also members of the British Commonwealth, more specific legislation was created which rendered more complex or replaced elements of the colonial penal code while continuing to be based on the British 'Prevention of Corruption Acts' of 1889–1916. For example, new crimes were defined, such as the outlawing of the acceptance of gifts (even if it has not been proven that they led to corrupt behaviours) by Kenyan officials (Law of 1956), nepotism was defined as a crime in Zimbabwe in 1985, and the principle of inversion of proof in cases involving an extremely affluent lifestyle was adopted in Tanzania. The concept of the presumption of corruption was introduced in Zambia in 1980 and in Botswana in 1994. Punishments also increased in severity (Coldham 1995).

Nonetheless, this intensive legislative activity was accompanied by an increase in the levels of corruption. In certain countries, such as Ghana, the signs of corruption had already begun to appear during the nationalist administration. From 1954, it was discovered that vehicles belonging to the Cocoa Purchasing Company were being used by party members and that the granting of loans to farmers was based on motives of electoral clientelism (Osei-Hwedie and Osei-Hwedie 2000). In his famous tract, *L'Afrique noire est mal partie* (1962), René Dumont pilloried countries like Benin, Republic of the Congo, Côte d'Ivoire, Gabon and Central African Republic just two years after they had gained independence. A comparative study on the functioning of the municipal councils of Kampala and Nairobi in the 1960s drew attention to the shady behaviour of local elected representatives (Greenstone 1966). In Zaire, the cases of embezzlement dealt with by the main court of Kinshasa increased from 70 for the period between 1958 and 1960 to 99 for the period between June and August 1960 alone (Mukenge 1973). Similarly, the number of cases of corruption recorded by the Nigerian police increased from 300 in 1967 to 1,191 in 1977 (Eker 1981).

For those authoritarian regimes that set themselves the task of constructing the nation-state shortly after gaining independence, corruption became, in effect, a mode of managing people that was identical in essence to the exercise and maintenance of power. Based on a clientelist type of redistribution, the neo-patrimonial chiefs succeeded in ensuring the survival of their regime and gave it an appearance of legitimacy, at least as long as the rent – both internal and external – did not start to dry up. One of the most telling examples of this logic of redistributive hoarding for the purpose of political stability is the Côte d'Ivoire of Houphouët-Boigny. The latter was a past master in the exercise of 'enlightened clientelism' (Conte 2004) through the deduction and redistribution of the rent from the cocoa and coffee industries in different sectors (expansion of the public service, guaranteed employment for graduates and immigrants working in agriculture). While corruption existed within this system, it was relatively well controlled by the single party monopoly (PDCI), whose control penetrated to all of the layers of Ivoirien society.

As opposed to this, the single party that was in power in Sierra Leone from 1968 to 1992 created a system of corruption tinged with tribalism. The All People's Congress under Siaka Stevens and Joseph Saidu Momoh, the former's successor from 1985, dominated the public sector, benefiting from the confusion between executive and legislative powers and systematically suppressing all challenges to their authority. The extensive personalization of political relations led to the distribution of key posts in the main ministries and in the administration of the public banks, police force, lottery and the state marketing offices among the members of the 'Ekutay' group – the natives of the same town as Momoh – and more generally among those from the Limba ethnic group. The commission of inquiry established by the military regime of Valentine Stasser in 1992–93 had three major scandals in its sights: 'Vouchergate' in 1982, 'Squandergate' in 1984 (concerning the embezzlement of government payment orders for personal ends) and 'Milliongate' in 1987 (concerning the fraudulent division of public funds between public servants and business men) (Kpundeh 1994).

The ideologues of Kwame Nkrumah's Convention People's Party (CPP) in Ghana argued that the single-party-rule system was capable of reducing corruption due to the weak politicization of the administration and the absence of expensive electoral campaigns. However, it was under this regime that corruption penetrated to all levels of the state in Ghana and gained ground within both public companies and local traditional authorities. The single party owed 90 per cent of its budgetary receipts to illicit payments (between 5 and 10 per cent) levied on procurement contracts. Companies like the National Development Corporation were used to collect and manage money obtained through corruption. The ministers were not outdone by this: it was a known fact that the minister of commerce demanded commission on import licences (between 5 and 10 per cent of the value of the licence requested) (Werlin 1972: 252). Nkrumah himself had gold bars which were the property of the National Treasury exported to Cairo, and a massive operation involving the smuggling of cocoa, food products, minerals and wood to Côte d'Ivoire, Burkina Faso and Togo was orchestrated with the complicity of the customs (Osei-Hwedie and Osei-Hwedie 2000: 48).

According to Médard's analysis (1998, 2002), the neo-patrimonial mode of regulation found in most authoritarian regimes ensures relative political stability as long as corruption reproduces itself in situations characterized by an – admittedly precarious – balance be-tween extraction and redistribution. Thus, according to the scenario for the assimilation of elites described by Bayart (1989), patronage constitutes the cement that binds the emerging ruling classes. How-ever, when economic growth ceases and the circuits of redistribution dry up, the political elites may adopt purely predatory attitudes out of concern for their short-term survival. The unprecedented oil boom from which Nigeria benefited in the 1970s was quickly mortgaged as a result of the very poor management of the Second Republic (1979–83), which culminated in Muhammadu Buhari's *coup d'état* of 1983; the latter was in turn ousted by Babangida in August 1985. The traditional channels of public patronage weakened during the rampant economic crisis of those years, being undermined by the drastic decline in government contracts, subsidies and employment. During this period the country underwent a transition from a 'de-centralized patrimonial regime', or prebendary (Lewis 1996: 80),[14] to an essentially predatory regime characterized by the concentra-tion of personal power exercised through coercion and violence, the erosion of central public institutions (which were progressively replaced by a limited circle of ethnical and personal loyalties) and large-scale corruption, to which were also added smuggling and drugs trafficking thanks to the complicity of the military leaders (Lewis 1996: 101).

In Côte d'Ivoire, the final years of the Houphouët regime were marked by policies of structural adjustment and by the drastic reduction in the prices paid to cocoa producers in 1988. When Houphouët-Boigny died in 1993, Bédié had to deal with slower growth, the devaluation of the CFA franc and the pressure of clienteles which had become too extensive relative to the insufficient level of income. The refocusing of redistribution on the populations of the south, and the Baoulé in particular, the mobilization of populations around the topic of *ivoirité* (i.e. Ivoirien identity) and the rupture with the north were not sufficient to halt the decline of the clientelist system, which, according to Conte (2004), became 'impoverished'. The *coup d'état* by General Gueï in 1999 took place in a country whose foreign debt was approaching 6,250 billion CFA francs. The military junta launched a series of reforms and an anti-corruption 'clean hands' operation, but quickly found itself cornered by the demands of an army which believed itself to have been marginalized by Bédié.

The aforementioned examples show, furthermore, that even if the reform of public life is always one of the main arguments used to justify the seizure of power by the army, military regimes that are not tainted by political and administrative corruption are rare. Some military chiefs actually had to leave office as a result of adopting the very illicit practices they had castigated, for example General A. Ankrah who gained power in Ghana in 1966 and had to resign in 1969 for having accepted a 'payment' (Osei-Hwedie and Osei-Hwedie 2000). Two exceptions to this rule are often cited: the revolutionary regimes of Sankara in Burkina Faso and Rawlings in Ghana, which gained a reputation for integrity while launching inter alia spectacular and repressive anti-corruption campaigns, based, for example, on inquiries into suspected illicit material enrichment; Sankara tried and condemned 200 former regime leaders and Rawlings executed 700 individuals convicted of corruption (Sarassoro 1990: 202; Gocking 1996). However, some military regimes did not engage in such dramatic crusades; nevertheless, even though they did not succeed in curbing corruption, they at least gave the impression that they were seriously concerned with the quest for public integrity. This was the case in Niger under Seyni Kountché. From 1974, 'the man who never smiled' (Amuwo 1986: 296) embarked on a crusade for reform based on discourses condemning the 'commercialism' of public servants and the diffusion of symbols and slogans intended to demonstrate the involvement of the new regime in the reform of the mentality of public actors: 'New order, new attitudes', 'Halt the commercialism of state officials' (Amuwo 1986: 291, 292) and 'Trust does not exclude control'. The general's distrust of the public administration prompted him to entrust its supervision to military personnel. Military power was also applied to a presidential security network led by Oumarou Amadou, known as 'Bonkano', who orchestrated unexpected raids based on intimidation and blackmail and mainly involving the lower levels of the administration, while allowing the high-level military officials and administrative officials to devote their energies to illicit affairs. Bonkano himself, who became very prosperous, would later become the subject of multiple accusations of corruption and illicit material enrichment during the National Conference.

Under some authoritarian regimes, in terms of both discourse and practice, corruption is definitively monopolized and controlled by those in power: as Anders (2005) stresses in the case of Malawi, the single-party regime of Kamuzu Banda is viewed as having been far less corrupt than the current democratically elected regime. However, it should be considered that under Banda the subject of corruption was taboo and that the integrity for which his administration is reputed was not the result of the stringent application of the law, but of a brutal system of oppression which exercised complete control over public servants. The appropriation of the state was limited to a tight circle around Banda while the low-level bureaucrats operated in constant fear of being fired or imprisoned.

Democratic processes and corruption

At this point we would like to consider the impact of the wave of democratization throughout the 1990s and the 'good governance' measures that accompanied it (Szeftel 1998). The view that corruption appears to have increased in the course of this period is generally undisputed in the literature. This observation concerns countries as diverse as the Congo (Blancq 1994), Malawi (Anders 2004; Khembo 2004; Anders 2005), Mozambique (Bertrand 2003;

Hanlon 2004), South Africa (Lodge 1998; Lodge 2002), Zambia (Szeftel 1982; Chikulo 2000) and Uganda (Langseth 1997; Flanary and Watt 1999). Even Botswana, a country reputed to have been relatively free of the phenomenon of corruption, was shaken by a series of scandals concerning the awarding of public contracts, illegal property transactions and the clientelist allocation of housing (Good 1994; Theobald and Williams 1999).

First, the popular aspirations for greater state integrity appear to be associated with ambiguous demands. In the early 1990s, countries in the Sahel like Mali and Senegal were besieged by movements demanding greater transparency and 'cleanliness' in the management of public affairs. In Mali, the public desire to have done with the dictatorship of Moussa Traoré was primarily the expression of a desire to have done with corruption. The streets of the main urban centres resounded to the cry in Bambara of *kokaje*, which literally translates as 'wash to make clean' and expresses both the idea of purification and transparency and of the punishment of the authors of economic and political crimes (Lange 1999: 123). In Senegal, the *set setal* ('make clean' in Wolof) movement saw young city-dwellers clean and decorate their neighbourhoods and expressed a similar desire for the cleaning up of political morals (Diouf 1992). More recently, public opinion in Burkina Faso was mobilized against the impunity from which political crimes benefit.[15] However, these claims, which are very much in tune with the donor organizations' idealized images of 'civil society', are accompanied by demands on the part of the same 'lowly' actors for more equitable access to the fruits of predation (Fay 1995: 24) and for the 'right of all to engage in prevarication' (Lange 1999: 128). In countries like Malawi, in which the lower levels of the bureaucracy were tightly controlled and relatively shielded from illicit access to public resources by authoritarian regimes, political liberalization had the effect of giving rise to the democratization on all levels of the forms of appropriation of state resources (Anders 2005: 204). In this new context, the human rights are equated with a regime that endorses personal gain as 'the right to grab as much as you can' (205).

Once the euphoria of national conferences has passed, the true face of the processes of democratization is that of cleverly orchestrated

privatization, unbridled economic liberalism, the pursuit of staff cut-
back measures in public administrations and the denationalization
and transfer of competencies to exsanguine local bodies. Thus, new
spaces and opportunities for predation arise. For example in Nigeria,
the privatization policies put forward by Babangida on the advent of
the Third Republic were quickly controlled and taken advantage of
by political networks, such as those of the 'Old Brigades' and 'Money
Bags' in the north of the country (Reno 1993). Corruption also sullied
the privatization programmes of the Zambian state from 1992, with
the result that almost all of the parastate companies ended up back
in the hands of the pre-nationalization owners (Chikulo 2000). In
several countries, the decentralization process, whose stated aims
included the promotion of citizen participation in the management
of local issues, provides an example of the relocation of misappropriation, which has been redistributed among local clientelist
networks that were fragmented as a result of the establishment of
multipartyism (Blundo 2001b). The illicit appropriation of urban
property (see Bouju 2000 on Mali), wild privatization of national
land (Klopp 2000) and fiscal disobedience (Fjeldstad 2001; Fjeldstad 2003) are just some of the areas in which the new political
classes, both local and national, invest their energies. In the majority
of cases, democratization essentially means the re-establishment
of multipartyism; corruption and electoral clientelism are more
prevalent than ever as demonstrated by the case of Cameroon where
President Biya's party sought the electoral support of business people
in exchange for contracts of fiscal exoneration, made numerous
electoral promises (new districts created a week before elections,
roads started and abandoned after the ballot, etc.) (Fombad 2000)
and competed with the opposition parties in the organization of real
'electoral banquets' (Socpa 2000).[16]

Public opinion in South Africa estimates that corruption has
increased since the advent of democratization in 1994. According
to a national survey carried out in 1998, 55 per cent of the people
interviewed believed that the majority of public servants take bribes
(Lodge 2002). Where documented for the apartheid era, corruption
remained on a modest level and limited to the post offices, police
officers (Brogden and Nijhar 1998) and the legal system. For the white

population 'experience of corruption would have been exceptional rather than normal, and concentrated in municipal rather than national state agencies' (Lodge 2002: 410). However, towards the end of apartheid, the proliferation of independent governments in the homelands increased the opportunities for illicit administrative transactions which were promoted by a local administration influenced by values extolling solidarity, reciprocity and the exchange of gifts. When the homelands' administrations were incorporated into the regional governments these practices became more widespread: between 1994 and 1999, eleven members of regional councils were involved in affairs of corruption. The political changes also gave rise to other opportunities: incompetent and ignorant ministers and managers failed to implement the rules for the awarding of public contracts, non-meritocratic procedures were adopted for administrative recruitment (due to certain excesses in 'Affirmative Action') and nepotism was associated with forms of political solidarity (militantism during apartheid).

Independent since 1975, Mozambique was immersed in civil war until 1992. While the first five years of independent government were characterized by a fervour of construction focusing on values of integrity, the early 1980s saw a turn to the West with corollary measures such as privatization, structural adjustment, transition towards a market economy and increase in international aid (from $359 million in 1985 to $875 million in 1988). This paved the way for the emergence and consolidation of an elite which 'captured' the state (Hanlon 2004). In the first half of the 1990s, the restrictions imposed by the IMF resulted in the reduction of the salaries of the petty bureaucracy by two-thirds while senior officials received large payments for work carried out within cooperation institutions or benefited from significant expenses for attending workshops. The 'little men' resorted to a corruption of survival while the 'big men' luxuriated in a 'climate of donor-approved corruption' (Hanlon 2004: 751). Eager for the adoption of measures to promote economic austerity and liberalization, the World Bank and the International Monetary Fund paradoxically supported the predatory behaviours of the elites in power who, while appearing to accept the proposed measures, distorted them to their own advantage. Thus, the members of FRELIMO (Liberation Front of Mozambique), in particular, controlled property transactions, the repurchase of denationalized companies and the allocation of commercial licences, and 90 per cent of the loans granted by the World Bank to small businesses were never paid. The association of predatory behaviour and the pangs of structural adjustment produced what Mozambicans refer to as *cabritalismo* (Harrison 1999).

The era of 'good governance'

It is not possible to analyse the reproduction of corruption in Africa without considering the role played by the international coopera- tion institutions. Today, development aid accounts for 90 per cent of public investment and 30 per cent of ongoing state expenses in sub-Saharan Africa (Cooksey 2002: 47). While a considerable proportion of development aid now takes the form of support for anti-corruption programmes (for a recent analysis, see Michael 2004),[17] it should be noted that, whether 'participatory' or liberal in spirit, no development project is limited to the neutral transfer of technology, money and institutions. Projects are embedded in complex social and political realities, in which actor strategies are implemented which tend towards the appropriation of the symbolic or economic resources of external intervention, which, as a result, becomes an entirely separate local political factor.[18] 'Aid, in the form of project loans in particular, creates many opportunities for patronage, including project location, hiring project staff, train- ing opportunities, procurement and purchases, and consultancy' (Cooksey 2002: 47). Some studies have shown how the large-scale and often competing intervention of aid organizations gives rise to the emergence of overpaid and functional bureaucratic 'enclaves' at national level, thus extending the gap with the state administra- tions, in which absenteeism is becoming more widespread and the seeking of additional revenue, be it legal or illegal, is becoming the norm.[19] In other cases, the massive financial support granted to countries with the best reputations for the implementation of neoliberal reforms has provided certain governments with the means of redynamizing the channels of patronage. This phenomenon was clearly demonstrated by Mwenda and Tangri (2005) in their scathing criticism of the perverted effects of international cooperation in Uganda. However, the most rewarding perspectives on the forms of corruption and opportunities to engage in it that arise wherever development projects are implemented are mainly provided by recent ethnographic research focusing on local contexts.

In his study of the informal and unofficial organization of a family planning programme in Nigeria, Smith shows that the project is perceived locally as an occasion for converting external resources into local wealth 'in people' (2003: 709) – that is, into people one can control. The author also describes the routine and open practice of patronage and corruption: for example, the clientelist allocation of jobs based on the obligation to reward the 'nominators' from the Ministry of Health by retroceding them part of the project resources (a practice that corresponds to our concept of *'rent-based commission'*; see Chapter 3); the granting of generous expenses to senior officials for participation in weekly seminars that they actually only attend for a few minutes (Smith 2003: 709–10); the 'sharing' of project equipment with sectors of the administration excluded from the intervention; and the embezzlement of project funding through the inflation of local contracts and underpayment of personnel. The workshops constitute the strategic location of the local reappropriation of the project: for the aid organizations they represent a sign that the programme is working and that its messages are getting through to the beneficiaries, and for the local leaders they represent an opportunity to receive 'gratitude' in the form of commission and gifts from local suppliers and traders and to benefit from reciprocal gestures on the part of the invited individuals (Smith 2003: 713). These observations are easily applicable to the majority of development-cooperation programmes in sub-Saharan Africa.

In spite of their superficial involvement in the war against corruption, the aid organizations are reluctant to acknowledge that their projects are pervaded by the phenomenon they claim to be fighting and are indirectly encouraging. In effect, this would run the risk of their intervention being challenged.[20] Bähre's (2005) study, which focuses on the case of a programme for the construction and fitting out of underprivileged neighbourhoods in the city of Cape Town, illustrates this attitude clearly. The project committee in the Indawo Yoxolo neighbourhood operated like a kind of mafia. Payments were demanded of the project beneficiaries and houses were taken away from residents and allocated to friends of the committee. Spontaneous demonstrations against these abuses by some residents were quickly silenced, eventually through the murder of one of the protesters. The institutions involved in the programme – Dutch cooperation and a private company called Future Dwelling – underestimated the gravity of the situation; they treated the complaints like simple rumours and continued to preach the importance of the committees in the context of community participation. Most of the protestors left the neighbourhood as a result of the violence. The murderer, a member of the project management committee, was sentenced to one year in prison and rejoined the committee on his release. According to Bähre, corruption in cooperation programmes is ignored or minimized by the participants for different reasons: first, because the repercussions of accusations are important on the social level, it is difficult to express one's opposition to the organization in which one works; second, because some aspects of a project work well and corruption is relegated to the level of a secondary effect or necessary evil; and, finally, it is difficult to admit to the gap between the ideology of participation and actual practices on the ground. This case study also shows that

> not only the state is involved in the maintenance and neglect of corruption. Private companies, NGOs, and mafia-style community leaders are equally involved, and in some instances they are so much intertwined with one another that it is unclear where the state stops and the market or society begins. (Bähre 2005: 118)

For this reason, the distinction that was made for a long time between state structures (or structures controlled by the state) and institutions formed by 'civil society', in terms of the first being corrupt and ineffective and the second being endowed with every possible virtue, should be qualified. This is clearly demonstrated by Dahou's study on the chaotic and factional management of external resources tapped by an 'endogenous' farming organization in the Delta of Senegal (Dahou 2003), which easily bears comparison with the embezzlement reported by Hamer (1981) in his study on the co-operatives created by the Kenyan state in Bukusu country.

Due to their disillusionment with the economic and social crisis, the urban classes and minor state officialdom in African countries were driven to perceive the democratic process 'as the process of democratization of access to state financial resources or external aid' (Lange 1999: 128).

As correctly noted by Szeftel (1998), the neoliberal approaches, according to which the idea of the reinforcement of civil society and the simultaneous diminution of the role of the state would enable a clearer separation between the public and private spheres, are coming to an abrupt end: it is difficult to believe that the role of controller and critic of public affairs will be assumed by a civil society comprising NGOs based on external sponsorship and frequently run by senior civil servants or their relatives. Moreover, to insist on the need to reduce the size of the state is sometimes to forget that African states are weak and need to be reinforced before they can implement reform properly. Thus the combination of weak states and weak civil societies enables the domination of the electorate and state institutions by smaller political machines which function on the basis of the logics of factionalism, patronage and regionalism.

The 'everyday' state

The size of the public service: the oversized state

An important element of the debate on the African state concerns its hypertrophied character: in an extensively quoted article, Larry Diamond (1987) defined the 'typical' African state as a 'swollen state', characterized by a disproportionate development of the parastate sector following the nationalization of foreign companies established during the colonial period and by excessive expansion in terms of administrative personnel. According to Diamond 'the larger the state – the greater the proportion of resources it controls and economic activity it regulates – the greater will tend to be the level of political corruption' (1987: 584). Moreover, the 'swollen state' gives rise to systematic political corruption on a large scale, which in turn promotes the birth of a dominant class attached to the state. This class, which is closely dependent on the control of the state, sets its sights on a subsequent expansion of the state and a greater diffusion of political corruption (1987: 585). While the theory of the hypertrophied state provoked quite a significant response in the specialist literature (Asibuo 1992) and constituted the basis of the policies for the reduction in the numbers of public-sector employees promoted by the Bretton Woods institutions from the mid-1980s, recent comparative analyses show that the public wage bill in Africa is not as excessive as tended to be believed (Goldsmith 1999).

Of course, while the administration restricted itself to functions essentially involving the maintenance of public order and the collection of taxes during the colonial period, the attempts to construct a modern state in the post-independence period gave rise to a rapid increase in bureaucratic apparatuses during the 1960s: the public service in Ghana grew by 67.7 per cent between 1960 and 1965 (Werlin 1972); whereas at independence Kenya had 63,000 public servants for a population of 10 million, by 1979 their number had increased to 258,000; in Nigeria there were 72,000 public servants in 1960 for an estimated population of 40 million inhabitants and in 1974 the federal administration consisted of 275,000 officials, while the educational administration and the police force had a further 383,000 employees. In the majority of African countries, the early 1980s marked the peak in public recruitment, with three times the number of employees as compared with the 1960s. In Kenya, the public sector was significantly oversized until the late 1990s (Bigsten and Ove 1997), and in 1985 the Guinean civil service was clearly overmanned with 80,000 employees, although this number was reduced by 50 per cent two years later (Morice 1987). It should also be noted, however, that the African population grew by 70 per cent during this period. In reality the percentage of public servants in relation to the total population is the lowest in the world: 1.5 per cent in Africa as compared with 3 per cent in Latin America and 2.6 per cent in Asia (Goldsmith 1999: 527–8). The two African countries with ratios of 5.5 and 5.8 per cent respectively, Mauritius and Botswana, are also those in which the state functions most efficiently.

The question of salaries

Another factor that is very often used to explain the prevalence of corruption among public servants and is found throughout the literature we surveyed from the early 1960s to the present day is that of the poor working conditions and low salaries of public-sector workers in Africa.[21] In effect, recurrent economic crises resulted in a considerable deterioration in the salaries of African public servants: in the decade 1975–85, the purchasing power of public servants in Nigeria, Ethiopia, Kenya, Somalia, Sudan and Zambia shrank to virtually nothing (Hope 2000).

Nonetheless, it is necessary to look beyond these laconic shortcuts, which would have us believe that poor salaries are the main cause of corruption (Sarassoro 1990). As Mbembe notes, in Africa salaries merely represent an 'allocation of a purely ascriptive nature' (2000: 73). They do not reward productivity and therefore do not establish any correlation between what is earned and the work carried out; they are more an instrument through which the state purchases obedience and gratitude. On the other hand, in contexts characterized by the absence of policies in the area of social security and by economic insecurity, the salary is equated with a privilege. Along with the other advantages granted to civil servants (for example, advances on their salaries, payments for training and expenses), it represents what is referred to in Malawi as the 'Holy Trinity of the good civil servant' (Anders 2005: 130). Moreover, the beneficiaries of such privileges have found themselves being attributed a status by society which, while enabling them to create and maintain a clientele, is accompanied by burdens, obligations and material requirements, for which the structure of salaries in Africa has always been inadequate. This is demonstrated by Price (1975) in a sociological study of Ghanaian public servants: even if the bureaucratic classes were significantly better paid than the rest of the population, the state employees viewed their salaries as very low in view of the demands of their status, requirements which the author evaluates as exceeding by a factor of two or three those associated with the same posts formerly occupied by Europeans. Based on a questionnaire carried out among 434 state employees at all levels of the hierarchy, Price shows that 80 per cent of the informants were responsible for people apart from their immediate families and that a third of them had at least three or more dependants. He also shows that over 80 per cent believed that it would be appropriate to their position to possess

Western consumer goods (Price 1975: 152–3). According to Price, their corrupt practices result from the incapacity to satisfy these needs from their official income (159).

As a result of the jeopardizing of the public service, in which a population that was sufficiently educated to abandon manual labour but deprived of sufficient education to obtain a professional qualification, found 'a vast social service for recuperation' (Sarassoro 1990: 200), and the degeneration of the middle classes, which traditionally stemmed from the public service, the quest for complementary income, be it legal or illegal, became more widespread. As Morice noted almost two decades ago, obtaining a post in the public service simply made it possible for the officials and their dependants to maintain a position in the context of the profitable activities of the official and informal economies (1987: 112). Under Mobutu, 90 per cent of public servants lived in uncertainty and were badly paid. It is estimated that temporary 'contractual' but de facto permanent officials represented between 80 and 90 per cent of the Zairean public service (Gould 1980: 69). Given the poverty among the officials in the lower levels of the administration, those who would have liked to remain honest and uncorrupted were faced with extreme penury. The others faced a limited range of options: they could either immerse themselves in corruption and embezzlement in order to survive or take up a second job and/or engage in 'moonlighting' (1980: 70–71). The section of Anders's study on the moonlighting activities of Malawian officials during and after office hours is particularly insightful (Anders 2005: 142–53). Even if the phenomenon of extra-salarial income has been documented since the colonial era,[22] according to Mbembe recent trends are contributing to the transformation of the very definition of post-colonial citizenship in Africa: 'henceforth, the individual who can access the networks of the parallel economic and the subsistence made possible by this economy is a citizen' (Mbembe 2000: 123).

For most African countries, the recommendation of an increase in public-sector salaries as a means of combating corruption is at best fanciful and at worst infeasible. On the one hand, the trend over the past twenty years has been to reduce the size of the public service and the blocking of recruitment. On the other, the traditional

frustrations with regard to the significant salarial discrepancy between the higher and lower levels of the administration (Werlin
1972) have been joined by new motifs for apathy in the awareness of
the salaries enjoyed by the employees of the development agencies
and NGOs, which are clearly unobtainable by those employed in the
indigenous public services (Anders 2004: 47). Finally, recent experience, for example that gained in the reform of the tax authorities
in Tanzania, shows that the improvement of salaries and working
conditions can merely be seen as a 'bonus' to be added to the existing illicit income. The creation of the Tanzania Revenue Authority
in 1995, which was manned by personnel significantly better paid
than the rest of the public sector, only momentarily discouraged
the corrupt practices of officials: the increase in salaries, which was
quickly absorbed by rampant inflation, was far from equivalent to
the illicit gains made possible by their position and its only effect
was to increase the requests for help made by the officials' families
and entourages (Fjeldstad 2003: 171).

The organization and functioning of administrations

In terms of the concrete functioning of administrations, the literature we examined provides a strongly consensual list of evils and
dysfunctions that afflict the African bureaucracies: 'permanent' and
'occasional' absenteeism (Nembot 2000: 298; Morice 1987); slow
administrative procedures (Sarassoro 1979); dilapidated administrations which are ill-adapted to social change (Asibuo 1992); rigid,
impersonal and ritualized implementation of the rules (Schwarz
1974); complex and opaque regulations that are difficult to apply
and that leave infinite scope for discretional powers (Fjeldstad 2003;
Hope 2000; McMullan 1961); the centralization of decision-making
processes and lack of delegation at subordinate levels of the administration (Cohen 1980); inadequate archiving or its complete absence;
poor division of tasks and functions in both spatial and sectoral
terms (Darbon 2001: 29).

Less common are analyses which, like this book, confirm the
'almost formal splitting of power' (Mbembe 2000: 117), which is
expressed by a hiatus between formal and parallel hierarchies, the
lack of correspondence between official functions and effective

powers and the primacy of the oral over the written. Considering that the opportunities for accessing illegal income are tending to become institutionalized, Sindzingre (1994) observes the creation of a parallel organization within the bureaucratic organization, in which posts are valued essentially on the basis of the illicit gains to which they provide access. In his empirical study on the Malawian administration, Anders proposes the concept of a 'parallel order' – that is, 'a set of basic moral principles and an unofficial code of conduct based on "respect for the master" that usually prevailed over official regulations' (2005: 207). This order is based on two central characteristics of social relations within the bureaucracy: asymmetrical power relations of maintenance and indebtedness (208). Without expressing respect and allegiance vis-à-vis superiors, it is not possible to hope to advance in one's career, participate in on-site workshops, obtain allowances and so on. This parallel and informal order does not resemble a classical clientelist pyramid linking the centre with the periphery, but is instead based on a multitude of unconnected clientelist relations: 'from the perspective of the individual civil servant each department, each school and each hospital was like a "village with its chief"' (211). LeVine (1975b) made the same observation in his research on the Ghanian administration: the ministries of the interior, agriculture and finance each functioned in an autonomous and isolated way and those in office only wanted to provide the services strictly associated with their own job descriptions. Each administrative position became in some way a '*situation acquise*' (LeVine 1975b: 56) and decisions were systematically deferred upwards to the top of the hierarchy. According to LeVine, the proliferation of administrative structures was at the root of this fragmentation of the administrative system:

> in a fragmented administrative system ..., the more officials are located in the same general area (bureaucratic density), the less likely they are to co-ordinate their activities even if they work in the same agency (i.e. link or articulate their activities), and the more likely they are to engage in acts of political corruption (1975b: 55).

The officials, their behaviours and representations

In the social science literature, the variety of general interpretations of the failings and dysfunctionalities of African administrations contrasts sharply with the absence of empirical studies on the social lives of public servants, their representations of the public service and their professional practices, so much so that Copans was recently able to suggest ironically that in black Africa there are 'states without civil servants' (Copans 2001). This lack of data is also reflected in the literature we examined, in which the African public servant is depicted in very broad brushstrokes, often to the level of caricature.

Some authors focus on the psychological and moral characteristics of public servants. Thus, while Brownsberger (1983) deplores the profound materialism of Nigerian officials, Sarassoro embarks on a disconcerting typology, making a distinction between the 'inexperienced', who ignore the rules for the management of the state, either on account of their sudden appointment after independence or their lack of education and inability to be trained at a later stage (1979: 28–9); the 'tempted', who know the rules, but are fascinated by easy money (29); the 'dissatisfied', who are drowning in economic and social pressures; the 'naive', who allow themselves to be taken in by marabouts and charlatans; the 'hung-up', the 'servile imitators of the colonizer' (31); the 'contaminated', who adjust their behaviour to that of their superiors (32); and, finally, the 'untouchables', the 'big fish' who have no anxieties. Other analyses focus on personal morality and on the quest to maximize positions by economic actors within an organization and stress that the behaviours of officials are determined by a particular political-administrative environment: first, the strong politicization of the public service, which gives rise to uncertainty and incites administrative actors to stagnate in the structure without taking any risks (Asibuo 1992) and profit from opportunities for illicit gain before being transferred elsewhere (Le Vine 1975b; Fombad 2000; Mbaku 2000a, 2000b; Osei-Hwedie and Osei-Hwedie 2000); second, an administrative context in which control is rare and whose innumerable examples of the impunity of corruption among the powerful compels their subordinates to act in the same way (Werlin 1972; Cohen 1980; Brownsberger 1983; Sindzingre 1994, 1997; Masquelier 2001; Fjeldstad 2003). Finally, reference is also made to the schizophrenic behaviour or 'cultural dualism' (Anders 2005) of African officials who are torn between contradictory or distant normative universes, between compliance with abstract administrative norms and the concrete expectations of their networks of social belonging (Andreski 1968, 1970; Wraith and Simpkins 1970; Werlin 1972; Price 1975; Nembot 2000). However, with the exception of Anders's study, which brings us straight to the heart of the daily manoeuvres by means of which public servants juggle between the contradictory systems of regulations and obligations, the articles and studies quoted do not go beyond the stage of the banal enumeration of what are presented as the immutable traits of African bureaucracies. As opposed to this, the studies on the professional cultures of bureaucrats recently initiated by Olivier de Sardan (2001, 2004) provide new perspectives based on empirical data.

Gaps, grey areas and new research perspectives

The nature of the available sources – the majority of studies are based on fragmented information – and the scarcity of empirical research have given rise to an abundance of publications which approach corruption in a general way and tend to focus on grand corruption and the analysis of policies to overcome it. As opposed to this, apart from a few exceptions – the studies on fraud and road traffic in Zaire (Emizet 1998), the tax system in Tanzania (Fjeldstad 2001, 2003), administrative law in Cameroon (Ngimbog 2002), the parastate companies in Senegal (Casswell 1984) and urban property in Central Africa (Piermay 1986) – there is a lack of studies focusing on a specific sector.

Other gaps in the literature would necessitate new projects and an increase in the number of case studies on: corruption during the pre-colonial and colonial eras; the emergence of NGOs and associative movements, which are immersed in the field of 'good governance', and their unintentional effects; the local appropriation and misappropriation of the discourses and policies of 'good governance'; the popular movements and initiatives and 'bottom up' micro-reforms; the connections between the different national and international levels; and, finally, the links between petty and grand corruption and between corruption and criminality.

A transverse empirical approach to these different issues could lead to an increase in the number of biographies and thus shed light on the processes through which an individual can gradually become 'corrupt' or 'dishonest'. In other words, it could instigate a process in the social sciences similar to that initiated by Achebe in the area of literature with *A Man of the People*.

3

Everyday corruption in West Africa

G. Blundo and J.-P. Olivier de Sardan

An identical system of corruption

The research we carried out in Benin, Niger and Senegal and in the
individual sectors surveyed (customs and transport, justice, health,
public procurements, local tax systems, development projects and
anti-corruption provisions) revealed an astonishing convergence
in terms of both informal administrative functioning and the various 'corrupt' practices – in the broadest sense – facilitated by this
informal functioning. Needless to say, we were expecting to discover
a number of similar behaviours in the different sectors and countries: our own day-to-day encounters with various public services
in Africa had accustomed us to certain 'similarities' in terms of,
for example, the disdain shown to users, the routine *pots-de-vin*
(bribes), the widespread charging of commission, the racketeering
by the police and the system of 'favours', which prevailed far beyond
the boundaries of individual cultures and regimes.

Nevertheless, we thought that countries following post-colonial trajectories as diverse as those of Benin, with its fifteen-year
'Marxist' regime; Niger, where the administrative chieftaincy has
remained in place from colonization to the present day and, at the
time of our fieldwork, is the only form of local power in rural areas;

and Senegal, which, renowned for its democratic experience and long-standing decentralization, would offer relatively contrasting and varied pictures of 'petty corruption' and its contexts. However, this was not the case: even if a Senegalese customs office is not quite the same thing as a Nigerien customs office, the Gaspard Camara hospital in Dakar bears no resemblance to the CNHU hospital in Cotonou, and Benin lawyers are more numerous and experienced than their Nigerien counterparts, we discovered the same 'dominant tendencies' everywhere: the same procedures of corruption (and corruption of procedure), the same unwarranted fees, the same 'arrangements', the same 'tricks'. Furthermore, all of these practices were embedded in the same weakness of the official state, the same widespread clientelism and the same impotence – and in part abdication – on the part of the political elites.

It should also be said that we encountered in many places officials who deplored the gravity of this evil and regretted their impotence. All of the officials we met who had experienced the desire to institute reform at one level or another – and many of them held positions of responsibility – openly acknowledged their failure. The reaction to the presentation of our findings (see Chapter 1) to the inspectors of state, inspectors of taxes, directors of other administrative bodies and other senior officials was revealing in this regard: far from contesting our findings, they tended to augment the analysis. Thus the first major conclusion of our study, which comes before the other less obvious, specialized and technical conclusions to be analysed later, comprises three complementary observations: a widespread system of corruption exists in Africa today (without doubt, at least, in the three countries under consideration[1]); this widespread system of corruption is embedded in an equivalent and widespread system of 'informal functioning' among administrations; and, finally, honest and competent officials who avoid these two systems in their personal professional practice are not currently in a position reform them.

These three elements are inextricably linked. The fact that the system of corruption is embedded in the administrative system renders any attempt at reform particularly difficult and also explains the marginalization of reformers. However, the first question that arises here concerns why the systems of corruption and administrative are more or less identical in all three countries. And the most obvious response to this question is that their historical, economic and political contexts are largely similar.

The same historical, economic and political context

The three countries in question are, in effect, former colonies of French West Africa and thus share the same kind of colonial past.[2] The influence of their colonial heritage with regard to the relationship between the administration and the populations should not be underestimated: the colonial bureaucracy was characterized by despotism and arbitrariness, a contempt for users, inordinate privilege, and the use of intermediaries, corruption and favours. These 'administrative habits' were extended and intensified after independence.[3] Furthermore independence, which was achieved in the context of the Cold War and *Françafrique* (i.e. the system of French neocolonial domination of its former African colonies), saw all three countries benefit from lenient and excessive loans, secured in the 1970s by various revenues from agricultural products and raw materials (e.g. peanuts in Senegal and Niger, cotton in Benin, uranium in Niger). Hence, the global economic crisis of the 1980s affected all three countries with equal force: a radical fall in revenues, the end of the loans, the increasing burden of both foreign and internal debt (non-payment of salaries in Benin and then in Niger; non-payment of suppliers), structural adjustment, downsizing of the public service, very weak recovery of tax, privatizations and devaluation, and so on.

The spread of pluripartism and the freedom of the press in the late 1980s, both of which are largely established and uncontested today,[4] led in all three countries to the emergence of complex forms of 'party-based clientelism', whereby the secret funding of parties (in particular by 'friends in business') plays a central role in political life, elections are largely associated with the large-scale distribution of money (often taking the form of 'vote buying'), and various manoeuvres and tricks are employed by all of the relevant players. The various informal sectors of the economy that elude any kind of taxation or regulation also play a very important role. Finally, the same 'project system', associated with multilateral and bilateral cooperation and NGOs, was established in the three countries for the management of the external aid which became increasingly necessary for the survival of these countries and their avoidance of bankruptcy. This system prompted the creation of privileged functional enclaves – the projects – and the proliferation of 'brokers' (see Bierschenk, Chaveau and Olivier de Sardan 2000) in a 'normal' administrative environment that appears increasingly compromised from the perspective of official norms.

It goes without saying that this summary is extremely brief and that other elements should be taken into account. However, it was necessary to review at least the broad outlines of this historical, economic and political context: although it may not have a determining influence on the corrupt phenomena we will now describe, it is certainly part of their general background.

The embeddedness of corruption

In reality, the *levels of embeddedness* of corruption in the most wide-ranging social, administrative and cultural contexts are multiple. The social phenomena of corruption and their environments can be visualized as a set of concentric circles. The basic forms of corruption – its fundamental mechanisms – are located at the centre. These basic forms are integrated into the more complex strategies of the actors who engage in corruption. The basic forms and strategies together constitute the corrupt practices. They, in turn, are 'set' in the routine functioning of the public services. Finally, all of this is embedded in a series of recurrent social, economic and political logics which themselves unfold in a wider socio-political and socio-economic context.[5]

The basic forms of corruption

The first inventory produced from the findings of our studies describes the fundamental mechanisms on which the common corrupt practices are based. What is involved here are some simple forms of 'corruption' (in the broad sense) which are widespread in the three countries studied and within their different administrations. (The scale of the corruption is the only thing that varies, based on the issues at stake, and these are also highly variable.) We shall now identify the seven 'basic' forms of corruption as they would appear from the perspective that is closest to the practices and representations of local social actors.[6]

'Commission' paid for illicit services

This form of corruption involves the payment of money by users of administrative services to officials who provide access to illicit advantages, exemptions or discounts. Thus the recipient takes his or her 'share'[7] for the provision of an intermediary service or for an intervention on behalf of the user; the payment often incorporates the idea of compensation for the risks involved. The intervention in question results in an unjustified favour being granted to the user, most commonly at the expense of the public purse – for example, the undervaluation of customs declarations – but sometimes also at the expense of competitors, as with the classic case of 'fixed' public tender procedures in which the party that awarded the contract is generally not the most competent or competitive. In other words, the official benefits in part from the illicit gain he helps the user to obtain. In most cases, the commission is 'transactional' – that is, related to the transaction in question; for example, it corresponds to a percentage of the transaction. It is keenly negotiated in some cases but standard in others – for instance, the famous 10 per cent that all recipients of public contracts must pay to the official who helped them to obtain the contract. However, when paid by an official who wishes to hold on to a post that generates an illicit income, the commission may also be based on a rent principle. Thus an appointment to an 'interesting' post which offers regular access to illicit benefits may give rise to the monthly payment of *enveloppes* (bribes) to the sponsor by the recipient. This is one of the most striking examples of systemic corruption.

> In Benin and in Senegal, for example, an appointment to a 'lucrative' customs post, which offers significant opportunities for the rapid accumulation of wealth, results in the periodic payment of sums which are

redistributed within the customs hierarchy. In Senegal, the informal office of assistant collector of market taxes generates a income, from which the collector, the overseer of indoor and outdoor markets and, in some cases also, the collector of municipal taxes also benefit.

Given that it involves mutually beneficial 'complicity' between the official and the service user, the illegitimacy of this practice, which is usually openly acknowledged in general discourse, becomes blurred in practice.

Unwarranted fees for public services

In this case, the official forces the user to pay for the implementation of an act associated with his office. In other words, he sells 'the service' he is supposed to carry out 'free of charge' from the point of view of the user.

> In the three countries studied, it is difficult to obtain a birth certificate anonymously without paying 500 or 1,000 CFA francs to the registry office official for his 'work'.

> In Benin, beneficiaries are 'billed' for the intervention of the police or *gendarmerie*, either indirectly in the form of a request for 'beer money' or 'travel expenses', or directly, for example, when these bodies established 'security contracts' with the private operators of the Free Port of Cotonou (for the surveillance of goods depots under the authority of the Customs and of motor vehicle fleets and for the direction of road traffic at the vehicular exit from the port).

This variant of the forms of internal privatization, which service users sometimes justify on the basis of the absence of salaries – or significant arrears in the case of Niger – is now established practice. It often exploits the diligence or zeal of users and generally takes advantage of their ignorance of the fees officially charged by the administration. Any file that is not 'padded' with a note will be systematically ignored and subject to an indefinite delay. The cost of the service is sometimes clearly stated and defined, and sometimes it is left to the user's discretion and remains entirely unstated.

> The patient will be 'charged' 100 CFA francs by the nurse for a free vaccination.

The temporary secretaries at the Senegalese courts create artificial shortages of forms and administrative documents and then make the users pay, claiming to be willing to 'help them out' by pretending to obtain the documents from other services.

In this case, the fact of paying the official directly 'for the deed' does not equate with an unwarranted illegal service; it is a service that is normally provided free of charge, on which a private charge is imposed. It is the user who pays this private supplementary cost.

Another variant of this form of corruption is 'over-billing' – that is, in the case of a service for which a specific fee is charged, the official adds an additional, illegitimate, fee to be paid by the user.

The health record, which is needed for all consultations, is sold at double the official price by the receptionist.

When giving birth, for which a single all-inclusive fee is charged, the mother will end up having to pay two to three times in excess of the official fee.

When recognized as such, these unwarranted payments are generally condemned by the users of administrative services and they will voluntarily refer to 'rackets' in this context.

The 'gratuity'

While the unwarranted fee – like the 'commission' – is generally based on an *ex ante* transaction, the gratuity is given *ex post* and appears as a spontaneous gesture on the part of the service user. Gratitude is shown to a public official who has 'done his work well' by offering 'something', the sum or form of the gratuity being left to the discretion of the user.

Thus, a nurse who has treated a patient with kindness will receive her *'cola'*; the family of a patient that is satisfied with the treatment prescribed by a doctor at the local health centre will offer some notes which will not be refused.[8]

Obviously, this practice only makes sense in the same administrative universe as that which creates the above-described 'unwarranted fee'. The simple fact of an official doing his or her work with diligence and, moreover, without making a request for payment in advance is generally exceptional and thus merits a reward.

From the perspective of the actors involved – the recipients and the donors – this phenomenon is far removed from corruption and is generally viewed as entirely legitimate.

> During the feed-back seminar in Benin, a customs official who claimed to play an active role in the battle against corruption reported how on one occasion, when he 'worked well' to clear a consignment of goods quickly and in accordance with the rules, the trader expressed his gratitude by giving him 500,000 CFA francs. The customs official contrasted this 'legitimate gift' with corrupt practices.

However, the line between a retrospective 'gift' offered at the discretion of the user and an anticipated, solicited or expected gift, or a favour that knowingly prompts a gratuity, is a fine one. Sometimes users complain about these gifts that they feel obliged to give. In reality, the routine and trivial nature of these gifts would suggest to us that they are more akin to a customary 'tip' than an exceptional 'gift'. Irrespective of this, as a result of its social legitimacy, this practice of offering gifts undoubtedly contributes to the covering of tracks and results in the reintegration of certain forms of bureaucratic interaction into the multiple forms of social exchange.

'String-pulling'

There is universal agreement among users with respect to the fact that the administrative systems in the countries studied are entirely dominated by favouritism at the expense of competence and efficiency. From nominations and appointments, to training, education and the provision of services to users, 'string-pulling', cronyism and 'recommendations' are routine and persistent phenomena which can be found at the heart of all administrative practices. A system that can be described as the 'general exchange' of favours prevails which is as vast as the networks that exist between officials and representatives of the administration.

The general perception of favouritism is highly ambivalent. On the one hand, it is frequently denounced – either in impersonal terms as a system, or in personal terms when the informant in question is or has been a victim of it. On the other hand, however, those who practise it appear to perceive it as being endowed with a profound social legitimacy: the refusal to 'do a favour' for a relative or someone recommended by a relative carries the risk of strong familial and social disapproval. In fact, to the extent that in order to obtain satisfaction the user of a public service must either 'know someone' or 'give something', favouritism is the other side of the coin of corruption. The general view is that the successful procurement of an administrative service without the payment of a bribe or help of a relative constitutes an enormous stroke of luck.

The levy or 'toll'

Unlike the commission and unwarranted fee, the levy or 'toll' is extorted without any kind of intermediation being made or service being supplied, be it legal or illegal.

> The Customs' 'flying squad' collects an 'informal tax' from all hauliers passing through its area for not having to fully unload their vehicles for checking.
>
> A patient presenting at a health centre has to pay a fictitious 'examination fee' to the receptionist.
>
> The pensioner has to 'give something' to be able to withdraw his or her pension.
>
> In order to obtain the start-up payment, the businessman must pay a 'special tribute' to the Treasury official.

This form of corruption is by far the most widely condemned by users in so far as it is perceived as pure and simple extortion. As in the case of unwarranted fees, in this context, users frequently use the term 'racket' (a term that arises frequently in the three countries studied) and even refer to the 'taking hostage' of their time – for example, the 'toll' paid by a driver buys him the freedom to travel in his car.

The 'gombo', petty 'white-collar' theft and the 'sideline'

Petty 'white-collar' theft involves the use of company materials and resources by workers for the completion of private paid work, for example the use of company computers by secretaries for typing academic theses for payment – either during or outside of official working hours. This practice is widespread and systematic in the three countries studied: that is, work premises and resources are widely used by personnel for private ends, either during or after working hours.

The sideline partly corresponds to what is referred to as a *gombo* in the Côte d'Ivoire – the fact of state officials having a supplementary source of income outside of that arising from their official job, which is earned either on top of or in conjunction with their official salary. This supplementary activity is sometimes carried out at the official place of work and sometimes elsewhere, and is frequently pursued to the disadvantage of official tasks, which are temporarily abandoned. The sideline and *gombo* are widely practised throughout the countries studied: health personnel provide private 'consultations' at the public dispensary or at home; more use is made of work telephones for informal business than for actual work-related conversations; Grade A officials seek consultancy work during their holidays, but also during official working hours, and so on. This can be seen as a vast extension of the 'perks of office' involving the – sometimes legal or tolerated – private use of the state's time and resources (e.g. the private use of official cars provided for certain senior officials, the use of the office telephone for personal communications, engagement in consultancy activities, etc.). However, these 'perks' have a strong tendency to become excessive due to their widespread abuse and may even become marketable as a result of being sold to third parties. Nonetheless, this form of corruption is considered as largely legitimate by those who benefit from it.

Misappropriation

What is involved here is not simply the private use of public resources (i.e. 'white-collar' theft), but an actual act of appropriation whereby the public origin of the commodity in question is concealed. Such misappropriation may involve materials – the transition from the 'petty theft' of small items of office supplies to the more serious theft of larger items tends to be a smooth one – or cash, in which case what is involved is a classic case of the 'misappropriation of funds', which is undoubtedly common, but clearly more risky; thus it is seen as very important not to 'get caught'.

> Light pieces of equipment (blood-pressure gauges, thermometers) and heavier ones (electrocardiograph and ultrasound devices) tend to 'escape from' the public hospitals and maternity units only to resurface in the various private clinics in the capitals.

Closely related to theft, which is always viewed negatively, but reluctantly tolerated when perpetrated within family contexts or networks
of acquaintances and severely condemned when anonymous, misappropriation is clearly deemed illegitimate in general discourses;
however, like unwarranted fees, it becomes far more admissible
when the informant knows the perpetrator and, in particular, if the
latter has shown generosity in their family and social circles and
the 'victim' remains an abstract entity, such as the Treasury, aid
donors, the state. In effect, while the forms of extortion described
above involve the dispossession of the individual, misappropriation
involves the dispossession of the 'collective', which is difficult to
present as a victim.

The first four forms of corruption identified above – the commission,
the unwarranted fee, the gratuity and string-pulling – involve *transactions* of either a monetary or a material nature or transactions that
are based on emotional or identity-based ties. This does not apply to
the last three forms, which instead involve forms of extortion (levy
or 'toll') or privative appropriation ('sideline' and misappropriation).
The first four forms of transaction are often interlinked; in other
words, they are hybrid and ambiguous forms frequently encountered
in daily reality: the *ex post* gratuity may be 'expected' or 'solicited'
in so far as it is more akin to a form of unwarranted fee or commission; the over-billing of a medical service may involve not only a levy
but also an unwarranted fee, and, similarly, the 'toll' may conceal
a commission, and so on.

> When a haulier is intercepted by the customs 'flying brigade' and, like
> all hauliers, pays a 'toll' of 10,000 CFA francs to avoid the unloading
> and checking of his vehicle, if he is not 'above board' this 10,000 CFA
> francs may be perceived as a 'commission' paid to the customs official
> for 'turning a blind eye'.

Links may also exist between monetary and non-monetary transactions; that is, a commission or toll may also be paid in kind.

> If a 'development project' finances the renovation of a minister's house,
> it may be interpreted not only as a form of 'misappropriation', but also
> as either a 'commission', i.e. for the adoption by the minister of the
> role of intermediary who will enable the project to benefit from favours

granted by the administration, or a toll which is paid for the simple freedom to operate.

Certain aspects of such transactions are more or less spontaneous, at least from the perspective of the actors involved, for example the gratuity and string-pulling; others are the outcome of negotiation and bargaining, for example the commission and, sometimes, the unwarranted fee; and others again are an expression of an outright power relationship, for example the 'toll'. We also noted that all of these forms of corruption are viewed ambiguously, depending on whether the informant has a direct or indirect relationship with the practice in question. Nonetheless, this does not prevent each individual form of corruption from occupying a specific place on the scale of legitimacy/illegitimacy.

Finally, even if these basic forms of corruption do not directly coincide with the legal categories in force in the three countries studied, the gratuity and the commission can be said to involve largely the offence of 'corruption'; the practices of imposing unwarranted fees and tolls mainly correspond to the offence of 'extortion (by a public servant)'; 'string-pulling' and, more generally, the availing of favours are referred to in legal language as 'influence peddling'; while the 'sideline' is related to the offence of the 'misappropriation of public money'.

Corrupt strategies

These basic forms of corruption generally belong to various medium-term and long-term strategies shared by officials and service users. We will now examine the main modalities at work here.

Corrupt investments

The corrupt investment involves giving some kind of 'anticipatory gift' to a public servant which enables the creation of a kind of – at least symbolic – debt on the part of the latter vis-à-vis the 'benefactor'. A number of corrupt practices are based on such anticipatory gifts or 'investments':

> A newly appointed judge will receive a welcoming gift of an air conditioner from the main local businessman or lawyer. Conversely,

Table 3.1   The basic forms of corruption

Form of corruption	Type of interaction	Degree of legitimacy	Legal category
Gratuity	Spontaneous transaction	Legitimate	Corruption
Commission for illicit service	Negotiated transaction	Highly ambivalent	Corruption
String-pulling, favours, nepotism	Spontaneous transaction	Legitimate	Influence peddling
Unwarranted fee for a public service	Negotiated transaction or extortion	Predominantly illegitimate	Extortion (by a public servant)
Levy or toll	Extortion	Illegitimate	Extortion (by a public servant)
Gombo, 'white-collar crime', sideline	Appropriation	Predominantly illegitimate	Misappropriation of public goods, abuse of social goods
Misappropriation	Appropriation	Highly ambivalent	Misappropriation of public goods, abuse of social goods

another judge may put himself into a situation of indebtedness vis-à-vis the businessmen whose generosity he solicits in the run-up to the festival of Tabaski.

The practices of evergetism[9] are based on this model and generate an obligation of acknowledgement on the part of the beneficiary or, again, a 'right' of recuperation on the part of the donor.

> In Niger when an official who is a native of a village pays for the repair of the pump, it is considered that he has a right to pocket the income it generates.[10]

> In an effort to compensate for the dilapidated state of its fleet of vehicles and its meagre monthly petrol allowance (around 70 litres for an entire brigade), the Senegalese customs administration borrows vehicles and money from large businessmen or hauliers. When fraudulent goods are seized, these private 'sponsors' can then recoup their investment, by

benefiting from the lucrative sale of the goods by public auction, by obtaining a direct return on the seized goods or by obtaining substantial discounts on customs charges when completing import procedures.

The formation of enduring relationships

Participants often try to perpetuate corrupt relations or, in other words, transform them into stabilized social relationships of a 'clientelist' nature. Thus, the exchange of services or favours and daily interaction generate systems of reciprocal obligation between these participants, which, in turn, facilitate the formation of dyads between officials and users, or between officials and intermediaries, which are often highly conducive to corruption.

> Individual hauliers or traders (such as the *Njogaan* in Senegal) will refer to 'my customs man'. They will expect him to be on duty when they cross the border and they will foster a relationship with him that goes beyond a merely 'commercial' one, becoming, for example, a 'joking relationship',[11] or one involving the exchange of small favours or gifts above and beyond any corrupt transactions that may take place.
>
> Similarly, a pregnant woman will try to build personal relations with a midwife, who will become 'her midwife' and who will monitor her labour and deliver her baby.

These enduring arenas of collusion are also favoured by the fact that in certain sectors, such as the law, customs and civil status, the controllers and the controlled – that is, the state authorities and private users of its services – share not only the same locations but also the same normative arena, the same education and the same type of activities.

> We only have to think of the close-knit links between the officials of the registry office and the lobbyists ('*agents d'affaires*') in Senegal; or again, in all three countries, between lawyers, prosecutors and prison guards, and between the customs officials, traders and official or ambulant customs brokers.

This situation has two consequences. First, it is not possible to hold the agents of the state solely responsible for corrupt relationships. In fact, it is more often the users who produce or reproduce these relationships in so far as they benefit from them. Thus, there is widespread mutual agreement on the fact that 'stealing from the state is not stealing from anyone', and that the parties will benefit mutually at the expense of the excluded 'third party' (see Meyer-Bisch 1995). Second, 'parochial corruption' and 'market corruption' cannot be presented as absolute opposites, as Scott (1969) suggests: in the three countries we studied, a permanent tendency to establish social proximity within the context of monetary transactions can be observed.

The rapid accumulation of wealth

The fact of obtaining a 'lucrative' post in any kind of public service is mainly perceived as an opportunity that must be profited from as quickly as possible and to the maximum possible extent; such posts do not last forever and, as we shall see later, the rapid rotation of appointments in administrations fosters this behaviour. Thus, what is involved here are short-term strategies based on the perception that any way or means of accumulating wealth as quickly as possible is good. Given the precarious nature of certain appointments and the pressure emanating from family and social circles, the illicit acquisition of wealth is viewed with a certain level of indulgence by public opinion. Paradoxically, someone who does not avail him- or herself of an opportunity of this kind that presents itself is considered 'crazy', or is suspected of having selfishly 'devoured' the fruit of his or her putative illicit activities.

> In 1999, Senegal was shaken by the discovery of the embezzlement of around 3.5 thousand million CFA francs by a network of seven Treasury tax inspectors. The individual sums embezzled ranged from 132 million to a thousand million CFA francs. Our enquiries revealed that no one in the villages in which the network operated was shocked by the level of wealth acquired by these Treasury officials because they had distinguished themselves in terms of their generosity and largesse.

The mutualization of corruption

In some areas, the agents of the state and the auxiliary agents who assist them in their everyday administrative tasks support each other in their corrupt practices because the existence of an overtly hierarchical chain necessitates the redistribution of such benefits, because their functioning as a team enables the creation of a 'horizontal' partnership, or, again, because the monopolization of the

opportunity for corruption would expose the corrupt official to the
risk of being denounced by colleagues who have been excluded from
the illicit transaction.

> Thus, in the three countries studied, the customs officials divide the
> income obtained from seizures of fraudulent goods on the basis of their
> 'official' salary scales, and in Senegal the members of commissions
> for the awarding of public tenders carefully divide up the bribes paid
> to them by the businessmen. Similarly, many of the duty teams in
> maternity units distribute the proceeds of 'sales' or the over-billing
> of their services.

The manipulation of regulatory regimes

Contrary to what might be expected, illicit transactions and practices
are not associated with an ignorance of the law or regulations on
the part of officials. On the contrary, such practices involve mani-
pulative activities which are facilitated by a good command and
knowledge of the relevant information. Thus, for the most part,
it is only among users that ignorance of the relevant regulations
leads to the acceptance of corrupt practices based on the creation
of unequal power relationships. For the professionals, however, the
manipulation of such regulations is central to the imposition or
provocation of corrupt practices.

The administrative services in the three countries studied have at
their disposal an inadequate or imprecise – and sometimes excessive
– arsenal of rules for the exercising of their functions in the area of
control, sanction and authorization. This is particularly true of the
customs sector. Thus the laws and regulations often leave scope for
extensive discretionary powers. A cheat may be punished or have a
blind eye turned to his activities if the value of the fraudulent act
in question is modest. Alternatively, it may be decided to impose a
sanction on the perpetrator while negotiating with him the sum of the
fine to be levied. In such contexts, in which the laws and regulations
of the administration are rarely made accessible to a wider public
and remain alien to the country's citizens, a situation arises whereby
the monopolization of technical-bureaucratic knowledge combined
with the low level of responsibility assumed on the part of officials
vis-à-vis the public enables the daily negotiation of the powers of the
administration. Thus the lack information available to users about

public services and procedures, combined with the selective application of the regulations, could explain why they tend to adopt a number of circumvention and anticipation strategies as well as account for the emergence of various forms of corruption racket.

However, more sophisticated forms of corruption can also be observed which go beyond the exploitation of users' ignorance of the law and regulations and which identify and exploit the weaknesses in the regulations, thus creating a form of corruption that retains a semblance of legality.

> The case of the allocation of public tenders in Senegal is an example of this form of legalized corruption: by availing themselves of a system of exemptions and the loose interpretation of certain legal texts, the socialist powers (and there is nothing to indicate that the situation has changed with the new regime) were able to allocate contracts for several billion CFA francs without publishing official invitations to tender and based on the establishment of private 'informal' agreements.

This has obvious consequences in the context of the battle against corruption and, like the increasing number of anti-corruption rules and measures, campaigns for the information or training of public servants are not necessarily effective in preventing such activities.

The discursive strategies

Rhetorical skills, including the ability to haggle or bargain, constitute an essential resource in the overall context of corrupt transactions (the importance of popular semiology in the context of corruption is explored in Chapter 4). Corrupt relationships often involve a strong element of bargaining, and this bargaining process concerns not only the sums of money involved but also the rules to be applied or ignored. Thus it could also be said that a minimal command of the 'two languages' – the language of official rules and the language of 'informal' practices – is required. Corrupt transactions are not brutal and anonymous in nature; they have their codes and 'practical rules',[12] their skills, decorum and etiquette. Thus corruption is learned 'on the job': a progressive process of initiation, which constitutes an essential part of the process, must be undertaken.[13]

> Apprentice truck drivers learn not only about mechanics on the 'course' but also about the various practices of petty corruption.

Furthermore, corrupt practices are incorporated into enduring strategies of justification and accusation: justification of the corrupter's own behaviour and accusations concerning the corrupt behaviour of others. In fact it is possible to identify two axes in this context: one extending from legality to illegality and another extending from extreme legitimacy to extreme illegitimacy. Each corrupt practice is perceived by each actor as situated on a certain point along these two axes; however, this perception is not necessarily stable and can vary according to positions and contexts. In other words, the discourses on corruption refer more to 'a negotiated classification of behaviours than [to] an ... inherent quality of behaviours' (Chibnall and Saunders 1977: 139). Thus, the actors in a given social or professional universe may adopt a 'situational' morality in line with their objectives and the informal criteria of interpretation that are shared within this universe. Of course, in the majority of cases they will not fail to recognize the illegal or amoral character of such actions and will simply decide to ignore it or underestimate it (Chibnall and Saunders 1977: 141). Actions that are taken for granted, for example, in the context of the relationships between business people and decision-makers – such as the exchange of favours and gifts and the arrangement of informal meetings outside of the workplace – only become unacceptable when subject to scrutiny in a courtroom.

Similarly, all corrupt individuals are not judged by the same yardstick. Corruption has its own ethics; the customs official and tax collector are perceived as irredeemable because they live from illicit gains. However, this widespread condemnation derives from their 'taxation' and extortion practices and not from their eventual willingness to enter into 'arrangements', however illegal. Thus, while the 'bad' customs officer may be generally perceived as corrupt, the 'good' one is not necessarily characterized as honest and upstanding. He will also 'negotiate' the application of the regulations with the client; however, instead of brutally imposing obligations and prevarications, he will readily exploit 'emotion', affinities and common understanding. Because of this, the bribe he receives from the user is not considered as a levy imposed under constraint; instead, it is seen as a legitimate gratuity paid in acknowledgement of the officer's display of indulgence. Similarly, the embezzler who redistributes his illicit gains will not be widely stigmatized. We also observed that a contrast exists between the general discourses on corruption, which tend to be more critical, and accounts referring to concrete situations or specific actors, which, with the exception of situations in which the informant considers himself a victim, tend to be more tolerant.

The embeddedness of corruption in administrative practices

It is impossible to dissociate corrupt practices, both basic forms and strategies, from an entire configuration of broader practices that are widespread within administrations and state services and determine the real functioning of public services in the three countries studied. In other words, the corrupt practices are embedded in a context of 'daily governance', from which they are more or less inseparable. The routine management practices within administrations and public services 'accommodate' and foster corruption. Thus it makes sense to present the most important elements of this public management which not only concerns the characteristics of individual agents of the state, but is also the product of the interaction between officials, users and intermediaries.

The institutionalization of voluntary work and recourse to administrative brokers[14]

In all three countries studied, the structural adjustment policies and increasing competition between parallel bureaucracies generated by the development cooperation system have undermined the administrations, which frequently lack motivated personnel and have difficulties in fulfilling the main functions of the state. Thus recourse to voluntary services is essential. However, even when state officials are sufficient in number, they still hand over part of their work to unpaid auxiliaries. For their part, these unregulated and unpaid workers, who do not feature in any organizational charts, find indirect means of subsistence – for example, small gratuities from personnel and users, sidelines, commission – and also hope to find formal employment in the administration at some point.

All of the services studied managed to function thanks to the support of non-administrative personnel of ill-defined status, who are sometimes engaged in a 'voluntary' capacity for around twenty years and fulfil secretarial tasks in the courts, drive vehicles for customs officers, provide numerous services in health centres and collect municipal taxes on behalf of the official collectors.

These auxiliaries, who are joined by an equally informal multitude of 'administrative brokers' (lobbyists, canvassers of clients, etc.), have a triple role to play:

1. They would appear to play a functional role in facilitating processes involving the users of state services or the tasks of the official personnel: they help to accelerate procedures (at the cost, however, of users who do not have access to their services) and sometimes contribute to their 'humanization'. They may protect their clients by trying to prevent the imposition of a sanction or by increasing their chances of winning a case or asserting their rights. They also facilitate the personalization of administrative processes and thus provide reassurance for the citizen in the face of an administration perceived as 'all-powerful'.
2. They reproduce the 'local professional culture'[15] with its habits, improvisations and tricks. Whereas the officials come and go, they always remain in place and hence constitute the 'memory' of their services.
3. They highlight the 'informalization' of the public service and heighten the blurring of the boundaries between the administration and the marketplace, between public and private services and between the informalization around the state and within the state. While they may not always be the vectors of corruption, they can nonetheless contribute to the euphemization and spread of illicit practices. As well as facilitating corrupt interaction between actors who are highly unequal from a statutory point of view, the intervention of brokers makes it possible to cover tracks and conceal the proof of illicit transactions,.

The dividing of the administration

This phenomenon, which is the corollary of the informalization of the public service, is particularly observable on two levels.

The futility of formal hierarchies   The gap between the information about administrative hierarchies provided by the organizational charts and the actual division of labour within these bodies is often spectacular. In reality, it is almost impossible to find out who actually does what by consulting lists of personnel and focusing on the official status of state officials. In some cases, officials are overqualified and carry out tasks inferior to their levels of education and expertise. More common, however, is the phenomenon of underqualification, which often extends to cases whereby the incumbent is entirely unqualified to carry out the task assigned to him or her.

> In the course of our study, we encountered municipal tax collectors who featured as 'office boys' or 'junior clerks' in the municipal organizational chart, court drivers acting as interpreters at hearings, ward orderlies assisting at births, temporary secretaries assuming the role of registrars, canvassers passing themselves off as lawyers, and stretcher-bearers or unskilled workers acting as medication advisors and directing patients to unofficial pharmacies.

Overall, an upward 'shift' can be observed in the hierarchies as well as in an unwarranted valorization of minor positions, which are characterized at the same time by their polysemy.[16] Within the administrative arena, it is a small step from the valorization of the officially sanctioned voluntary worker to the toleration of the informal broker (canvasser, *agent d'affaire*). This shifting of functions obviously creates a considerable air of vagueness around the terms and conditions associated with a post or status, and around the rules that are supposed to regulate professional behaviour. The resulting law of improvisation is conducive to the proliferation of illegal transactions.

The 'emic' classification of administrative posts   In addition to the functional and spatial classification of bureaucratic organizations, state actors have added a classification which is based on their day-to-day experience: all customs officials, gendarmes, Treasury officials and court employees can distinguish with ease between 'lucrative' posts and 'dry' posts. The former provide access to a high level of transactions, whereby the holder has direct contact with users – that is, posts in the field as opposed to strictly administrative posts.

They enable the very rapid accumulation of private income and their allocation is subject to fierce competition and is often based on logics of political reward and/or private commission levied on the associated income.

> Thus, for the customs official who is close to retirement, a posting to the Free Port of Dakar represents a primary aspiration; however, failing this he may be happy with one of the Gambia border posts.
>
> As opposed to this, the appointment of a Nigerian customs official to the Niamey oil authority is perceived as being akin to being thrown on the scrap heap.

In contrast, the 'dry' posts, which offer few opportunities for earning extra income, tend to be located in remote isolated corners where the quality of life is mediocre and where officials run the risk of being quickly forgotten by the hierarchy. As a result, postings to such locations are perceived as banishment in atonement for transgressions, professional errors and political disgrace.

The creation of queues

One of the main manifestations of the structural indifference of bureaucratic organizations[17] is the way that they force their users to adapt to their schedules and to submit to or accept the timetables set by their officials: 'the user's time is not as important as that of the official' (Hertzfeld 1992 : 162). Thus the personal schedules of users are seriously disrupted by different forms of bureaucratic indifference, such as instructions to return the following day or the impossibility of predicting the duration of administrative procedures. In other words, it is the officials who control the duration and speed of interaction with users. While time may be a resource availed of by all administrations to 'pace' the supply of public services, in the context of a dysfunctional bureaucracy it becomes a central strategic resource to be exploited in corrupt exchanges.

Thus, while the lack of qualified personnel results in an excessive burden on state services and the unavoidable formation of long 'queues' for the completion of the most insignificant of procedures, it is also possible for officials to create bottlenecks deliberately. Therefore, in addition to the classic excuse of the file languishing at the bottom of the pile, administrations have several other options for 'hijacking' their users' temporal resources and then offering a faster individual service for payment. In the case of control bodies, such as the customs, police and gendarmerie, this situation usually involves the threat of the application of certain 'weapons' in their regulatory arsenal.

> The delays caused by checks and controls (escorts, unloading, systematic searches) are the cause of significant economic losses for traders and taxi drivers. The officials, who are fully aware of this, abuse their authority and oblige drivers to 'give something'. In Senegal, even passengers contribute so that the vehicles they are travelling in can avoid such delays.

The administrations can also play on the 'natural' complexity or slowness of procedures, as illustrated by the following examples taken from our study of the machinery associated with the legal and public procurement systems.

> In the three countries, successive deferrals of hearings, for which the judge has sole responsibility, mean that hundreds of detainees are left rotting in jail while awaiting judgments.
>
> In Senegal, due to the delays that arise in the production of the first authentic copies of court judgments by the offices of the court clerks, the defendants end up paying bribes to the court clerks (on top of the official documentation fee) so that they can have their judgments removed from the piles of judgments awaiting processing.
>
> In Benin and Senegal, the stages leading to the receipt of a final payment constitute a real obstacle course for business people. Opportunities are created for illicit payments at every stage (signature of confirmation of receipt and control, processing of the file by the financial services, payment of the sum by the Treasury) through the staging of delays, hold-ups, financial problems, etc.

Finally, the functioning of the administration can also be hindered by various forms of structural, organized and simulated shortages of money.

> In the Benin health system, actual or fictitious breakdowns in the supply of medication are exploited, recurring breakdowns of the radiology equipment at the CNHU are simulated and a fictitious shortage of hospital beds is created by nursing auxiliaries so that they can reserve beds for their private clientele.

In Dakar, the businessman who avoids entering into an illegal arrangement with the commissions which award public tenders will find himself faced with fictitious breakdowns in the supply of tender documents. Having been forced to make several visits to the department before finally obtaining the documents, he will not have enough time to complete his tender application correctly and will, therefore, be heavily penalized.

The personalization of administrative relationships

The contact between service users and the administration is indelibly characterized by distrust and uncertainty. The need for protection against possible prevarication or obstacles always forces users to seek to establish relationships with the officials. They never address the official behind the hatch directly and make no attempt to find out about 'normal' procedures, but start by finding out about the real or fictitious relations they might be able to establish in preparation for the procedure to be completed. In brief, the users adopt these strategies to try to personalize their administrative relationships because they are otherwise characterized by an extreme ambivalence, ranging from harsh and inhumane treatment to total solicitude, with various forms of clientelism in between.

Ambivalence: dehumanization and 'over-personalization'   In effect, anonymity is a factor of exclusion when it comes to public services, irrespective of the specific service involved. The anonymous user is ignored, badly received, often humiliated and sometimes harshly treated. Despite the fact that, according to the administrative regulations, the standard functional relationship between public officials and users should be anonymous in nature, the only kind of relationship that actually works is the personalized one. The anonymous user is treated 'like an animal' while the 'recommended' user is taken in hand, assisted and sometimes even made a fuss of.

Thus pregnant women who present to the maternity services of large hospital centres in Benin face two scenarios: on the one hand they can receive humiliating, insulting and negligent treatment, and on the other a personal and relatively efficient service thanks to the 'sponsorship' of the midwives. The 'sponsored' mothers will be presented and entrusted to colleagues as 'protégés'.

Thus two extreme relational universes exist, and the officials in the field move between them with complete ease. Little scope remains for neutral and purely technical and professional relationships. One characteristic of corruption is that it can act as a bridge between these two extreme universes. It can intervene at both the level of the anonymous relationship and that of the personalized relationship. Corruption is, in effect, a means of 'overcoming' the handicap of anonymity or compensating for it. However, it also offers a way of 'personalizing' a relationship to the extent that a marketable relationship or commercial transaction is not at all at odds with a personalized relationship. On the contrary, the two can be entirely compatible, as can be observed every day at the market where clients will have their 'own' vendors. The giving of a 'gift' or 'commission' to an obliging relative, willing friend or a benevolent acquaintance is standard practice. As opposed to this, the imposition of a 'toll' is reserved for anonymous contacts.

Clientelism   In the world of personal relationships, some relationships are clearly more 'horizontal' and others more 'vertical' in nature. The systems of allegiance that exist within the administration are multiple and dense. They range from personal debts for services rendered (and the more senior the actor the more services he 'renders'), through familial and regional networks to the enormous influence of the political parties. Because of this, few officials are truly independent. They are all subject to pressures which they are generally unable to resist due to their involvement in a regime of debt or obligation.

With the democratization processes of recent years, the three countries examined in our study have seen a spectacular increase in the significance of political clientelism:[18] when it comes to appointments, from top ministerial level to that of the lowliest office boy, a membership card of the party in power is a more important qualification than professional competence. The 'acknowledgement' of services provided to the party infiltrates all political and administrative acts. Of course, political clientelism does not make the other forms of clientelism disappear; it joins them, encompasses them and often dominates them. Corruption clearly benefits from clientelism. It follows in its tracks, surrounds it and even reinforces it.

Impunity

Impunity is a direct consequence of clientelism, which can defeat any attempt at reform, in particular on the level of the war against corruption. In effect, the imposition of any sanction will pose a problem because the individual being sanctioned will be integrated to a greater or lesser extent into a protective clientelist network. Thus, anyone who tries to impose sanctions will immediately find himself targeted by multiple 'interventions', or even threats, from his peers or from more senior actors. In most cases, he will also find himself being repudiated by his own hierarchy, which will order the release of the perpetrator or suspension of the punishment. This is an important factor that dissuades actors from implementing the regulations as intended. Furthermore, an official who is sanctioned is generally only guilty of acts which numerous other actors in his network also engage in. Hence, the sanctioning of one individual represents a threat to an entire system.

> In Senegal shady tax collectors who get caught in the net of the municipal police are immediately released by order of the mayor. The collectors, who are selected from the mayor's political clientele, pay over part of their illicit gains into the informal funds of the municipalities.
>
> Similarly, the *'agents d'affaires'*, i.e. lobbyists, who lurk around the corridors of the courts and sell temporary rights or false birth certificates, are never definitively removed from these locations because they constitute the intermediary link in the corruption chain, between those subject to the law and the men of the law.

This is why impunity is the rule and sanction the exception. Thus the question arises as to whether the occasional implementation of the laws and regulations which are otherwise ridiculed on a day-to-day basis by all and sundry is not based on motivations that have nothing to do with justice or the smooth running of services – that is, the settling of accounts, elimination of nuisances, refusals to pay up, redistribute or show allegiance and so on. This represents a serious problem in the context of the war against corruption.

The absence of controls and 'every-man-for-himself-ism'

Each official lives in a kind of bubble, which he sometimes shares with one or two others and in which he organizes his activities in a way that appears most convenient to him. He does not have to provide detailed reports on his work – the hierarchy is generally content with the 'absence of problems' and sometimes in receipt of a small income from its subordinates. In general, the quality of the services provided by an official is not subject to any form of control. General meetings of services are virtually unknown, professional emulation does not exist and the discussion of practices and collective organization is non-existent. Like professional negligence and disdain towards users, corrupt practices can prosper in each individual 'bubble'. So long as there is no threat to the comfortable existence of colleagues or superiors, there is no accountability to them. In fact, 'team play' is either entirely or almost completely lacking within the public service: everyone 'goes his own way' and does not authorize anyone to comment on his style of play. It has come to a point where involvement in the work of another, even that of a subordinate, is widely viewed as improper, inappropriate and even dangerous. It should be stressed that this culture of 'every man for himself' is clearly linked with the 'culture of impunity', and, at the level of corrupt practices, is reinforced by the human and material underresourcing of the various internal control bodies created by the governments of the three countries studied in their attempts to fight corruption (see Mathieu 2002: ch. 9): derisory petrol supplies, defective vehicles, non-replacement of employees when sick or retired and the complete absence of career structures, which sometimes lead to the identification of public posts as dead ends.

'Privilegism'

Certain posts within the public service come with a number of 'perks', such as a car, a house, bonuses,[19] which are often stretched as far as possible and sometimes excessively so. However, to the extent that they signal a distance between the user and the official, these 'perks' also act as forms of 'distinction'.[20] They draw attention to the fact that one is dealing with a man (or woman) of power, an important person, someone 'who is not just anybody'. This can be referred to as 'privilegism'. By extension, access to a public post, even a minor one lacking the advantages of official function, becomes synonymous with access to extra resources and, hence, to a 'superiority' vis-à-vis mere users that should be clearly demonstrated. Furthermore, the generally low official level of salaries, in particular as compared with the salaries of the expatriates dealt with regularly by the indigenous public, results in even greater emphasis being placed – both symbolically and materially – by officials on the advantages of their office and on the privileges associated with a post, which tend to be perceived as a legitimate 'due'.

Sometimes this 'privilegism' is combined with a significant margin for manoeuvre granted by law or regulation to the holder of an office, for example the 'deep-seated' conviction of the judge, the transactional powers of a customs official, the freedom of choice of doctors with regard to the treatments they choose to apply. This reinforces considerably the arbitrary exercise of official functions and the privileges associated with them.

The social and cultural logics

In addition to providing fertile ground for the perpetration of corrupt acts, the administrative customs and habits presented above belong to a group of 'ordinary' rules, practices, representations and behaviours that are part of social life in general, and, although they do not involve corruption in themselves, they 'communicate' with corrupt relationships, 'facilitate' or tolerate them. Were it not for the risk of heading in the direction of more or less explicit 'culturalism', which in shifting the responsibility for corruption to local cultures would be both unjustified and incorrect, it would be possible to refer here to a 'socio-cultural' environment which favours corruption in certain ways. Instead, we shall content ourselves with providing a list of 'socio-cultural logics'[21] – for the most part non-traditional, that is they were adopted or developed under colonization or after independence – which, *in certain circumstances* (for example, in the case of the pre-existence of a minimal level of corruption or the showing of bad example by elites), may contribute to the extension or legitimization of everyday corruption. We are treading a fine line here between the excessive attribution of blame to the 'customs' in force and, conversely, the untenable negation of any link between corruption and current practices.[22]

Normative pluralism

The importance of normative pluralism, both in Africa and in other places,[23] has already been highlighted. It fosters negotiation not only within a consensual system of rules but also on the rules of the game, which are never unique. In other words, it is rare for a single system of rules to be established, and it is more common for actors to navigate between several possible applicable rules based on their resources, strategies and contexts. It should also be added here that there is a significant gap – which exists everywhere, but is more obvious in Africa – between the official or publicly assumed rules (themselves plural in nature) and the 'real' rules based on local professional cultures, bureaucratic customs, traditions and routines, accepted ruses and practical knowledge, skills and other '*coping strategies*'.[24]

Normative pluralism can also be found in the context of both social life 'outside of work' (see the disputes concerning marriage ceremonies or conflicts concerning land) and professional life in the public sector, in particular, which itself is permeable to external rules. Thus the clear and fundamental separation between public rules (relating to the public function and public service) and private rules (i.e. social norms in force outside of the service) inherent to all bureaucracies is permanently eliminated. This fluidity and variety of both formal and informal rules – what is involved here is not an absence of 'rules', which would be indicative of anomie, but instead an obvious excess of rules, which open the playing field to the maximum – is clearly favourable to the dissolution of the boundary between licit and illicit practices and between so-called 'white', 'grey' and 'black' corruption (see Heidenheimer 1990).

The widespread exchange of services and 'putting the person before the institution'

The relational capital of individuals is particularly extensive in Africa. This has been noted frequently in the context of the extended family; however, it also applies in other areas, for example one only has to consider the importance of '*promotionnaires*' (a term that covers the personal networks established from the stage of secondary or even primary school). The investment in sociability is both a resource and a constraint, and it has to be reactivated in numerous festive, ritual and familial circumstances. Given the numerous obligations involved in the maintenance and reproduction of all kinds of relational networks, they are a source of incessant preoccupation in the context of daily life. One of the properties of these relational networks is that the exchange of services takes place not only between relatives and friends but also between 'acquaintances', in the widest sense, who include anyone 'recommended' by a relative or friend, by a friend of a relative, or by a friend of a friend. This obligation 'to render service' is supported by an entire social moral code and this leads to a widespread system of services and counter-services, in which each individual is 'involved'.

Thus we can see here how the above-described 'favouritism' in the public services is part of the wider systems of favours and counter-favours that punctuate the entire arena of social life. As a result, its exclusion from professional life is made difficult, if not impossible, without insisting on a complete rupture between normal social life and professional life. That is because, to the extent that the institutions and organizations gradually disappear behind the people and the procedures behind the actors involved, in a way professional life is modelled on social life.

Intermediation and brokerage

More than in other parts of the world, a number of social activities in Africa, ranging from amorous relationships and marriage, magico-religious practices and the exercise of power, to service and small business activities, involve the intervention of 'intermediaries'. The activities associated with development aid are not immune to this, indeed 'development brokerage' is a thriving activity (see Bierschenk, Chauveau and Olivier de Sardan 2000), and we have already seen how the relationship between the administration and these, often informal, intermediaries, who proliferate in front of customs offices and around the law courts, works. It is clear that this social extension of brokerage, not only on the doorsteps of the public services but also in the context of a very wide range of social activities, creates a situation conducive to the spread of brokerage in the context of corruption, which in turn paves the way for corrupt activities.

Endless gifts and presents, ostentation and 'over-monetization'

The proliferation of occasions in the context of everyday social life on which people are obliged to put their hands in their pockets, and the increasing monetization of the small gifts offered on these occasions, including those given to close friends and family members, have prompted the widespread consideration that the 'small sums' paid to state officials for carrying out their functions are merely a variation on these standard gifts and an extension of the 'oblative propriety' that permeates daily life. Added to the significant number of dependants who have to be supported, this need to 'maintain one's rank' – on pain of being affected by 'shame'[25] – or simply to demonstrate a minimum of good manners and generosity, which go hand in hand, means that public servants and other socio-professional groups are under constant financial pressure, especially in view of the gap between these endless demand for cash and the very low salaries they are paid. For convenience, and not from a desire to introduce specialized economic terminology, we shall use the term 'over-monetization' to describe this pressure that fuels the permanent quest for cash – that is, for loans, 'a helping hand', small jobs and corruption.

Along the same lines, the prevailing spirit of ostentation and 'ostentatious generosity' constitutes an additional source of financial pressure that tends to be exerted directly by the immediate family – parents, spouses and children. Thus it is possible to observe the serious inflation of the 'gestures and presents' expected in family and close social contexts, ranging from small everyday gestures – for instance the inevitable 'taxi money' that must given to visitors – and more exceptional and astonishing contributions, such as the millions of CFA francs that funerals cost in some places and marriages cost everywhere, to the footing of the bills for the new clothes and finery required for every festival or a parent's pilgrimage to Mecca. The payment of the costs of health care also adds to these financial pressures: the cost of treatment of a common disorder easily exceeds 10 per cent of a secretary's monthly salary.[26]

The social cost of integrity

These diverse logics constitute an undeniable and ongoing presence in the social life of Benin, Niger and Senegal and form a virtually imperceptible continuum with corrupt practices. They do not obligate, and are clearly compatible with honest behaviour. However, they contribute to the high social cost of honest behaviour, to the extent that according to these logics the refusal to engage in corruption is perceived as a lack of propriety or a break with 'normal' solidarity. It is our belief that one of the main problems revealed by our studies can be identified here: complete integrity is a luxury or virtue that is beyond the scope of the majority of the citizens of Benin, Niger and Senegal under current circumstances. Or, to put it in oversimplified terms: only the rich or sainted can allow themselves the luxury of integrity. The pressure created by the surrounding social environment pulls people in the other direction; it is pushing the spread of corrupt practices and their integration into standard behaviour. To refuse a 'gift' is to offend the donor; to refuse a privilege or special favour to a 'recommended' person is to contravene the fundamental rules of courtesy; to refuse to benefit from the 'advantages of office' that have been hugely extended by colleagues is to show arrogance towards them; not to accept the usual little tricks that help round off family finances at the end of the month is to trigger domestic scenes, and so on.

The following two anecdotes, which arose in the context of other studies, are particularly illustrative in this context:

The two old women   Two old women in a Nigerien village, Kouli and Kouti, were in charge of selling the water from the foot-operated water pump by the bucket. They were appointed by the committee for the management of the pump. They were both given nicknames. Kouli, who refused any favours and did not allow a woman to take water without paying, was nicknamed *'ceferia'*, the ungodly one, and Kouti, who was more flexible and accommodating, became known as *'alsilaama'*, the believer.[27]

The well-rewarded doctor   A general practitioner in a public health centre in Burkina Faso receives a patient to whom he announces a piece of good news: according to the test report, the patient does not have AIDS. After the meeting with the patient, he receives me [i.e. the researcher]. The doctor has a 5,000 CFA franc note in his hand. He shows me his gift: 'Ah! You see, I am truly happy, he has just given me a present.' He opens the door of the office and shows the note to the patients waiting in the waiting room. 'Ah! truly, he must be thanked, he has just given me a present. Thank him for me.' The patients thank the benefactor and give their blessings. The doctor returns to his chair; he pockets the note and tells me that one day he went home with 60,000 CFA francs.[28]

Corruption and the transformation of the state

The privatization and informalization of public services

Embedded in a 'dysfunctional' context of the supply of public services, and legitimated by social and cultural logics, the corrupt practices outlined here are ultimately part of the profound process of transformation under way in the African state. This transformation is currently heading in the direction of the progressive privatization and informalization of public services. In other words, we are witnessing the emergence of new forms of *informal privatization* and the *progressive institutionalization* of the informal as a means of the day-to-day management of the state. The processes of informal privatization differ enormously from the formal privatization policies currently being implemented on the African continent – whether or not they are freely chosen or a response to external pressures is of little importance. We are not interested here in the public initiatives undertaken by the state, which involve the seeking of assistance from private companies and the delegation of some of the state's former functions to these companies, as is the case with the partial privatization of the customs administration (see the transfer of the control of customs valuation to the SGS in Senegal, Cotecna in Niger and Bivac in Benin) and the privatization of public companies in a number of sectors (e.g. water, electricity, telecommunications).[29]

The formal process of delegation of state functions to private actors is being joined or substituted by an informal phenomenon involving the private appropriation of procedures and means which remain the prerogatives of the state in appearance more than in reality. Thus, what we are witnessing here is the de facto informal privatization of administrative action, which can be triggered either internally, by being carried out on the initiative of state agents, or externally – that is, arising from interference of an economic or political nature in the machinery of the state by external actors. It is also the result of localized negotiations and arrangements that are relatively autonomous with respect to the centralized power, although widespread throughout the territory. What is involved here is the privatization of the administration 'by segment' (Hibou 1999: 18).

Internal informal privatization

Obviously, this category of privatization includes practices such as the private use of public material, in other words the practice of petty 'white-collar' theft (see above) and the directing of users of public health structures towards private clinics controlled by public health officials – an activity that is clearly related to the offence of 'insider trading', to the extent that a relational capital and social capital acquired as a result of the holding of a public office are exploited for private interests – and the different forms of unwarranted payment solicited by public officials for provision of a service that they would normally be expected to provide free of charge as part of their official duties (see above), and extends right up to the 'leasing of a public service', such as the personalized protection programme proposed by the police and gendarmes to the economic operators of the Free Port of Cotonou. These practices rest on the idea that the services supplied by the public administration may be 'appropriated', 'leased' or 'sold' by its officials for their own benefit.

Other more underhand and less visible practices implemented in the context of the internal informal privatization of the state involve the *self-financing of administrative services* by their officials.

In view of the lack of operating resources at their disposal, some heads of customs brigades in Senegal invest private resources so as to enable the service to continue operating. More than a straightforward reflection of dedication or excessive zeal, this is motivated by the competition between customs brigades, career advancement and access to the bonus system and to sources of illicit wealth.

The same principle guides the local representatives in Senegal, who pay the deficit in the rural tax collection on behalf of those liable for tax so as to obtain from the state a fund awarded to communities that achieve 100 per cent tax recovery. The fund in question is then redistributed among the counsellors, who consider it a legitimate payment for the work carried out.[30]

In Benin, the public health centres use private medication obtained by the health-care workers using their own 'personal resources', who then pocket the proceeds from their sale.

Thus the administrative post becomes de facto a simple tool for the accumulation of wealth that must be maintained and invested in so that it can perform well. This is not very far removed from the 'venality of office' of the French *Ancien Régime*. However, this end is obscured by the fact that the public servants appear to be trying to overcome the dysfunction of the administration.

External informal privatization

Similarly, this form of privatization arises from the destitution, unproductiveness and inefficacy that are characteristic of the public administrations of the three countries studied, which solicit certain services from private operators: for example, the Senegalese police, gendarmerie and courts use the drivers of public transport vehicles to distribute their administrative mail. Similarly, these vehicles are borrowed by the court police for transporting detainees and for the organization of raids. The same practices are found in Benin. The administration must return these favours and curry favour with its sponsors and informal service providers, for example by author-izing the overloading of vehicles or by waiving charges on drivers who cause accidents. The same privileged but informal relationship between public agents and private operators underlies the modern practices and interests of *evergetism*, whereby, for example, large business interests finance the operation of customs offices and re-ceive in exchange privileged access to goods that are seized by the customs authorities and resold at auctions, which are merely public in name.

Finally, the widespread presence of *administrative brokers* (who may or may not be included in the administration's organizational charts) and *auxiliary personnel* also represents a form of informal privatization of the state. Their omnipresence within the bureau-cratic machinery indicates that, given that they are equally indis-pensable to both the service users and the bureaucrats, these are actors who cannot be ignored. This progressive institutionalization of informal phenomena in state structures paradoxically facilitates their continued existence and continuity of function. However, it also contributes to the reorientation or delegitimization of the actions of administrative services which are subject to the new rules of operation imposed by the *'agents d'affaires'*, *klébés*, canvassers and other auxiliary personnel.[31] These forms of – internal or external – informal privatization have the following characteristics in common:

- they are not the exclusive domain of the agents of the state, but the product of the interaction between officials, intermediaries and the users of public services;
- they originate in sporadic arrangements facilitated by the recourse – shared by different public, private and intermediary partners – to 'practical rules', behaviours and logics that are alien to the public arena;
- this group of rules, behaviours and logics has something to do with ways in which the so-called 'informal' sector of the economy functions. Bargaining and haggling are the preferred modes of operation in this sector; low profit margins are accepted (i.e. modest bribes), agreements are regulated in a friendly manner and on the basis of the principle of orality (see Niane 2000: 7) and procedures are replaced by personal relationship;
- this gives rise to the widespread dispersal of the decisions taken by the administration (see also Hibou 1999: 22).

The criminalization of administrative structures

Along with the mechanisms of petty corruption, we encountered other crimes and offences perpetrated against the state, which, although they do not qualify for comprehensive inclusion in the 'complex of corruption', maintain close relationships with it. In effect these crimes and offences sustain corruption while, at the same time, they are a product of it and bear witness to an ongoing process of criminalization of administrative structures.[32] Analysis of the journalistic documentation uncovered during our research in the field highlights the significance of fiscal fraud and all kinds of forgery in the three countries studied – for example, trafficking in foreign currency, the printing of counterfeit notes, the forgery of official documents, trafficking in false passports, the sale of medical certificates and the forgery of examination certificates.

In Senegal there is nothing easier than obtaining the certificates and documents necessary to create a company 'which exists on paper' and which can submit for and win 'fixed' invitations to tender. In Senegal, again, a Kaolack businessman who belonged to a fraudulent network that was dismantled in 1999 and had embezzled the Public Treasury of over 1.5 thousand million CFA francs was able to leave Senegal a free man thanks to the purchase of a diplomatic passport.

Thus 'fakes and the use of fakes' are common currency and practice. This is a cause of corruption of public officials and in turn facilitates the concealment of embezzlement and other irregularities. For, as several inspectors and auditors said to us, most of the time everything is normal and perfectly documented on paper. It has often been said that in Africa the administration operates on the basis of orality. This does not mean that it does not produce written documents, but that the most 'real' contracts, most solid agreements and most respected regulations remain on an oral level – the level of the given word, the unwritten ethic of corruption. The written report, financial report and official record of deliberation serve to maintain the formal appearance of compliance with administrative procedures, which are hence stripped of their original content. The written word is often falsified to varying extents. This 'petty criminality'[33] sometimes overlaps with 'petty corruption', but the two should not be confused; similarly, serious crime often overlaps with large-scale corruption, but the two are not identical.

The vicious circle of corruption

The spread of the observed practices, their deep-rootedness in the public service and their embeddedness in the social logics that contribute to their legitimation have undoubtedly led to the emergence of a kind of vicious circle. From the perspective of the user of the administration, corruption is often a way of managing and overcoming uncertainty; however, at the same time, it contributes to the intensification of this uncertainty. As we have seen, the uncertainty is permanent and arises from a number of factors: the impenetrability of the regulations adopted by administrative services and the endless scope for their manipulation; the normative pluralism that permeates both society and the administration; the ambivalence of the relation-ships between state officials and the public, which is often abused (if the user is anonymous) and sometimes fostered (depending on social or political status, potential for corruption and how close the person in question is to the official in question); interventionism on the part of political and/or religious networks which can influence decisions in the area of justice, lead to the granting of procurement contracts, close or open prison doors; and the enormous financial pressure on individuals to meet social obligations ('over-monetization'), which obliges everyone to engage in a constant quest for money.

For the user, the defence available against this feeling of pre-cariousness consists in making sure of one's protectors and guides to the nooks and crannies of the bureaucratic system and the in-termediaries who intercede on one's behalf. On some occasions, it will be possible to benefit from relations, friends, acquaintances, clientelist and dependency links, on others it will be necessary to buy protection, to pay the 'price of the *cola*' and 'grease someone's palm'. The fact that everyone believes that they must protect themselves against the dysfunction of public services using favours or corrup-tion means that everyone exploits their personal relationships or indulges in corrupt practices all the time. Thus, the more widespread and common corrupt practices become, the greater the dysfunc-tion and uncertainty that prevails with respect to the outcome of administrative procedures and the greater the reach of corruption. If corruption is everywhere, in order for the individual to protect himself or herself he or she must engage in it on a preventive basis. The proliferation in the three countries studied of marabouts and charlatans specializing in the supply of talismans that supposedly provide protection against the corruption of others and conceal the holder's own corrupt practices is proof of the extent to which this vicious circle of corruption has become rooted in the daily lives of their citizens.

Conclusion: what kind of state is involved?

Most of the elements we have analysed at the different levels of embeddedness of corruption are not 'specifically African phenomena' and can all be found, to a greater or lesser extent, in the countries of the northern hemisphere. The perception of the prevalence of unwarranted payments, favours, string-pulling and normative plurality also exists, for example, in France and the United States. In terms of the simple 'presence or absence of acts' there is little or nothing that distinguishes African corruption or its embeddedness in the administrative arena and social life from European corruption. However, the scale does vary considerably, as well, of course, as the 'style' (i.e. codes and manners) and the forms of legitimization used. It is the scale and the widespread nature of these features, and not their mere presence, that are unique to African countries. They characterize a 'petty corruption' that is not nearly as widespread in Europe, but may be found in similar forms on other continents. There is a kind of qualitative threshold that is overstepped. Thus, if petty corruption and the informal functioning of the state are contained and relatively limited to certain spheres (as is the case in Europe) or extremely widespread (as in Africa), it can be assumed that the states in question are no longer of the same type.

The case of 'large-scale corruption' is obviously different, to the extent that this is a globalized phenomenon with its preferred sectors – construction, public works, arms, and communication links with international criminal trafficking and other organized crime networks. Africa undoubtedly plays its part in this kind of corruption through the shamelessness and greed of certain predatory regimes and the significance of their links with former colonizers.[34] The examination of this issue lies beyond our competencies in terms of empirical research.

The following question remains to be answered: against the background of the criminalization and privatization of the state (see Hibou 1999), neo-patrimonialism (Médard 1990, 1998) and 'the politics of the belly' (Bayart 1989), exactly what kind of state are we dealing with here? The state in Africa clearly does not function like that in Europe or North America; however, it has obvious affinities with the former Communist states as well as certain Asian, Middle Eastern and Latin American states. An entire body of political science literature is devoted to the pinpointing of this difference and to the creation of a label for the contemporary African state.

There is no shortage of adjectives in circulation: neo-patrimonial, imported, feeble, phantom, predatory, kleptocratic, and so on. What these analyses all have in common is that they are seldom based on empirical studies of the 'actual functioning' of African states and rely instead on generalizations drawn from secondary sources (in particular the print media). Thus, in the context of these analyses, the state largely remains an 'abstract entity'. The obvious question here is whether our approach to three African states, which is based on empirical study and 'bottom-up' in nature, will enable us to contribute to this debate. The honest answer is yes and no. No, in the sense that the conceptualization of the modern African state involves a specific discipline, comparative political science, which is not our subject, is beyond our expertise and can manage perfectly well without us, just as we can develop our own research without reference to it. Yes, in that the insights based on the everyday informal functioning of the state analysed by our team enables us to engage in a dialogue with at least some of the positions supported by our colleagues in the political sciences,[35] even if we do not share all of their conclusions.

It is necessary to choose, and we shall refer here essentially to the argumentation presented by Hibou (1999). Hibou's work can be summarized in two points: a position and a theory. The position, which we share, consists in taking the African state 'as it is' and avoiding its normative characterization with reference to the Western state, which usually leads to the underlining of its 'deficits' as compared with this model. We agree: it is necessary to start with the 'real state' and avoid the trap of occidentalo-centrism. However, we must express our reservations on an important point: the fact that the *official* African state is a Western-style state (structure, organization, definition of posts and careers, laws, regulations) is also part of the 'real state' and must be taken into account in the analysis. Similarly, the fact that a number of African citizens have this largely familiar Western model in their minds and themselves assess the functioning of their 'real state' in this light (a fact to which Hibou also refers) is another factor that must be considered. This is not a normative judgement on the part of the researcher. In other words, *as researchers*, we must avoid projecting our normative judgements onto the African state; however, we must also take the normative judgements produced by local actors and the African state itself into account in our analyses.

In our view, Hibou's actual theory is more contestable as it supports the idea that, far from deteriorating, the African state (like its post-Communist equivalents and others) is becoming stronger through the hold enjoyed by political personnel and actors associated with the state on a large part of the informal economy (embezzlement, fraud, criminal economy) and the formal economy (privatizations, holdings, etc.). Even if the activities involved here are not officially state activities, but very personal 'business' carried out by the agents of the state and their friends, all of these 'private' activities of the political class in the widest sense are 'attributed' to this new type of state, which, as a result, is increasingly invading society as a whole. Hibou concludes that the state can only be reinforced, at the cost of an a priori confusion between the state as an institution and the political (or, in this case, political-economic) class. She brushes aside the distinction between the public and the private. Any act carried out in connection with a politician would, therefore, be imputed to the state.

Thus, it is our belief that the *reinforcement of the political-economic class* and its hold on the country, as understood by Hibou, is not at all incompatible with a *decline of the state* as an institution providing public goods and services. On the contrary, the 'informal privatization of the state' as it emerges overwhelmingly from our studies well and truly indicates an increase in the private profits of the agents of the state, and *at the same time* a deterioration in the supply of public goods and services *from the perspective of the user*, as well as that of the observer.[36] This is confirmed in the following chapter, which is dedicated to the popular representations of corruption and the words used to designate it.

4

The popular semiology of corruption

G. Blundo and J.-P. Olivier de Sardan

The statements and words relating to corruption that were recorded systematically in the course of our interviews[1] describe, as it were, the symbolic, ideological and argumental landscape of corruption in Benin, Niger and Senegal. What is essentially involved here are widely shared representations[2] that exist beyond the individual variations associated with the context of delivery, the status of informants and their professional milieu.[3] These views can be found in the familiar expressions that refer to corrupt transactions and the know-how associated with them, and in the widely held estimations or 'explanations' of the phenomenon, its consequences and causes. It must be borne in mind here that corruption is not only an everyday practice lived (and hence 'spoken') by one and all; it is also a recurring element in both public discourse[4] and private debate. For the sake of convenience, we shall approach our analysis of the popular semiology of corruption at two different levels. The first is the level of constructed discourses based on an argumental mode – in other words, discourses that lead to the *ideological configurations relating to corruption*. The second involves the level of the vocabulary used, which brings us to the *semantic field of corruption* – in other words, the symbolic embeddedness of corruption.[5]

Justificatory utterances

Two major modalities of normative discourse on corruption can be found in our corpus: the first tends to justify, or even legitimize, corrupt practices while the second stigmatizes it. Contrary to the findings of Johnston's pioneering 1991 study on the popular conceptions of corruption in the United States, which analysed variations in judgements on the basis of actors and their direct experience of the phenomenon, our corpus clearly shows that actors shift continuously from one modality to the other, not only in accordance with the context of delivery but also on the basis of the argumental sequences within one and the same context. In other words, speaking about corruption involves an incessant alternation between condemnation and tolerance. This ambivalence is constitutive of the remarks made about corruption in the three countries studied and cannot be interpreted as a double-edged rhetorical game in which, for example, the 'truth' of the justification would contrast with the 'pretence' of the stigmatization: the actors must be credited with good faith and everything points to the fact that their condemnation of corruption is just as sincere as the 'comprehension' they express in this regard.

Nonetheless, the utterances that intend to legitimize corruption are not based on the same types of rules and norms as the accusatory-type utterances. While the latter tend to reflect 'official' rules and an ideal conception of public management,[6] the former are closer to the prevailing 'practical' norms.[7] The discourses surrounding stigmatization are also closely associated with political rhetoric. All regime changes involve the proliferation of such discourses – a number of *coups d'état* were justified by the desire to bring an end to corruption – and all opposition forces make extensive use of this register. Even the powers that be do not refrain from resorting to it occasionally. Of course, accusatory statements also incorporate forms of 'explanation' of corruption which are entirely negative – greed and venality, declining professional ethics, moral weakness and so on. What is of sole interest to us in this context, however, are the justificatory and legitimizing discourses that are most revealing in terms of the integration of corruption into everyday practices.

The 'archetypical' justificatory argument includes some 'grand utterances' in which corruption is sometimes a question of recovery – of what is seen as 'one's due', 'good manners', privilege, social pressure, redistribution, mimesis, defiance or as mere 'borrowing'. Each of these 'grand utterances' in turn incorporates a number of different variants.

Corruption as a means of recovery and survival

For the public servant or user of public services corruption may represent a means of 'recovering one's due' and thus being compensated for an injustice, to which the perpetrator believes himself or herself to have fallen victim. In the case of the public servant, illegal payments and other informal 'salary supplements' are legitimized in terms of the inadequacy of the salaries paid by the public sector as compared with those paid by the private sector (or the fact that they have not been paid at all), 'projects', foreign cooperation and international organizations. The justification of corruption in this context may also draw on the register of 'just remuneration'. Thus corruption is portrayed as a kind of compensatory allowance that is levied automatically, a well-deserved supplement to the normal salary paid: 'My position and responsibilities mean that I am owed something that is not given to me through the normal channels.'

> I believe that the corruption at the town hall can be tolerated up to a certain level. Because it is [perpetrated by] officials who are badly paid and are the victims of many social problems. (Public sector employee, Kaolack)

In the case of the users of public services, corruption would appear to provide a means of compensating for levels of taxation or levies that are perceived as excessive and do not translate into high-quality public services.

It may be noted that this argument can be expounded in a register of 'survival' wherein corruption is seen as a vital necessity involving *coping strategies*: 'without it I cannot feed my family'. This is referred to in the jargon of the Senegalese traffic police as *ligeey depaas* ('work to cover expenses'). It involves the traffic wardens' practice of positioning themselves in locations that are not heavily monitored for the purpose of carrying out unofficial controls, squeezing 'a few cents' out of the road users and then disappearing again. More generally, several informants established a clear causal link between poverty among officials and the temptation to misappropriate public resources. The frequently proposed solution to this problem was seen as the entrusting of management of public goods to the rich, who would be in a better position to redistribute them.

Corruption as 'good manners'

Another widespread notion about corruption is that it is based on kindness or propriety. Here, too, the argument is expounded in several registers: compassion, good manners, common courtesy. On the one hand, the argument of compassion comes into play when a public servant knows when 'to take pity on' the user and gives in to certain people's entreaties and supplications.

> Sometimes it is not humane to see an old woman with her table of goods not even worth FCFA 400 and give her a ticket for FCFA 100 every day, says a market levy collector who prefers to accept a lower sum from her which he will pocket without providing a receipt. (A.D., Kaolack)

On the other hand, the obligation to accept a tip from the user who is satisfied with the service rendered is a question of politeness and good manners.

> Sometimes I provide a service, I simply provide a service.... The guy sees that I made a big effort, but all that is part of my job and I am paid for that. But afterwards he takes out some money, he forces me [to accept it], he gives it to me, I refuse, but he puts it into my pocket. It is also a problem with the mentality of certain Senegalese here. (Public servant, Kaolack)

Finally, a mode of seemly coexistence (or a form of *joking relationship* – an established jovial mode of communication between or within ethnic groups) may exist between regular professional partners. This is a courteous mode of interaction between business/work contacts – that is, people who share the same working space (according to the Wolof saying *ñuuy rotaando ñoy laxaso goj*, literally 'those who draw water from the well together get their ropes mixed up') and thus become 'familiar' (*miin* in Wolof) – and is demonstrated by the

following testimonies of Senegalese police officers, which describe
the forms of mutual support that frequently exist between the police
and the drivers' associations:

> Often, what happens is that people pay me some *cola* [i.e. a bribe], some
> cigarettes, but then again I work with them ... me, I squander money, I
> smoke cigarettes. When they give me *cola*, it's to satisfy them ... there
> again, it's because they make my work easier. I have to take [it], even if
> I don't want to ... but when someone gives me money, I do not take it ...
> but that person, if he gives me cigarettes ... to be honest with you, I take
> them.... But we are Africans, I'm with them. From seven in the morning
> until seven at night, I'm with them. All day ... I'm with them the whole
> time. They often call me, even to come and eat in their vehicle, but the
> person there, if he calls us twice, three times and you don't come, he
> will say something to you; he will say to you, 'I called you twice, three
> times to come and eat, you don't come.' He says *'mann duma dëmm'*
> ['I am not a sorcerer']. 'OK!' *'Xaw ma loo may bañee'* ['I don't know
> why you hate me']. (Police officer, Kaolack, 3 May 2000)

> My feeling is that it is the administration that forces us to be corrupt....
> All of the mail belonging to the administration is involved: police,
> gendarmerie, court, prison, transport service, commercial service....
> All of the mail [is entrusted] to the drivers, we are obliged to degrade
> ourselves, otherwise they may refuse. When you ask them, tomorrow
> they will ask you for something that you will not be able to refuse.... To
> bring people to court, the court approaches the garage officer to look
> for a vehicle to go to the remand centre.... But if someone lends you
> their vehicle and its fuel to transport criminals free of charge today,
> you cannot refuse him a service the following day! It is the driver
> who invests his money with the bowing and scraping of the police
> officer. You want to talk of corruption or that those people there do
> not respect.... It is the administration that does not respect. (Police
> sergeant, Kaolack, 8 June 2000)

In all three cases the monetary counterpart of the transaction
is systematically equated with a 'gift', the social expression par
excellence of good manners, which, it is often argued, has nothing
to do with corruption.

> Yes, often when I sort out people's problems on a social level, they come
> to me with small gifts. But that too is in the nature of the Senegalese.
> It's how the Senegalese are. If you are satisfied with a guy when he sorts
> out your problem, eh! ... tomorrow you arrive with a kilo of rice or even
> a kilo of peanuts, but that's the nature of the Senegalese. Me, if someone

does something for me, if I have a mate or a friend ... who manages to sort out my problems, the first thing [I do] is to try and return his money. It's nothing at all. (Police officer, Kaolack, 3 May 2000).

When a shopkeeper offers to give you [a gift of] the goods you came to buy, it is difficult to know if it is an impartial gift or an investment. The guy who is corrupt is not necessarily bad, sometimes he is mistaken. (Regional director of customs, 26 April 2000, Senegal)

Corruption as privilege

Corruption is sometimes compared to a kind of 'perk of office' and thus represents the natural extension of the official's status. In effect 'privilegism' is an extreme form of extension of the 'perks of office' and can be found in all African administrations. In the popular representations used by officials to justify their pursuit of such privileges, the authorities are seen as being appointed to their position by God (*Yalla mo ko fallu* in Wolof): they deserve respect and they must also accept the tokens of honour offered to them by the citizens. Moreover, as a Wolof adage states, *ndawu buur buur la*, 'he who is sent by the king is himself a king'. The receipt of money from users and the misappropriation of public goods or monies is, therefore, merely one legitimate privilege among many others that expresses the appropriation by officials of the space, facilities and materials of the services for which they work. The enjoyment of the privileges of power gradually becomes a habit and is thus perceived as an irreversible process. This is again clearly expressed by another Wolof adage: *nag su mine yaq, dotul ànd ak nag yi* – 'the cow that is accustomed to causing damage will no longer follow the herd'.

> For example, the ambulance belonging to a Niamey maternity unit is basically used to collect the midday and evening meals from the hospital's main canteen, which are intended exclusively for the nursing staff, and for doing the errands of the head of the maternity unit (including taking her children to school, or for use at marriages and baptisms). The petrol allowance is used for this. If a patient is discharged and the ambulance happens to be there, the [patient's] companions have to pay for the petrol.

Corruption and social pressure

> A Senegalese doctor reports: 'Just to show you how difficult it is, I told my family that I no longer have a stamp, I lost my stamp [for validating

medical certificates]. Simply to avoid having to stamp whatever. You are going to tell me that this is weakness on my part. But it's the only way I found of having a clear conscience. They make me sign everything; if I refuse, there are problems. My aunt will come or my sister will say that "you refuse things although it is nothing, you refuse, but your colleague will do it" etc. Honestly, I have so many problems that I said I had lost my stamp and now I am left in peace; I have the stamps at the bottom of my drawer.'

This social pressure may be exerted equally by family, friends, acquaintances and colleagues. In all cases, the pressure from family and peers obliges the person of whom the request is made to abandon any personal 'anti-corruption' scruples he or she may have in favour of a group ethic that promotes favours and ostentatious redistribution.[8] This comes very close to a 'cultural' justification of corruption.

The obstacles can only be the same ones, that is emotion, pressure. You can only try to put obstacles in the way of the functioning of the law or administration when there is pressure.... Pressure from the boss or pressure from these people or those people, there can only be a breach [of discipline] when there is pressure. And, for me, the only way to stop the pressure is to say no. That means accepting that you are unpopular.... Look, there are different ways of exerting influence and putting the pressure on. Someone says to you: *diw de, toopatol ma ko, suma nit la* ('Mr So-and-so, take care of him, he's my man'). Thus, if you don't want to be disagreeable and unpopular with this person you risk not acting as you should professionally. Our problem [is that] the check on public-spiritedness is emotion, it is the pressure, and that is Senegalese.

It is our flaw, it is our flaw, emotion is our flaw. Me, I mix emotion and pressure, it's the same objective, to promote or try to prevent an inevitable event. That is the aim of emotion or pressure. (Retired head court clerk, 25 May 2000, Kaolack)

Corruption as redistribution

Although closely related to the previous arguments, the question of corruption as redistribution nonetheless differs in several respects. In this case, the justificatory mode insists specifically on the use of the fruits of corruption. The corrupt party does not deny having engaged in illicit transactions or having embezzled public money, but justifies his actions and tries to minimize their scope by arguing that he was not the direct beneficiary. The case of the public confessions of Ablaye Diack, one of the most important figures in Senegalese political life during the socialist domination[9] and one of the first politicians to have shifted allegiance to Wade's PDS party, which emerged victorious from the elections in March 2000, is a recent and particularly significant example of this phenomenon.

> In the course of a political meeting held in Kaolack on 16 April 2001, Diack is supposed to have declared: 'I can say that I deserve some credit. I do not have any foreign accounts. The Inspectors from the DIC [Criminal Investigation Authority] carried out investigations everywhere and did not find anything on me. But, to be honest, I cannot say that I have not embezzled. *Sacc naa* ['I have stolen']. But I shared everything that I stole with the people of Kaolack. God alone is my witness.'[10]

The perpetrator of corruption buys the silence of colleagues or the benevolence of the population through his generosity. Again, it is a question of conforming to the etiquette that informs the world of corruption. The fact of having *bouffé* (literally 'devoured' – that is, lined his pockets) is not enough to prompt his stigmatization. To be stigmatized, he would also have had to have acted in a selfish way, to have been guilty of greed and arrogance and to have excluded others from the benefits of the act of embezzlement.[11]

Corruption as mimesis

In this context, it is a question of 'doing as everyone else does' so as not to end up a laughing stock. The example of corrupt behaviour comes from 'above'. The ruling classes lead the way; they are the biggest thieves. Thus, anyone who chooses not to follow their example could only be described as foolish. A more professional variant of this phenomenon involves shifting the responsibility for corrupt practices to the hierarchy that engages in such practices. Thus the spread of corruption is the product of an aggregation of individual strategies that inevitably gain currency. Several of our informants among the law-enforcement agencies (i.e. customs officers, police officers, gendarmes) in all three countries studied asserted that it is best to profit from the opportunity for corruption whenever it arises

– that is, quickly to negotiate an arrangement with a smuggler or driver who is at fault rather than to sanction them in the normal way. If they impose a sanction, they run a significant risk of attracting the disapproval of their superiors – who will revoke the sanction – and of being excluded from the benefits of any illicit arrangements that may take place on a higher level in the administrative hierarchy.

In certain professions, this mimesis has been elevated to an actual professional imperative. It is very possible that a police officer assigned to traffic duty will not remain in this position for very long if he refuses to enter into 'arrangements' with drivers who commit traffic offences. In any case, it is difficult to see how he could otherwise pay his superiors the 'share' they expect as their due. While corruption may be 'optional' in certain sectors – such as the legal system – it is 'compulsory' in others, for example policing, and this obligation provides its perpetrators with an optimum justification for their activities.

Corruption as challenge

Engaging in corruption always carries risks, however minimal or improbable. Even if controls are rare or lax, perpetrators are never entirely immune from the risk of denunciation by a political adversary, the treachery of a disappointed colleague or the envy and jealousy of their social circle. The fact of 'knowing how to profit' from one's position (*profitoo* in Wolof) is thus perceived as a sign of character, strong personality and daring (*dëgër fit*). As long as fortune smiles on him, the individual who knows how to excel in this art is respected for having risen to the challenge and for standing out from the crowd. Moreover, the corollary of this admiration, which was barely veiled in our informants' accounts, is a kind of inversion of moral values leading to the ridiculing of integrity. Thus, a person who has benefited from a 'lucrative' position is no 'fool', but alert and bright (*doful, ku yeew la*). By contrast, the official who does not know how to 'moralize' with the people (i.e. how to negotiate) not only 'lacks dignity' or 'personality' (*defa ñàkk fulla* or *faayda*), he is even unpleasant (*ku soxor*) because he does not believe in work (*gëm liggéey*) and does not go in for the jokes (*amul caaxaan*). Against the background of a situation dominated by economic uncertainty, individual capacities for negotiation (*waxaale*), the ability to reach consensus (*maasla*) and to 'get by' (*lijjanti*) are held in very high regard.

Corruption as borrowing

The legitimization of corruption as an act of 'borrowing' basically concerns the misappropriation of money, which, as we know, is commonplace at all levels of society. The unscrupulous manager believes that instead of lying around doing nothing, the unused collective funds for which he is responsible may be used to bail him (or those close to him) out, and that he will reimburse this 'loan' when better times come. The newspapers are full of articles about treasurers and other managers of public funds who fall easy prey to *faux marabouts* (i.e. bogus Islamic clerks) who claim to be able to 'multiply' bank notes. The former entrust large sums 'borrowed' from the funds they manage to these charlatans in the hope of seeing them quadruple. In contexts in which the collection of large sums of cash is commonplace ('over-monetization'[12]), this 'borrowing' is an everyday activity practised by all and sundry, and the maximum possible postponement of repayment is one of its rules. The system of 'borrowing' from collective or public funds is based on that of the granting of loans to individuals, which are often not repaid, or to institutions; bad debtors are rarely pursued by the mutual credit funds, the cooperatives and even the banks.

> The establishment of the Société Nationale de Recouvrement (SNR) [National Society for Debt Recovery] in Senegal in 1991[13] to assist the state in recovering significant debts was a failure. The seven banking institutions, in which the state was a major shareholder (USB, BSK, SOFISEDIT, BNDS, SONAGA, Sonabanque and Assurbank), expected the restitution of almost 300 billion CFA francs. The main creditors of the Senegalese banks include religious and traditional chiefs (4,022 million), judges (672 million), lawyers, notaries and bailiffs (457 million), ministers (324 million), members of the military (309 million), members of parliament (279 million), diplomats (244 million), civil administrators (96 million), etc.

These different lines of argument are indicative of a kind of 'sociology of common sense'. This 'sociology' does not represent any threat to 'professional sociology', as some have suggested. Indeed, professional sociologists cannot afford to ignore it, particularly because the 'explanations' it provides often coincide with their own analyses. However, the mechanisms at the root of the different justificatory discourses differ somewhat. Using the arguments based on the concepts of 'privilege', 'social pressure', 'redistribution', 'mimesis' and 'challenge', actors aim to legitimize practices which – as they well know – are illegal or frowned on socially. Thus, their practices would appear to be motivated by need (for money or the acceleration of procedures), the obligation to respect the social norms of reciprocity and network solidarity or the need to 'maintain one's position'. As opposed to this, the other discourses mentioned above (i.e. 'recovery', 'good manners', 'borrowing') tend to neutralize[14] the negative connotations – in terms of the legal situation or everyday morality – of corrupt acts using processes that could be described as 'euphemization'. Thus, corruption is either transformed into a mark of kindness or compassion or disappears entirely, as is the case when someone asserts that they have 'borrowed' money from the kitty with the intention of repaying it or someone claims to be merely recovering resources of which they have been unfairly deprived. Thus, it is possible to draw the following provisional conclusion: due to their extensive proximity to or interpenetration with common and 'normal' social practices, corrupt practices are largely 'justified' or 'excused' in the eyes of the actors. We shall now corroborate this through our analysis of the associated semantic field.

The semantic field

Here our focus of interest is no longer on the arguments constructed around corruption, but on the simple 'words' of corruption – that is, the expressions used by everyone to talk about, describe and practise corruption. Standard French has its own vocabulary for corrupt acts, which is not short on metaphor: for example, *graisser la patte* ('to grease somebody's palm'), *donner un 'dessous de table'* (literally to give an 'under the table', i.e. a bribe) and *verser un 'pot de vin'* (literally 'to pour a drink of wine', i.e. pay a bribe). Thus, of interest to us here is the kind of terminology used in both African French and in local languages. This subject is relatively uncharted territory in analytical terms. The few anthropological studies that have been carried out on corruption are surprisingly limited when it comes to exploring the local vocabulary associated with illicit activities. And even when the topic is taken into account, as for example in Gould's (1980) book on Zaire, it is relegated to the annex as though to underline the anecdotal nature of the exercise. Thus, our study is the first attempt made to analyse a corpus of vernacular expressions and terminologies closely or distantly related to corrupt practices. Some of the most obvious limits of this exercise should, however, be pointed out: by classifying words, expressions and proverbs in different semantic registers, we were forced to remove them from their natural context of delivery. Having 'flattened' the data in our corpus in this way, we refrained from formulating hypotheses on the choices available to the informants between different expressions within one and the same register and between different registers based on the speakers in question and delivery context. Moreover, we do not take gestural semiology into account in our analysis. We are, however, clearly aware of the importance of the performative dimension of corrupt transactions as already highlighted by Gupta (1995).

Apart from terms that refer to corruption as an idea and general phenomenon (for example, the Wolof term *ger*, i.e. to sweat, to corrupt, which is not widely used nowadays, and the Arabic term *rashawa*, corruption, which is sometimes used by Hausa-speaking informants), the vast majority of the terms, expressions and turns of phrase currently in use in the three countries studied may be divided into six registers: manducation, transaction, begging, sociability, extortion and secrecy.

Manducation

The most familiar terms[15] in this register are *manger* (to eat) and *bouffer* (French slang for eat, devour, guzzle, etc.), and some local formulations that have been derived from them, for example *mange-ment* ('eating'). The same expressions exist in both Wolof (*lekk*) and Zarma (*ngwa*). It is said of the perpetrator of an act of embezzle-ment that he has *mangé la caisse ou l'argent* ('eaten the till or the money') or that he is *un mangeur d'argent d'autrui* ('the devourer of other people's money'; *nooru waani ngwako* in Zarma and Dendi). The adjective *rassassié* (i.e. full or sated, *a kungu* in Zarma, *rees na* in Wolof) is used to describe an individual who has been paid his share of the proceeds of a corrupt act, or an official who has embezzled funds. Various other derivatives may be added to this list: for example, *mangeoire* (trough; *lekkukay* in Wolof) is used to refer to an 'interesting' appointment or posting – that is, one that offers significant potential for corruption; *postes juteux* ('juicy', i.e. lucrative, posts; *nangu teeyey*, 'new/fresh places', and *nangu kan ga mansi*, 'sweet places', in Zarma; *post yu tooy*, 'wet posts', as opposed to *post yu woow*, 'dry posts', in Wolof); 'to grease one's mouth' (*me fisandiyan* in Zarma, from which the expression *a mee fisi* is derived, meaning 'his mouth is greasing', he is corrupt; similarly the Dendi expression *ji tuusu mee gaa*, 'to rub butter on the mouth'); to give someone his *portion* or *part* (to share, *ba* in Zarma; *wallam* in Wolof) or give 'the share of the eye' ('*mo baa*' in Zarma, meaning the share one gives to someone who sees you doing something corrupt); 'to move one's hand over one's beard' (i.e. the gesture involved in moving hand to mouth; *kabe daaruyan* in Zarma); 'make drink' (i.e. to water; *hangandi* in Zarma); to prepare a bait (*kooto* in Dendi). The Dendi expression *dii ka dan me*, which translates literally as 'take that and put it in your mouth' and means 'that's your share', is also very common. Similarly the practice of petty corruption may be described in Wolof using the verb *macaat*, 'to suck the leftovers at the bottom of the plate'. A number of proverbs are also used in this context: the well-known African French saying *la chèvre mange là où elle est attachée*, 'the goat eats where she is tied up', also exists in Dendi, as *hancine si kuurun kala nan kan i na talala*, and is echoed in a very similar register in Zarma, *bor si duru ka jang gamba*, 'he who grinds does not fail to take a mouthful for himself'.

The vocabulary of manducation is often referred to in studies on African political modernity.[16] However, our research shows that it is merely one of a number of possible idioms available in reference to corruption in the three countries studied. We shall return later to the position occupied by this register in the moral economies of corruption.

Transaction

The linguistic repertoire relating to the theme of transaction is no less extensive than that of manducation. This register includes terms and expressions that refer to the vocabulary of both commercial transactions and the phenomena of intermediation and brokerage. While *gagner*, which means literally 'to earn' or 'to win' but is used in the sense of 'obtain' in the context of corruption, is undoubtedly one of the most widely used terms in this register (along with equivalents in Zarma, e.g. *duyan*), other French terms are also used intermittently, such as *faux-frais* ('incidental costs'), *frais de route ou de voyage* ('road or travel costs'), *petits-débours* ('minor outlay'), *à-côtés* ('incidental expenses'), *quota*, *taux* ('rate'). These have also been translated into expressions in the local languages (e.g. the Dendi expression *zaa Kpaaraku kala Taasi ii na too jisi no*, meaning 'from Parakou to Malanville, they [the gendarmes] have set their rate'). Certain expressions are used directly by actors to convey their availability to enter into illicit exchanges: thus, when an official says *ñu gisee* in Wolof ('we shall see'), he is indicating that he is open to negotiation (*waxaale*, a term mainly used to refer to 'haggling' at the market), and this sends a very clear message to the user. The same meaning is conveyed in Niger using the famous French verb *s'arranger* ('to come to an arrangement'; *ajara* in Hausa, *hanseyan* in Zarma). Bus and bush taxi passengers are also called on to pay a 'contribution' (*dan dan cere*, literally 'give everybody', in Zarma and Dendi) at each control post along the road. The term *bizineeti* (pidgin English for 'business' in Benin) means 'to do business' and, in a specific context, can signify entering into an illicit arrangement with someone.

Some of the other expressions involving the language of transaction which originate in the local languages are more difficult to translate: for example, *kalam deene* ('the pen [literally 'the tongue'] in the pen holder' in Zarma), which refers to a kind of advance given to a marabout consulted by people to write verses of the Qur'an, with the understanding that if his 'work' takes effect he shall be paid, and can be loosely translated as the 'the price of the ink'. The idea of giving an advance to an official so that he will do what is requested of him also derives from this. Other similar terms include *jaara* in

Zarma, which refers to the small supplement requested of a seller on merchandise that has just been purchased (i.e. 'a baker's dozen'); *laada*, meaning 'custom' in Zarma, which is actually a gift given to the witnesses of a corrupt transaction; and the closely related Wolof term *neexal*, which literally means 'to please' and refers to the act of 'buttering someone up', for example when one needs to ask a favour. Terms based on the basic concepts of commercial transactions are also used in the local languages: for example, 'buying' (*deyyan* in Zarma, *jënd* in Wolof), 'selling' (*neereyan* in Zarma, *jaay* in Wolof); 'paying' (*banayan* in Zarma) and 'profit' (*riiba* in Zarma). The expression 'to prepare oneself' (*ni ma soola* in Zarma), which is used to refer to the act of getting together the sum necessary for an expense, would be understood in an ad hoc context as an invitation to plan in advance for the payment of a bribe. Overbilling is sometimes expressed in Dendi as *deeke nooru bon*, meaning literally 'to put on the money'– that is, 'increase the price'.

Gratification and begging

L'argent du café ('coffee money'), *l'argent des condiments* ('condiment money'), *l'argent de l'essence* ('petrol money'), *l'argent de l'eau fraiche* ('money for cold water'), *l'argent du pain* ('bread money'), *l'argent du taxi*, or *du transport* ('money for the taxi or for transport'), *l'argent du thé* ('tea money'), *l'argent de la bière* ('beer money'), *l'argent de la cola* ('money for *cola*'), *le sucre pour les enfants* ('sugar for the children'; *sukaru xaale yi* in Wolof), *faire un geste* (to 'make a gesture'; *yugu yugu teyan* in Dendi), *faire quelque chose* (to 'do something'; *hay fo teyan* in Zarma): these expressions are all widely used in African French. They all originate in local languages: for example, *goro*, or *gooro* in Zarma and Dendi; and *guro* in Wolof – that is, *cola*; *foy giney nooru*, the 'money for the ingredients of the sauce' in Zarma; *toyal céeb* in Wolof, something 'to wet the rice'; *njëgu ndogu* in Wolof, *mee fermey* in Zarma, something to 'break the fast' during Ramadan, referring to a certain form of 'request' (*ngwaareyan* in Zarma, meaning 'to beg' and also 'to pray') or to words spoken when offering a gift to a dependant or poor relative. The Zarma expression *kayeesi* (literally 'Happy New Year') and the Wolof term *saricë* (a gift given by someone on return from a trip) are also used, as is the expression that someone *cherche* ('is looking'; *ceeciyan* in Zarma – this term describes the quest for food or money during a time of shortage). Furthermore, the fact of claiming the 'price of the *cola*' or the 'price of the tea' also alludes to these small offerings and gifts distributed on the occasion of family ceremonies (marriages, baptisms and funerals), or when an agreement is being sealed between partners. By making this small offering, a man who approaches a woman with a marriage proposal, or seeks a compliant attitude on the part of a customs official, expresses his satisfaction while inviting the beneficiary of the offering to respect the obligation that has been entered into.

> In Benin, the collectors at the markets of Malanville and Kandi say in reference to their daily activities: 'I took my *cola* (*gooro*) and I left.' A thief caught in the act says to the gendarme he is trying to soften up: 'Chief, that, look at it, it is some *cola*.' In Kandi, to 'arrange' a business transaction, it is said 'whatever the problem, I'll do my utmost, you have this little *cola* here'. A tax collector from Malanville is thus hailed by a taxpayer 'Hey, it's *cola*, just close your eyes.'[17]

Finally, we observed that everyday transactions with the local administration trigger complex forms of intermediation which necessitate recompense for the service provided. Thus, one would give a *njukël* ('what one gives to someone who helped us' in Wolof – that is, a reward), one would do *teranga* (this Wolof term refers to the rules of hospitality or marks of honour; however, in corrupt transactions it is used in the sense of gratification), or quite simply do a *xewël* ('favour' in Wolof).

These expressions remind us that corrupt interaction alternates between the pole of extortion, based on the model of the relationship between the predator (the public servant) and the victim (the citizen-user), and the pole of the gift or begging, based on the model of a relationship between a client (the public servant) and patron (the citizen-user). Thus the latter will hear the following expressions from the mouth of the official: 'you cannot come here empty-handed' (*bor si kaa kambe koonu* in Zarma) or 'empty hands do not open a door' (*loxoy nen du ubbi bunt* in Wolof). Such predatory attitudes trigger thinly veiled contempt on the part of service users: thus a Senegalese trader describing the eagerness of municipal tax officials to control merchandise says that they *courent comme des talibés*, 'run like marabout's disciples'.

The vocabulary of religion or ethics is also widely used: *bienfait* ('kindness'; *gomni* in Zarma), *bénédiction* ('blessing'; *albarka* in Zarma), *aumône* ('alms or charity'; *ma defe la ngir Yàlla*, literally 'I do that for you out of love for God', in Wolof), or *pitié* ('pity'; *yërëm* in Wolof). In the same context, the Dendi proverb used by beggars *fuuru banda ka garu jine* ('throw something behind you so as to cross ahead later') evokes the sense of a reward in the afterlife for charity shown in this life, and can also be used in the context of the corrupt investment.

Sociability

Corrupt negotiations may be punctuated with various terms of address borrowed from the realms of family or kinship: *mon père* or *ma mère* ('my father' or 'my mother'; *ay baaba*, *ay nya* in Zarma, *suma baay*, *suma yaay* in Wolof); *mon frère* or *ma sœur* ('my brother' or 'my sister'; *ay arma*, *ay wayma* in Zarma, *suma mag*, *suma rakk*, 'big brother', 'little brother' in Wolof); *mon enfant* or *mon petit enfant*, *mon fils*, *mon esclave* ('my child', or 'my little child', 'my son', 'my slave'; *ay ko*, *ay kociya*, *ay izo*, *ay banniya* in Zarma). The register of the joking relationship or *relation à la plaisanterie* (*baaso tare* in Zarma, *kal* in Wolof), which is generally used in the context of the relationships between ethnic groups and sanctions familiarity and 'friendly insults' associated with mutual interaction and support, is also used.

Various expressions used in the context of corruption are also based on the vocabulary of solidarity: for example *kambe-diyan* ('to take someone's hand' in Zarma), *faabayan* ('to rescue' in Zarma), *gaakasiney* and *dimbalante* ('mutual assistance' in Zarma and Wolof[18]) and *kambe hinka no ga cer nyum* ('you need two hands so that one can wash the other', in Zarma). Other expressions refer to the worlds of reciprocity, the exchange of favours and indebtedness: for example, the Wolof expressions *fete ma fii ma fete la fii* ('when I do something for you, you owe me something'), *loxoy kajoor dañuy jawatloo/weesaloo* ('the hands of the people from Kayor intertwine') and again *ku la neexal nga neexal ko* ('do something for he who does something for you'). On some occasions it is also necessary to ask for patience (*suurandiyan*, 'to make someone be patient', in Zarma), mutual comprehension (*ir ma faham nda cere*, 'let us understand each other', in Zarma), or trust (*alkawlu* or *alkawaali* in Zarma and Dendi); to refer to the fact of trusting someone (*ay ga ay bon talfi ni gaa*, 'I trust you', in Zarma), or to take the side of the person making a request (*kaa ye se* in Dendi, *fur ay se* in Zarma – 'put yourself in my hands/on my side'). Reference is also made to 'getting one's foot caught' (*ce diyan* in Darma – more or less 'reserve a fiancée'), in other words to enter into a 'special relationship' with someone.

Finally, we have the area of political influence, protection and recommendation, which plays a key role when it comes to surmounting the complex twists and turns of local bureaucracy. Thus, expressions sanctioned by use in the local French dialect, such as *il a le bras long* ('he has a long arm') and *il a une ceinture de sécurité* ('he has a safety belt' – that is, a well-placed protector) have their equivalents in the African languages: 'he has access' (*defa am bunt* in Wolof) or, in the slang of students, 'he controls networks' (*borom rézo la* in Wolof). One particular Wolof adage, *ku am kuddu du lakk*, meaning 'he who has a spoon does not burn his fingers', featured regularly in our informants' accounts. In Dendi, asking the question 'Did you come of your own accord or did someone bring you?' (*ni kaa no wala i kaanda ni no?*) is a reminder of the fact that anyone who approaches a service should be capable of bearing the necessary costs.

Extortion

The register of violence and extortion also features the context of corruption: to steal (*zeyyan* in Zarma, *sacc* in Wolof), to take by force (*komyan* in Zarma, *doole* in Wolof), to dupe (*zambayan* in Zarma), to put pressure on or wear someone down (*sonnal* in Wolof). Statements that stigmatize egoistic acts of misappropriation make use of the verbs to spoil (*yaq* in Wolof) and to waste or squander (*sank* in Wolof). Anodyne expressions mask the pressure exercised by police officers on drivers on the roads:

> It is the policemen ... who propose arrangements. One of them has just said to you 'Quickly, pay 6,000.' You say to him 'I don't have 6,000.' He

says to you, 'Just do it quickly!' [*kon gawal!*] So this 'do it quickly', what does it mean? You just take out 1,000, which you give to him. He lets you go. (Motorist, Ndiaga-Ndiaye, 9 May 2000, Kaolack, Senegal)

As a result, corrupt officials are referred to in less than complimentary terms: dog (*hansi* in Zarma), hyena (*koro* in Zarma, *bukki* in Wolof), or quite simply hypocrite (*munaakifi* in Zarma) and pagan (*ceferi* in Zarma). Of a 'very corrupt person' one would say *zey beeri* ('big thief') in Zarma. Thus, in Senegal – as in the other countries – the customs official and the tax collector are seen as accursed individuals who live off the work and efforts of others (*ñaxu jambur*), becoming rich on the backs of the weak (*dañuy lekk allalu néew doole yi*). Their gains are ill-gotten (*ribaa*) and for this reason hell awaits them at the end of their lives (*dina ñu dem safara*).

> You call someone a 'hyena' [*kuuru* in Dendi, *kooro* in Zarma], when you approach him to help you sort out a problem and all he thinks about is that he is going to 'eat', get his *cola*.

The 'ransoms' charged by public servants (in the sense of unmerited income) may also be referred to rather more benignly as 'excessively easy food' (*faala ngwaari* in Zarma and Dendi) and as 'eating something that was not produced by one's own sweat' (*lekk lu dul ñaqam* in Wolof).

Secrecy

Finally, there are expressions that convey the notion of secrecy and hence the illegality surrounding corruption: for example, *nuku ganda* in Zarma ('to give a small dig from below'), *seele ganda* in Dendi ('to pass underneath'), *moo dabuyan* ('to turn a blind eye' in Zarma), *gooru* in Zarma ('to sting/bite'), *jaxaase* in Wolof ('to obscure the trail'), a term used to deplore the lack of transparency in the administration. The expressions *dii ma si ci* in Zarma and Dendi ('take [this] and don't say anything') and *han ni mana di* in Zarma ('here, you did not see anything') will also be heard in this context. An expression like *Kundum nya feejo* in Zarma (literally 'the sheep of Koundoum's mother'), which is used to refer to an object whose identity one wishes to conceal from those present, may also be used in situations involving corruption. The Dendi expression *buka bu* ('the doe is dead' – that is, 'the objective has been achieved') may also be used to signify the successful completion of a corrupt transaction. The Zarma and Dendi expression *mun a se ganda* ('to pour/pay it underneath') is used to request that 'something be given secretly'. In Wolof, secrecy is expressed using the term *mbuxum*, 'under the table', which, according to our informants, refers to the notion of secrecy, the act of folding banknotes so as to conceal them in one's pocket (*boxom*) and to give something to someone discreetly (*buux*). The Senegalese expression *nuyoo murit* ('Mouride greeting'), which refers to the manner of greeting members of the Mouride confraternity and describes the act of sliding money into the hand of the person one is in the process of greeting, should also be included in this list. This expression is echoed by the Zarma and Dendi expression *kambe kukuni ka no*, which means 'to close one's hand to give'.

Of course not all of the terms in our corpus can be classified in the categories we have defined. For example, it would be difficult to categorize phrases such as *tondi dekeyan* ('to fill a file' in Zarma), *poser une pierre sur un dossier* ('to put a stone on a file' – so that it does not 'blow away'; in other words, so that it will be dealt with correctly); *nuune wiyan* ('to put out the fire' in Dendi and Zarma – that is, to escape sanction) and, finally, *toucher* (literally 'to touch', a euphemism meaning 'to receive money'; *laal* in Wolof). As we have seen, several of the categories involve the introduction of words denoting corruption into the generally positive vocabulary of daily routine: sociability, commerce, begging. Two others concern practices that are in no way exceptional but are, nonetheless, negative: extortion and secrecy. Here we find both the ambiguity or ambivalence of the representations of corruption referred to at the beginning of this chapter and, simultaneously, the tendency inspired by justificative discourses – the embedding of corruption into normal social practices and representations. Finally, we have the category of manducation, which is examined in more detail below.

Corruption and witchcraft[19]

Popular discourse and concepts are not the only source of interpretations and semantic associations in terms of everyday corruption in

Africa. While this emic level that we have highlighted may certainly not be ignored and while it is both a source of unique data and presents a certain register of interpretation, it clearly does not enjoy a monopoly of meaning, even of meanings 'close to the data'.[20] In effect, based on our data, it would be possible to propose other possible meanings that are not emic representations as such, but may, however, take these into account. We shall limit ourselves here to a particular comparative domain which represents a traditional area of inquiry in the context of the anthropological tradition:[21] that of the relationship between corruption and witchcraft. Three levels of relationships are possible: the emic level, a plausible external interpretive level, and an (in our view) implausible external interpretive level.

1. Like the majority of daily activities and, to an even greater extent, those involving power or money, corrupt processes encounter magic on the emic level of popular representations and practices. In the three countries studied, as elsewhere in Africa, the recourse to charms, talismans, *gris-gris*, 'safeguards' and other 'arms' or 'chemical weapons'[22] on the part of traders, politicians and senior officials is very common in situations involving business, elections, governance and important decisions. Thus it comes as no surprise to encounter direct links between corruption and the mystical world for the purpose of ensuring impunity or self-protection against competitors on an everyday basis.

> Other businessmen turn to the marabouts and sprinkle *safara* before the public meeting for the opening of bids. Once, I awarded a contract to someone who was not supposed to be used and his name was the only one we managed to pronounce. I think we were bewitched. (Developer, 23 September 2000, Kaolack)

> We are in Africa. There are powers that can hypnotize in specific cases. This means that he does not see anything at all. They turn to the marabouts who give them talismans and, for example, the guy will not be able to spot something, embezzlement. They do everything so that the guy will be otherwise engaged, so that he himself will ask to be otherwise employed. (Manager of the tax office, 3 October 2000, Kaolack)

A Senegalese consultant who came to Niger had his marabout come from Senegal to 'close the eyes' of the report sponsors so that they would not see how phoney he was and [would] not ask for an explanation.

Magic and criminality would even appear to be combined on occasion, as in the Senegalese case of a series of suspicious 'accidents' that befell members of the Cour contre l'enrichissement illicite (Court against the illicit acquisition of wealth and corruption). These accidents were interpreted as proof of an attack of witchcraft on the part of corrupt individuals targeted by the Court's inquiries and dissuaded judges from putting themselves forward as candidates to replace their dead colleagues. The Court has not been replaced since and is now dormant.

2. A second interpretative level exists, which is not emic and does not feature in either the arguments or the words of actors, but which, in our view, can nonetheless offer a certain degree of intelligibility. Corruption functions in a system of closed self-justificatory belief that provides a prefabricated mode of explanation for an entire series of everyday problems. As has long been noted, the same applies to witchcraft.

- Reference to the corruption (of others) enables people to find a reason for the dysfunction of the administration or decline in public services, when someone fails to obtain a public contract or has lost a case in court, for the impunity of offenders or the arrogance of officials, and so on. Accordingly, the attribution of illness or personal failure to some kind of magic or witchcraft represents a convenient explanation that is always available. Similarly, the rapid accumulation of wealth can be ascribed to suspect behaviour and recourse to the practices of magic or witchcraft.[23]
- The 'belief' in the general nature of corruption is, moreover, a factor in its generalization, as everyone thinks that it is necessary to defend themselves using the same methods, hence the high level of demand for 'string-pulling', various kinds of protection, corrupt and complacent officials, and so on. In the same way, magical practices feed belief in witchcraft and sorcery and the absolute need to preserve oneself in an identical register.

- On the other hand, just as witchcraft is empirically nothing but 'accusations' (explicit or in the form of rumours – one knows that X or Y accuses W or Z; one does not know exactly what W or Z actually did), likewise corruption exists above all on the level of suspicion and allegation (the almost permanent absence of proof dissolves the materiality of corruption and makes it scarcely more real, at least on a legal level, than sorcery and witchcraft). Both corruption and witchcraft are located in a social realm of suspicion which they share.
- Finally, both the sorcerer and the perpetrator of corruption arouse ambivalent feelings, a mixture of fascination and repulsion, envy and rejection.

3. Another possible external level of interpretation, which is not ours, compares the manducation of witchcraft (the sorcerer, consumer of souls, devours his victims – at least metaphorically) and the embezzlement of public goods which are jointly integrated into the concept of *bouffer*, 'to eat or devour'. Thus the 'politics of the belly' joins the 'politics of the cannibal witch' and the cupidity of politicians evokes the witch's hunger for human flesh:

> In Africa, this theme of the belly is based on two original cultural registers which are, moreover, closely linked: that of munificence which, for example, makes physical corpulence into a political quality and, above all, that of the invisible, i.e. the nocturnal world of the ancestors, of the dream, of divination and magic, of which the gut is the actual centre. When the Africans assert that their leaders are 'eating' them economically through excessive extortion they lend this assertion a disturbing connotation which haunts them from infancy and obsesses them until their death: that of the spectre of an attack of witchcraft which generates prosperity for the aggressor and failure, illness and misfortune for the victim. (Bayart 1992: 69)[24]

Hence, a kind of 'syndrome of consumption' is believed to unite sorcerers and the perpetrators of corruption in one and the same symbolic group. However, in our view this parallel is based on summary and contestable semiology which generally assumes that the verb 'to eat' and its synonyms are being used in a similar way in the registers of both corruption and witchcraft. Any close examination of the semantic field of the verb 'to eat' in African languages would demonstrate, however, that this word can have completely different meanings: thus, for example, in Zarma, the expression *habu ngwa*, meaning 'eat the market', is used in the sense of 'doing one's shopping at the market', and *fuula ngwa*, literally meaning 'to eat the hat', refers to the act of becoming an official chief. Conversely, the act of *lekk kés bi* in Wolof, 'eating the till', may also be expressed as *këpp kés bi*, 'overturn the till', without the implicit notion of embezzlement being changed in any way. If it is unacceptable to contain a 'natural metaphor' excessively,[25] where several natural metaphors are constructed on the basis of one and the same term, it is even less acceptable to select only two of them – that is, those that suit the point being demonstrated – while ignoring all of the others which, in fact, render the comparison invalid.

Conclusion

In our view, the analysis of the semiological field of corruption as presented above clearly demonstrates that manducation is only one of the many registers used and that the key issue here instead concerns the variety of symbolic references associated with corrupt practices and their integration into everyday forms of sociability. Thus the words combine with the discourses in one and the same process involving the banalization of corruption.

Moreover, the actors simultaneously condemn the practices that they justify. How do they deal with this paradox? Without doubt, a number of different solutions are adopted here. The main one revolves around the expression *il ne faut pas exagérer* ('there's no need to overdo it'). One may 'profit' from the advantages of public office, use the telephone, the photocopier or ambulance for personal purposes, but *il ne faut pas exagérer*. One may sell medication to the sick, request a small 'token' from the user who wants a certificate of civil status, fine a driver whose vehicle is not in order, but *il ne faut pas exagérer*. Those who 'overdo it' are subject to the (indirect) criticism or (masked) reprobation of their peers. While a good appetite is normal, gluttony is deplorable. And everyone should allow others to have access to the plate.

This 'moral economy of corruption' is not, however, constructed on an 'all or nothing' principle; it does not follow a binary logic according to which an act would be necessarily either licit or illicit, or a practice would be either normal or corrupt. On the contrary, it is all a question of circumstances and scale.[26] To show 'pity' for a destitute user of public services or a poor person sometimes involves demanding less money from him than others, sometimes leaving him alone, sometimes helping him and sometimes giving him a little of what was taken from the previous clients. Thus, whoever 'overdoes it' forgets to show pity (*oublie la pitié*), and also forgets solidarity ('the social needs of distribution'), and may also 'overdo' negligence when providing a service – that is, not provide even a minimum level of normal activity.

This thrust in the popular arguments and expressions prompts us to think about the war against corruption. Bearing in mind everything we have just described, this war is faced with formidable and complex problems. The question that arises here is whether it should adopt a radical 'zero tolerance' type strategy, involving full-scale ruptures with the multiple and, in some cases, harmless existing 'arrangements', and thus run the risk of being unrealistic or impractical in demanding that everyone completely abandon their diverse habits, or whether it should instead advance in small steps, outlining steadily (negotiated or imposed) dividing lines between the acceptable and unacceptable, and thus risk gradually surrendering its substance, requirements or soul.

PART II

Sectoral Studies

5

Corruption in the legal system

Mahaman Tidjani Alou

S is a senior official in the Nigerien civil service. This year his eldest daughter is taking her first-year school entrance examination. The administrative formalities involved in the registration procedure mean that she has to obtain a certificate of nationality from the relevant department of the court. In order to save time, S decides to go to the district court of Niamey in person. It is Monday. On this day, there are a lot of people at the law courts. The courthouse is a large building dating from colonial times. All around the building the tea vendors and snack sellers are doing a brisk trade. There are aprons spread out on the ground with displays of delicacies, a variety of brands of cigarette and cola nuts. At the entrance to the courthouse, a policeman sits slumped in an armchair. S has brought along his identity card, thinking that it might be required for entry. However, this is not the case. The policeman is engrossed in listening to his small crackly radio, which is barely audible due to the racket all around. Groups of people chatter noisily on the front steps of the courthouse and in the area around it. It would appear that the crowd is made up both of people who have business at the court and of people who are just hanging around. S heads towards the main entrance hall of the courthouse, looking for the department responsible for issuing certificates of nationality. On the right, a few prison warders are seated with prisoners on a long metal bench in front of the judge's office. On the left, a long corridor runs the length of the building. There is a lot of coming and going. Small groups of two or three people are standing around talking in the hall, at the back of which it is possible to glimpse a courtroom. From time to time, a man in a black robe passes by furtively; he is clearly busy and is presumably expected in the courtroom or in the judge's office. There are no signs indicating to S where he should go. At this point he is approached by an affable smiling gentleman who volunteers to show him the way to the department that deals with issuing certificates of nationality. In a corridor off the hall to the right, the stranger introduces him to a middle-aged woman. She is also very friendly and obliging and says that she works in this department. The two people are obviously acquainted. 'She works in the public prosecutor's office. She has been here for a long time. If you deal with her, you'll have no problem, you'll get the papers you need quickly' the man assures S. S, doubtlessly relieved to encounter so much solicitude, gives her all the necessary papers: his daughter's birth certificate, the father's certificate of nationality, a tax stamp for 1,000 CFA francs and the 500 CFA francs for the signature fee. The woman asks him to come back in two days' time, on Wednesday.

On the morning of the appointed day, S asks his office boy to go and fetch the document, indicating to him where he can find the office of the woman in question. However, she refuses to hand over the requested document. S, surprised by this attitude, decides to go to the office to collect the document himself, on the afternoon of Thursday. When he arrives at the office, the woman is not there. He is told that she doesn't work in the afternoons. Thus, he has to come back on Friday morning. He finds her comfortably ensconced in her office, which is roughly 4 square metres in size and is shared with another woman, a secretary apparently. There are two desks. The office is lively. A continuous stream of women come in and out. S quickly realizes that the secretary is selling a range of goods – ornaments, various items of jewellery, grass skirts, incense. The women come to this rather out-of-the-ordinary office to sample and perhaps buy the range of goods displayed on the table. S goes up to the woman. He greets her politely and asks for his document but nobody pays him any attention. He has to repeat himself several times before managing to get a reply. He has the unpleasant surprise of discovering that the woman, who two days ago was so familiar and friendly, does not even remember him and has no recollection of having been given any kind of papers by him. As he is insistent, she acknowledges that his name rings a bell with her. The papers, she says, must be being typed up in the office of the vice-president of the court. S decides to go to this office himself, but the employees he finds there have no recollection of his file. 'That name means nothing to us', they tell him. He returns to the woman to tell her about his unsuccessful visit. This time she sends him to the office of the president of the court. When he goes to the president's office, he finds nobody there. The offices are empty. He goes back again to the lady in the public prosecutor's office to tell her that his enquiries have been unsuccessful. She then asks S to come back on the Monday of the following week. 'It's already the weekend', she says to him. She promises him that she will find his papers and reassumes the kind and courteous manner she showed him on the first day.

When he returns on Monday he is told that the woman has a day off. She will not be in the office today. Then S suddenly remembers that he knows a judge at the court, a childhood friend. He decides to go and see him. His friend tells him off: 'You know well that I was here, and yet you went and handed your papers over to somebody else. It's not very responsible of you!' S apologizes. 'I trusted the department. I didn't think there would be any problem, I thought that everything would go smoothly.' 'We'll sort it out', his friend the judge tells him. He goes off immediately to the court president's office in search of the file. He comes back a few minutes later, expressing his regret that he has been unable to find anything. 'You must go back to this woman and ask her who she gave the file to', he tells his friend. The next day, Tuesday, he sends the office boy, convinced that the lady will be as good as her word. However she refuses to hand over the papers. Knowing that she doesn't work in the afternoons, he goes back himself on Wednesday, convinced that he will finally obtain the document he needs. He finds her insouciantly ensconced in her office. 'What, you still haven't obtained your papers?' she asks him calmly. At this point he loses his temper. Embarrassed, she takes him aside. 'Young man, you mustn't behave this way. I could be your mother. Besides, I know your mother. We don't solve problems in this way here. What will my colleagues think? I've already told you I don't know where your papers are. I've done my work. Your papers got lost in the office of the court vice-president's secretary. I cannot do anything for you. And stop talking in such a loud voice, people might think you've given me money.' S returns to the vice-president's office. The secretaries, who have still not found the missing file, tell him that the woman to whom he gave the file is not entitled to issue certificates of nationality. 'She is in the public prosecutor's office. It's not part of her job to issue certificates of nationality. Basically it's a racket with her. That's how she rips off people coming up for trial. She's damaging the image of the law. She is known for doing that here. Our advice to you now is to present your papers again and you'll have your certificate of nationality in twenty-four hours.' At this moment the vice-president enters the secretaries' office. 'S what are you doing here?' he exclaims. It turns out that he knows the judge. He's an old schoolmate from secondary school. He eagerly explains his problem to him. The vice-president listens attentively. He asks him to take a seat in his office. He calls one of his secretaries and asks her to draw up the certificate of nationality sought by S. Five minutes later, the document is ready without S having to provide any new papers as the same secretaries had advised him to do ten minutes earlier when telling him to submit a new application. His file was probably lying around on their desks. The vice-president signs the document and gives it to him. S thanks his friend for his efficiency and leaves the courthouse, relieved to have finally obtained the document he needs.

Ten days to obtain a certificate of nationality in an established court of law: this situation is one faced by many users of the legal system in Niger. A lack of reception and information procedures, the impenetrability of structures from the perspective of the anonymous user, the diversity of roles within the judicial hierarchy (judge, public prosecutor, vice-president, president), the strategic role of the secretarial staff, the presence of unofficial go-betweens, the importance of personal contacts – all of these factors characterize the day-to-day functioning of the courts. Strangely, researchers in the social sciences appear to pay scant attention to these aspects of legal institutions (Soulier 1985: 511). In general, research in the legal field is dominated by lawyers, who only study the subject under the reductive prism of classical legal exegesis or normative analysis (Treves 1995: 201–25). Furthermore, in the vast literature produced on the African state and the democratic processes that have been developed within it in recent years, the everyday functioning of the legal system has not been the subject of any particular study (see Buijtenhuijs and Rijnierse 1993; Buijtenhuijs and Thiriot 1995: 58; Van Walraven and Thiriot 2002; Daloz and Quantin 1997; Chabal and Daloz 1999; Bourmaud 1997). Nevertheless, we are aware of the importance accorded to the legal system, at least in terms of political discourse, in the context of the construction of the constitutional state in Africa. However, seminars and conferences only highlight the thorny issue of the independence of the judiciary or the question of the accessibility of the law for the majority of the people. Also, the few reforms instituted have merely concerned the status of a judiciary seeking independence in relation to overweening political influences or the improvement of the legal infrastructure, which, in a way, introduces the question of access to the law.

In summary, researchers in the social sciences show little interest in the everyday operation of the legal system in Africa. Studies on the everyday functioning of the legal system and how it affects users of the courts are few and far between (Du Bois de Gaudusson 1990; Le Roy 2004). Although the legal system is rather distinctive as an institution, it is nevertheless a part of the state just like other government departments – for example, education and health. As is the case with the latter, the public service dimension of the legal system involves multiple interactions with the social environment, which have a considerable impact on its modes of regulation. This means that it is necessary to focus on the actors of the legal system and their individual and collective strategies, on the one hand, and on society in terms of the everyday relationships that the actors of the legal system maintain with users of the courts, on the other. Thus, we will endeavour to analyse and understand the legal system 'as it really works' on the basis of cases examined in Benin, Niger and Senegal.

The operation of the legal system involves a large number of actors. By virtue of the diversity of their roles and responsibilities, however, judges are the strategic actors in the system. Depending on their specific positions within the legal system, they commit defendants for trial, prepare cases for judgment and pronounce court rulings. They are invested with extensive powers; thus their role is both envied and feared. They are assisted by administrative staff, in particular the court clerks and the secretaries who work in the offices of the clerk of the court and the public prosecutor. The clerks perform administrative duties. They take minutes and manage the archives of the courts of law, and are also responsible for recording court business, contacting the parties involved in a case, drawing up official reports, documenting court rulings, receiving members of the public and providing them with information. The secretarial staff perform tasks that are essential to the production of legal documents. It must also be said that although the clerks, whose diverse functions effectively involve them in areas beyond the purely legal sphere, play an important role in facilitating access to the judge, the secretaries perform a vital role in the drawing up of official documents (certificates of nationality, extracts from police records, court declarations certifying approximate place and date of birth, etc.). The police and gendarmerie also perform legal duties and are, therefore, involved in the delivery of justice, mainly through the investigations they conduct under the auspices of the judges.

The members of the public who use the legal system must also be taken into account in this context. There is no 'typical user' of the public judicial system. Anybody can have dealings with the law, whether as a litigant, a defendant or simply to obtain a birth, death or marriage certificate. In addition, other, no less important, actors actively participate in the workings of the legal system. These are the 'auxiliaries of justice' who effectively act as an interface between the legal system and its users. A range of professions are involved here: barristers, solicitors, bailiffs, interpreters, lobbyists, the officials of the criminal investigation department, prison warders, and so on. Each occupies a specific position within the legal system which they share with the other formal and informal actors who populate the corridors of the court buildings.

The legal systems in the three countries under consideration are currently mired in various controversies. They are accused, among other things, of being institutions blighted by the cancer of corruption. Few, if any, sanctions appear to be incurred by corrupt judges or other tainted officials. It is as though the public authorities have decided not to fight a phenomenon with which they appear to have become quite comfortable. In reference to the legal system in French-speaking African states at the beginning of the last decade, Du Bois de Gaudusson noted that

> The legal system has been the subject of many accusations, all of which have resulted in a full, severe and uncompromising verdict: the lack of an independent judiciary, the subordination of the legal system to political interests, corrupt judges, inadequate training of judges, lack of financial and documentation resources in the courts, the excessive legalism of procedures and regulations, the remoteness of the legal system from the people. (Du Bois de Gaudusson 1990: 6)

While some progress may have been made, for example in the area of the training of judges and the improvement of legal infrastructure, the validity of this observation barely appears to have been undermined by the passage of time. The more recent picture painted by Fall is scarcely more positive:

> Few African judges today benefit from the concept of the court as it is usually and legitimately formulated, i.e. as an institution whose mission it is to uphold the law and to deliver justice. Their credibility is seriously undermined ... The judge or, more generally, the legal system, is decried and accused of all kinds of wrongdoing: the person whose highest mission is to settle conflicts and protect citizens against violations of their rights and freedoms and against all arbitrary charges on the part of the authorities, finds himself violently taken to task and suspected of bias, corruption, negligence and even, very often, of incompetence on a daily basis. (Fall 2003: 4–5)

However, it is not all that long ago that the description of corruption in the context of the legal system mainly referred to the restrictive clauses in the penal code which make it difficult for judges to penalize corruption of any kind as they are obliged to impose the same level of punishment on both the perpetrator and the victim of corruption (Sarassoro 1990: 196; Bio Tchané 2000: 64). Moreover, when judges are personally censured, it is mainly for their strong dependence on the political authorities, and rarely for their propensity for corruption, the issue that is currently in the spotlight.[1] For, although the phenomenon of corruption has spread to the legal system, just as it has affected other government departments, due to the existence of oases of integrity, its analysis is not entirely a straightforward matter. It is precisely these phenomena that we wish to examine here by considering that these corrupt practices reflect a more general situation, and the fact that there is no reason why the legal system should have remained impervious to a corruption which has become endemic in African government departments in recent years. Thus, the aim of this analysis will be to demonstrate the specific forms of corruption that exist in the legal system, which enjoys a privileged position within the state.

Our case is based on three interconnected hypotheses:

1. Corruption generates all kinds of practices that obstruct the law from fulfilling its proper function, which is to ensure that essential social rules are upheld. In a sense, the way that these practices emerge and develop prompts us to reflect on the true purpose of the legal system whose functioning is increasingly thwarted.

2. Corruption is based on various mechanisms which enable its production and reproduction. These mechanisms, of which only the most significant will be noted here, are connected with certain salient characteristics of the state as it has developed in Africa and within which the legal system merely constitutes a single segment. Furthermore, corruption thrives in government departments which have been greatly undermined by national financial crises and by institutional weaknesses which generate all kinds of dysfunctionalities. The legal system is no exception to this trend. In fact, not only are the conditions of legal work prejudicial to the development of a healthy legal system, but structural constraints encourage actors to invent rules that foster the development of all kinds of corrupt practices.

3. Corruption leads to changes in the legal institutions, which in turn result in the distortion of the original normative model. This is reflected in the particular forms assumed by the legal system in Africa in the context of its daily interactions with users.

Corruption and the functioning of the legal system

The relationships between the legal system and its environment foster the development of corrupt practices and the emergence of an alternative system of operational rules, and thus trigger legal insecurity among the anonymous users of this public sector. These practices have occurred on such a scale in recent years as to reveal a legal system that is seriously infected with the virus of money. Having first outlined some instances of corruption in the legal institutions, we will then endeavour to decode the ways in which it manifests itself.

Some instances of corruption in the legal system

The way in which judges perceive and acknowledge the existence of corruption vacillates between the acknowledgement that corruption does, indeed, exist in the legal system and a tendency to minimize the extent of the problem, which, depending on the details of each individual case, is relativized and dismissed as a peripheral phenomenon.

Thus, according to a young examining magistrate in Niamey in Niger, corruption exists within the legal system, but it is encouraged by the people who stand trial:

> The temptation does not just concern the judges; it is first and foremost present in the minds of the defendants. My experience of nine to ten months has taught me the bitter lesson that, in the mind of the people, justice can be bought.... There is not a single case where the family of a prisoner has not approached us and made us some kind of offer. When the member of the family comes to us, it is not with a view to knowing what their relative has done. Their first approach is to offer something to the judge, and I imagine that this approach is not something that has come about because of the specific financial difficulties which judges are currently experiencing, but that it is a practice which has been

around for quite some time. Therefore, I think that as far as temptation is concerned, everyone is tempted, including the defendant, because if you have no money, you cannot obtain justice in this country. (Young examining magistrate at the District Court of Niamey)

Another point of view can be presented that certainly does not point the finger at the users of the legal system, but nonetheless acknowledges the existence of the phenomenon.

You know that the question of corruption is a rather delicate issue; it is true that for a long time the attitude that prevailed within the legal system was to refuse to talk about corruption. However, I think that the situation has never varied; overt cases of corruption in the judiciary have always been penalized. In my view, this practice does not simply date from the times when what I might refer to as public discourse existed. Judges guilty of corruption were always punished in cases in which we had concrete proof that corruption had taken place. What I think happened at a certain juncture was that we also got to a stage where the cases of corruption had become very numerous, and judges in their courts were confronted every day with corruption laws concerning some of their colleagues.... We had reached a time, an environment, even a moment, I would say, where the atmosphere was a bit contaminated. Rumours of corruption were so rife that you ended up being suspicious about one colleague or another because of these rumours. (Deputy prosecutor, Dakar)

More reticent points of view can also be found: 'I cannot say that the legal establishment is totally untainted by corruption, but this phenomenon remains, in my view, a marginal one' (Examining magistrate, Kaolack).

For many, access to justice depends on social and economic status and the contacts that the user is capable of mobilizing and using to his or her advantage in the legal system. It is generally acknowledged that a poor defendant who has no contacts can spend several years in custody without benefiting from the assistance of a lawyer.

Until now, whether or not you got arrested depended on your social and economic status and that, in turn, depends on your relationship with a member of the judicial system. It is certain that a poor person who has no resources is going to spend years in custody. Obviously, if you are rich, you can afford to pay for a lawyer. The lawyer will get you out of prison. You will end up spending less time in custody because he will introduce an application for bail while someone else, who has no knowledge of the law, will not do so as he is unaware of his rights. (Trainee lawyer, Niamey)

However, corruption can also affect the rich in a particular way. In the context of an analysis of the legal system in Niger, Dan Dah (2000) highlights

a widespread idea according to which judges tend to systematically sentence those who can afford to pay, even if the law works in their favour in other respects.... Banks, insurance companies, financial organizations and large companies are systematically sentenced to pay large sums of money to former employees who have been dismissed for serious offences (theft or breach of confidentiality, for example), in some cases, and to clients who are, in fact, far from blameless, in other cases. Furthermore, it is not rare to hear some judges declare, 'they can afford to pay'. To crown it all, these rulings are often backed up by a provisional enforcement order, which means that they can be implemented despite the initiation of an appeal. When they are not accompanied by a provisional enforcement order, these rulings are quickly recorded and placed at the disposal of the party that has won the case. How can one not question the impartiality of judges in such circumstances?

Over time, the attitude that justice can be bought has become widespread among users of the courts:

In the courts, the person who has spent the most money is right; there is no justice, it's like a public auction. (User of the court of Kandi, Benin)

The legal system is corrupt, judges are more dishonest and corrupt than other civil servants. (Defendant, Kandi)

In the courts, money wins out. There are people who commit serious crimes and who deserve to be sent to prison for a long time, but they just spend two or three days behind bars and are then released. (Defendant, Kandi)

Thus the bribing of judges has become the classic modus operandi for defendants who want to have their cases dealt with speedily:

Honestly, people don't work with the law here. What I am critical of is the long delays, indeed the unjustifiable way in which things were held up and impeded progress on my case. Given that that is how things are, and it is said after all that a goat will eat wherever he is tethered, I prefer to be told if I have to pay something or not. I know that corruption is real today, and people say that when faced with risk of losing everything, you must try and preserve something. If I come to the conclusion that things are going to continue in this way, I will be obliged to sacrifice at least a million in order to hang onto the remaining seven million, as from 1994 to today is a long time. (User of the district court of Niamey)

When asked about this situation, some judges admit that an atmosphere of suspicion has developed over time that systematically casts doubt on the integrity of their office. However, their discourse is not unequivocal as the judges also denounce the existence of corrupt individuals within their ranks who tarnish the image of their profession:

> When you are preoccupied with your career, because you want to progress too quickly, you can end up doing things that are not right. You can be persuaded to violate people's rights, anything. In every case, what judges must understand is that the politicians .... whatever regime comes to power, they will know how to use judges for their own ends. And to attain their own ends, they give judges enormous promotions, bribes and a whole load of things. And judges who are interested in such things cannot perform their duties as judges. (Examining magistrate at the District Court of Niamey)

The registers of petty corruption in the legal system

Two main registers of corruption can be identified in the legal systems in Benin, Niger and Senegal: the first is a classical form of corruption, the kind that is found in most state administrations, while the second is more specific as it involves the distinctive forms of corruption that take root and develop in legal institutions.

Ordinary corruption

At least three scenarios can be identified in this register. One concerns lowly employees within the legal system who are involved in issuing the various certificates and documents which come under the remit of the legal authorities on a daily basis. A second concerns the judge in his various relationships with the social environment, and a third scenario involves the misappropriation of public funds, something which also occurs in legal institutions.

The payment of unwarranted fees Within the legal system, there is a constant and strong demand for birth, marriage and death certificates and so on, and for other legal documents, such as certificates of nationality, extracts from police records, court declarations certifying approximate place and date of birth. Moreover, requests for such documents are always communicated to the relevant legal departments as a matter of urgency. In addition, judges' rulings are only effective if the documents which set them out are delivered to the user. The task of issuing these certificates and documents generally falls to the secretarial staff. They have control over the drawing up of the documents and access to the signature of the judge. Thus, the everyday activity of issuing these documents is almost never an automatic one. The procedure is always deferred and liable to postponement and therefore engenders a sense of uncertainty among users. The secretaries always take a long time to issue even the most straightforward certificates.

The case highlighted at the beginning of this chapter is quite illuminating in this regard. Even when the user carries out all the required formalities, the only way of obtaining certificates in a reasonable time frame is to 'pay'. You always have to give 'something' to save time, or else have useful contacts. Such transactions are obviously never expensive. They take the form of small 'gestures', gestures which are obligatory for the client. Thus, depending on the circumstances, the relations that develop between the public judicial system and its users become either mercantile or personalized. Such practices are carried out quite openly and are now considered normal.

This form of corruption is essentially one practised by lowly employees, and can also be described as corruption that acts as a means of survival. An unofficial system of fees charged for the delivery of certificates exists, which is familiar to users. However, this fee structure is flexible since the amount, usually paid before the certificate is delivered, is left to the discretion of the user (Blundo and Médard 2002: 19). This practice has become so commonplace that it now tends to be the rule. Here we have a classic situation, already observed in the customs (Tidjani Alou 2002: 13–22) and health services (Jaffré and Olivier de Sardan 2003), whereby the department that issues these certificates has been unofficially internally privatized by the employees responsible for providing the service (Olivier de Sardan 2001a: 70).

The exploitation of personal connections with judges   Like all public servants who occupy a position of authority in their relations with users, judges are constantly exposed in the performance of their duties to pressure from their families, social circles and the various networks and groups to which they belong – political parties, circles of friends, neighbourhoods, ethnic groups, former classmates, professional associations, and so on. In fact, it is not rare for a relative, friend or acquaintance to intervene with a judge, either on his or her own behalf or on behalf of a defendant: 'It is true that a judge is subjected to a lot of pressure; this pressure can come from family, from a professional association (if he belongs to one) and even from his social circle' (Examining magistrate, Kaolack, Senegal). The person who intervenes in this way may remind the judge of favours they have done for him in the past, or of their friendship with him or his family: 'One doesn't say no to one's own family, so as not to appear churlish', admits a Senegalese judge.

It is not uncommon for financial inducements to be offered to a judge by friends or members of his family circle. Frequently, this type of financial transaction takes place outside of the legal system so as to protect its clandestine nature. People facing trial avail themselves of different methods to gain access to judges.

> Actually, we approached him through his family. You know, the judge's family and my in-laws are related in some way. We went through my family to give the 100,000 CFA francs to his family. Well, I don't know if he took the money or not. Indeed, when I thanked him, he didn't say anything. He just said that this is what he can do when family is involved. In fact, he was surprised when he learned that I had been sentenced to three years' imprisonment. (Former detainee of Niamey civil prison).

Intermediaries may also be remunerated for their involvement, unbeknown to the judge.

The resources used to influence judges are mobilized on a totally subjective basis. They are expected to be 'good judges'; that is to say, it is assumed that they will be obliging and understanding towards people they know and ready to help them, even if this involves violating the rules that constitute the basis of this work. This epitomizes the difficulties inherent in the work of judges, forever torn between the continual demands made on them by their social circle and the requirements of their profession which follow a different logic. In these conditions, the challenge of applying the law, doing one's work normally and preserving one's integrity becomes a heroic vocation and, consequently, entails a life choice that few judges can afford to take due to its social cost.

The misappropriation of public funds This also occurs in the legal institutions. Here, the phenomenon is illustrated more specifically by the misappropriation of funds earmarked for legal purposes, a racket in which many judges in Benin have been involved.

> Following the publication of a report by the commission of inquiry of the Ministry of Finance into the fraudulent embezzlement of public funds earmarked for the legal system, these officials were imprisoned for two years. The main charge against this embezzlement network concerned the system set up by the judges enabling them to be paid fees from monies that had been earmarked for judicial inquiries. More than eight billion CFA francs are said to have been misappropriated by means of various forms of complicity between 1996 and 2000. (FIDH 2004: 9)

Apart from highlighting a criminal offence, this case illustrates the existence of embezzlement networks linking various sections of the government administration, including the legal system. It also reveals the way in which petty corruption can become associated with far more serious corruption. An affair that might have been considered as belonging to the realm of petty corruption was literally transformed over time into a matter of large-scale embezzlement. Finally, this scandal contributed to the demystification of the image of the judge, which was stripped of all legitimacy and equated with an ordinary criminal. However, corrupt practices can also be identified that are more specific to the legal system.

A register of corruption specific to the legal system:
the negotiation of sentences

Corrupt practices in the legal system are based mainly on the manipulation of the rules that regulate the system of penal sentences. This sentencing system is underpinned by a range of statutes outlining the specific responsibilities of the judge and lawyer, of which the most well known are the penal code and the code of penal procedure. Naturally, the judge occupies a central role within this structure since it falls to him to implement the sentencing system designed to deal with offences against the established public order. The development of corruption in the legal system has led to the negotiation of sentences not on an open or public basis, but on the basis of clandestine dealings. These reveal the existence of alternative rules and procedures which are largely independent of those enshrined in the statutory legislation and intended to govern the implementation of justice. What results is a rather vague, flexible and unpredictable system of sentencing which often involves a selective application of the rules, depending on the actors concerned and the resources they are able to mobilize. Thus the legal system itself is an arena in which commercial transactions are continually taking place and where the stakes vary, depending on the position occupied by the strategic actors within the system. This situation provides numerous opportunities for corruption which are directly linked to the different powers with which judges are legally vested.

The termination of proceedings The decision to try a defendant or not demonstrates the power of the prosecutor. Thus, in the early stages of legal proceedings, the public prosecutor's office is the constant target of appeals and requests, the aim of which is to dissuade the prosecutor and his deputies from implementing their power to press charges. They may also receive an order from above to drop a case, just as they may be 'approached' by (or on behalf of) a potential defendant proposing that they halt the proceedings in return for remuneration: 'The prosecutor may drop a case and nobody can do anything about it' (Official at the court of Kandi, Benin).

The abuse of flagrante delicto As Blundo observes in the case of Senegal, the institution of *flagrante delicto* proceedings transforms the prosecutor into a veritable 'demi-god' as it results in the short-circuiting of the preliminary investigation. In such cases, the prosecutor has the power to make a committal order, which is usually the province of the examining magistrate.

> The public prosecutor's office has the following procedures available to it: (1) *flagrante delicto*, (2) direct summons, (3) judicial inquiry and (4) termination of proceedings; *however although all of this may be perfectly regulated, the prosecutor usually only avails of the flagrante delicto option* [our stress]. (Examining magistrate, Kaolack, Senegal)

The application of the *flagrante delicto* option combined with the power to compel people to attend hearings grants the prosecutor the actual power to negotiate the release of a prospective prisoner. In such situations, it is possible that prosecutors will openly defend the defendant in return for payment, whereas their actual role in the trial is to defend society's interests (Blundo and Olivier de Sardan 2001a: 187–8). As it happens, the importance of the prosecutor in such circumstances means that he has a key role in deciding on the punishment and the administration of the sentence; thus users tend to seek him out in the assumption that he alone holds the key to their liberty.

Prison living conditions   The overcrowding of prisons and deterioration of the prison environment mean that detainees and their families are prompted to attempt to gain access to conditions that will improve the prisoners' quality of life during their time in prison. A prison is a self-contained world with its own rules and its own dominant figures. These rules have nothing to do with internal regulations. They are enacted by and in a prison environment that has its own internal code of conduct, to which every new detainee becomes subject as soon as he arrives in prison. All of the data we collected highlighted the inhuman environment that prevails in the prisons:

> He (the prisoner) has to put up with bad conditions, and furthermore he is not respected; that is to say that everything that makes you human is taken away from you. (Detainee, Niamey civil prison)

Indeed, the quest for tolerable living conditions in prisons is the systematic reason for the large number of financial transactions, in which detainees or their families become involved, the main issues under negotiation being access to better living quarters in the prison (there are different categories of accommodation in prisons), on the one hand, and exemption from heavy chores (cleaning, dish-washing, laundry, etc.), on the other. The cost of this preferential treatment varies according to the social status of the prisoner and his ability to pay the sums of money demanded by the 'true masters of the house' (prison warders and some prisoners) in exchange for access to the 'humanized areas of the prison'. Thus the enforcement of court rulings largely eludes the prosecution, which only has limited control over this important aspect of the legal process.

Remand and police custody   This comes under the remit of the criminal investigation department. Here again, the prisoner's treatment will differ according to whether he has useful contacts or not and depend on his financial resources:

> When I was arrested, I didn't have these problems and almost all the influential members of my party went off and threatened the criminal investigation department, saying that if ever they touched a hair on my head, they would have to deal with them. Let's say they made a lot of noise and as a result I was never locked up; on the contrary, they even allowed me to continue my life as before, I was outside; in the evenings, if I needed to take a drink – for at the time I was a drinker – someone would go and buy it for me, bring it to me, and make up my bed outside. Let's say that I personally didn't have this problem, but I did see that other people were not as fortunate as me; first they were made to strip and then, at the end, they were locked up in their cells and it was really humiliating and degrading. Really, conditions are very bad in the criminal investigation department. It's terrible if you don't have anyone to make sure that you are not ill-treated. (Prisoner in Niamey civil prison)

A parallel legal system   It is also possible to observe that the powers of the criminal investigation department go beyond the domain of investigation and extend unofficially to aspects of sentencing. Many cases do not even get as far as the courts. They are settled at the door of the police station by police officers, sometimes without the knowledge of the judge and in return for money. In this instance, police officers use arbitrary powers of detention under cover of the custodial powers authorized by the law for dealing with the numerous incidents that they encounter at the police stations. The dread of being locked up in the insalubrious detention centres of the criminal investigation department often prompts people to bargain for their liberty by seeking an out-of-court settlement, even if they have been arrested with good reason. In the cases observed in Niger, this usurpation of power by the police at the criminal investigation department not only involves criminal cases. Strangely, it also extends to civil and commercial cases. Thus, straightforward personal or private disputes are dealt with on the basis of an informal penal code whereby the criminal investigation department exploits the person's fear of going to prison and the ultimate humiliation that this represents. These practices mean that the police officers assigned to the criminal investigation department automatically have the means of generating an extra source of private income.

The reduction of prison sentences and amnesties Reductions in prison sentences and the granting of amnesties to prisoners, which are envisaged first and foremost as 'humanitarian acts' sanctioned by the president on special occasions, also fall prey to the bargaining culture that exists in prisons. The issue of health is a particularly popular option in this context. Basically, the detainee has to 'buy' a medical certificate attesting that he is suffering from one of the serious illnesses regarded as grounds for appeal for an amnesty (AIDS, tuberculosis, leprosy). At this level, the networks of corruption inevitably involve doctors, but they also involve the active complicity of judges from the prosecutor's office, who again see them as an ideal opportunity to make financial gain out of their power to check the files submitted to them. Thus, the prosecution is at the centre of a complex network of potentially lucrative transactions, of which some judges do not hesitate to take advantage.

Bargaining for bail The supreme power of the examining magistrate is also up for sale in this bargaining process. Given the slowness of the legal process, the decisions reached by the examining magistrate are crucial. This is why the magistrate is constantly lobbied by users and defendants with all kinds of requests and offers and subjected to pressure, the aim of which is to get the judge to deliver rulings in favour of the defendant, which will spare him the anguish of imprisonment. The prosecutor has the power to 'drop a case', but the examining magistrate has the power to grant 'bail'. However, the obtaining of bail involves the exchange of a series of reciprocal favours between the principal actors involved in the trial. The lawyers play an active role at this stage, as it falls to them to set the process in motion, invoking for this purpose the sacrosanct principle of the presumption of innocence. However, the decision to release a prisoner on bail essentially depends on the examining magistrate, who initiates the process, and on the consent of his counterpart in the prosecution, who ultimately takes the decision to release a prisoner. Thus the power to release prisoners on bail has become a major source of income for judges, and the prisoners, who are well aware of this, exploit this situation to the full. When the judge refuses bail at a first hearing, transactions may be reinitiated at the level of the court of appeal. More detailed statistical information on the granting of bail by judges would be required to reach a clearer understanding of the extent of this phenomenon.

The misconduct of the defence   Lawyers are not immune to the phenomenon of corruption. In fact, they are frequently perceived as vehicles of corruption when they encourage clients, who are involved in a trial, to set aside 'the judge's share'. What is involved here is the purchase from the judge of a ruling favourable to the defendant. Thus the lawyers contribute to the propagation of a particular image of the legal system whereby it is seen as a public service that is 'marketable and venal'. However, depending on the circumstances, the misconduct of lawyers can also assume different forms: for example, the misappropriation of funds obtained from clients at the end of a trial and the 'buying of the lawyer by the opposing party', so that he will mount a poor defence of his client. In the latter case, the lawyer refrains from using 'all his knowledge and technical expertise to ensure that his client wins his case because, as a layman, the client is ignorant of legal procedures' (lawyer, Niamey). The methods typically used in this instance include the failure to invoke the right of appeal, to which every defendant is entitled, within the prescribed time limit, and the deliberate absence of the lawyer on the day of a trial, which puts his client at a considerable disadvantage.

Corrupt practices and their reproduction in the legal system

Several mechanisms contribute to the development and reproduction of corruption in the legal system. While some are linked to the social environment in which the courts operate, others are directly related to the weakness of legal institutions.

Justice and the social environment

The law is perceived as terrifying and unpredictable in its relations with society. This negative perception is not unconnected to the forms of intermediation that develop within the legal system.

Fear of the law

The law inspires fear, uncertainty and insecurity in people. In fact,

> As soon as people receive a court summons, they are alarmed, they don't understand. And they take it out on the bailiff just because the bailiff has brought them the summons. They think that the bailiff bears them ill will. (Examining magistrate, Niamey, Niger)

> The law is sometimes perceived as a 'convent' which is reserved for the initiated, a real 'jungle': to go to court is to go to war', according to a defendant in Kandi. (Blundo and Olivier de Sardan 2001a: 81)

> When you win a case, it means that the judge agrees that it is he who is right, because it is he who determines the truth in the final analysis and he attributes it to whomever he wants. (Blundo and Olivier de Sardan 2001a: 186)

If the user is well connected socially, he usually goes through a lawyer who negotiates directly with the judge. In this instance, the problem of access to the judge does not arise; the lawyer is a regular at the court, he knows the staff there and enjoys cordial and convivial everyday relations with them. He will also know the judge and will probably already have had dealings with him; he may even have been a contemporary at university. In the case of a trial, he will do everything to ensure that his wealthy client is spared severe penalties, and this includes 'coming to an arrangement' with the judge. However, the anonymous user almost never has access to the services of a lawyer. He is often forced to enter directly and personally into contact with the courts. When he gets there, there is nobody to guide him or show him where to go. He will have to search anxiously around a building occupied by many unknown officials. In fact, the mere act of locating the judge's office is often a demoralizing obstacle race, in the course of which he will be exposed to the scrutiny of numerous strangers. He will also have to contend with the indifference of secretaries and other auxiliary employees who work in the corridors of the courthouse and in the antechambers of the judge's office. Finally, he will have to meet the judge in his majestic gown and in the silence of his office. This interview is frightening because its outcome is always uncertain. For the user, it depends exclusively on the judge's goodwill, and not on the laws he is supposed to implement. This probably explains the need that users always feel to protect themselves in advance by availing themselves of either magic practices, which are supposed to ensure that the judge will be kind to them, or of the numerous intermediaries who operate in the arena of the courts.

Intermediation

Three main analytical axes can be considered here: the political interventionism perceived as fostering corruption in the legal system; the existence of institutional intermediation mechanisms, which operate, depending on the circumstances, through the functional duplication of official systems and procedures; and the emergence of informal mechanisms of intermediation, which operate through the monopolization and abuse of legal institutions.

Political intermediation: political interventionism This practice has its basis in the constitution, which enshrines the structural control exercised by the executive over the everyday operation of the institutions responsible for the delivery of justice. It takes effect through the actions of the minister for justice, who intervenes in the operation of the legal system through the medium of the public prosecution department (the public prosecutor, the state prosecutor and their deputies). The following remarks made by a deputy state prosecutor are significant in this regard:

> The most serious difficulties in the prosecutor's department arise when there is a lawsuit involving a legally defined offence and, because they know the perpetrators of the crime, members of the government ask that the case be dropped; that is to say, they ask us not to press charges. This generates frustration and paralyses the prosecutor in the application of his own legal expertise and judgement. Anyway, when a ruling has been made which has become definitive, you know the prosecutor's office is responsible for making sure that the law is implemented and that the court's decisions are applied, and when somebody asks for the application to be deferred, when all the guidelines and rules endorsing an indictment have been fulfilled and a stay of execution is requested, it's frustrating ... That's politics. (Deputy prosecutor, Niamey)

These are commonplace practices which, irrespective of the successive political regimes, have significantly tarnished the image of the legal system in the countries under consideration. The mechanism is quite simple. When they want to influence a court verdict to their advantage, governments ask the minister of justice to intervene with the prosecutor's department. Moreover, the formal hierarchies are not always respected. The minister can brief a prosecutor directly so as to indicate to him the course of action to be followed in a given case. The prosecutor then carries out a series of actions that depend on the various actors who occupy positions of power within the court: that is, the president of the court, the examining magistrate to whom the case is allocated, and the judge who will be responsible for delivering a ruling on the case. We clearly see here the extent of the significance the government attaches to controlling the legal system by appointing judges to the courts whom it has already won over to its own agenda. And it is no accident that the power to appoint members of the judiciary rests with the Conseil supérieur de la Magistrature, a body which is mainly composed of institutions that are under the direct control of the government of the day. In reality, governments always want to control the judiciary by placing their own appointees in strategic posts within the legal system.

If the government's intervention proves successful, the reward the judge can expect varies, depending on his position. The public prosecutor can expect a reward in the form of promotion, either within the legal administration (director, general secretary or minister)[2] or within the hierarchy of the courts, as well as symbolic gains such as the 'high esteem of the minister'. As for the examining magistrate and the presiding judge, they can at least hope to hold on to their positions, thus reinforcing their security of tenure. However, if they do not play the game, they run the risk of being assigned to a less interesting court, and one that is less attractive in terms of career prospects, or of being assigned to a dead-end job in the ministry. The chancelleries are full of judges who ministers no longer wish to see employed as judges for various reasons. Thus, it may be noted here that judicial appointments can be ambiguous in terms of their function: that is, depending on the circumstances, they can involve a penalty or promotion.

Institutional intermediation through functional duplication   In this scenario, those holding institutional positions within the judiciary use their official position to create clandestine personal networks of intermediation, which they exploit in their various relationships within the legal system and its environment.

- *Judges*   The judges use their influence with colleagues in charge of a given case to the advantage of their families, friends and acquaintances. In this instance, the transaction is not necessarily financial and may be analysed as an exchange of services between colleagues. Obviously, this type of transaction is only possible if the circumstances lend themselves to it. The judge who needs a favour will not ask just any of his colleagues. He will mobilize all of the social connections and advantages he has accumulated in the course of his judicial career – that is, with the judges whom he has helped in the advancement of their careers or in other areas and anyone else who is indebted to him for any reason. We can clearly see here all of the factors that contribute to the creation of networks of contacts and the importance of the way in which cases are assigned to judges at the level of preliminary examinations as well as that of judgments and rulings.

- *Lawyers* These 'auxiliaries of the law' often work in collusion with judges. Thus court rulings are frequently the outcome of a preliminary arrangement which sometimes has a financial basis. Lawyers and judges usually know each other and socialize in the same circles. Their close relations facilitate deals, preferential treatment and the corruption of the legal system. In a situation in which the defendant is ill-informed about his rights and about the way in which the legal system functions, a minimum of justice and fairness can only be guaranteed by the professionalism and probity of the lawyer–judge partnership.

- *Clerks* Clerks occupy a strategic position within the courts; they are responsible for the recording of court hearings. Furthermore, they keep the original documents of the judgments and rulings that have been delivered and, if necessary, issue copies of these, which are known as *grosses*,[3] certificates or authentic copies. They receive the defendants, bring them to the judge and take note of the hearings that he grants. Hence, from the outset of every case, their role places them at the interface between the judges and defendants. In the eyes of defendants, the clerks have considerable powers. When they receive the defendants, they calm them down and prepare them for meeting the judge. The fact that they record the details of hearings heightens the strategic nature of their position within the legal process. Defendants constantly ask them to intervene with the judge on their behalf. Hence, many corrupt transactions are negotiated through their intervention.

Since it's the clerk who writes everything down, the prisoners tell themselves that the clerk is much more dangerous than the judge. They think that their future depends on the clerk – if he decides to write something in their favour, they will be released. It is with this in mind that they try to see the people who prowl around here, who are not court employees, and sometimes the prisoners themselves act as the representatives of other prisoners, they are the ones who approach us, there is no shortage of offers. (Clerk at the office of an examining magistrate, Niamey)

Thus the intermediaries target the clerk in the hope that he will intercede with the judge on their behalf. A brokerage chain develops which includes the clerk and an unofficial broker acting on behalf of the defendant. The clerks readily admit that they are often offered bribes to intercede with the judge on behalf of defendants or prisoners – that is, to negotiate the reduction of a sentence in the case of a prisoner or to have a defendant's charges dropped for lack of evidence or have him released on bail. Therefore, due to their strategic position within the courts as a point of access to the judge, in the course of their work the clerks are exposed to a lot of temptation, before, during and after the indictment procedure and during the preliminary investigation of cases.

- *The secretaries of the clerks and public prosecutors* Given that the secretaries control access to the clerk and to the judge and also issue certain documents, such as birth and marriage certificates, they represent a fundamental link in the brokerage chain. When they reach a certain level of seniority in their posts, they acquire positions of power as linchpins within the court and capitalize on their seniority, which they exploit not only to inform defendants of a given judge's potential for corruption but also to advise judges not to refuse the overtures of people facing trial, 'because that's how it's always been. You have to take advantage of the situation as it is one that won't last. You can be transferred to less lucrative positions at any time.'

  Due to the stability of their jobs, the secretaries sometimes know more about the 'real' functioning of the courts than the judges. In some courts, they have become real vehicles of corruption. They even have resources at their disposal which some judges do not have available to them. Everybody in the courts knows them. It is easy to gain access to them. They are always pleasant to deal with, but their friendliness is invariably calculated. They never act alone, but with the complicity of certain judges who are their friends and whose motives they share. In this respect, they also fulfil the task of directing users to the judge. In summary, they oversee an extensive network of corruption in which all kinds of actors are involved, including judges and lawyers.

Hence, brokerage chains based on different configurations are formed within the legal institutions in this way. One such chain is characterized by judges and lawyers acting together on the basis of widespread patterns of collusion, which may extend into the criminal investigation department and the prison authorities. A second type is based on parallel networks which echo the conventional official hierarchies and function according to a logic of corruption: each link plays a vital role in the functioning of the network, at the end of which is the judge, without whom corrupt actions cannot systematically become established within the legal system.

Unofficial intermediation: the monopolization of the courts Several types of informal intermediaries have been identified, all of them characterized by the fact that they are external to the legal system. Their main resource is constituted by the relational capital that they are able to activate, either directly or indirectly, within the legal system. They prowl around the courts and offer their services to the lost and intimidated anonymous users of the court. However, they play other less visible roles in relation to the judges, who tolerate their presence in the courts. To show that no scenario is typical in this context, three different types of informal intermediation are presented below. These tend to vary according to the specific court and the type of user involved.

• *Prominent local figures acting as intermediaries in Benin* The emergence of these intermediaries is directly connected to the weakness of the legal infrastructure in Benin. Combined with the absence or extreme rarity of representatives of the law, this fosters the growth of complex networks of contacts and relations between various local actors in secondary towns: these include employees of the legal system as well as prominent figures in the local community who, due to their social position and attendant influence, form an interface between some defendants and the law. The case of public figures acting as intermediaries in a medium-sized town in northern Benin is quite illustrative in this regard. Due to the nature of their professional activities, these people are generally well-known in the town. For example, R is in charge of the linguistic subcommittee for the Fulfulde language and a former member of parliament; Z is an interpreter at the court. Both have a fairly high profile locally and people come running to them when they have to deal with the law.

As it happens, the skill and effectiveness of these intermediaries reside in their ability to create solid relationships with those working within the legal system: for example, by meeting them in the context of local politics and by offering gifts at christenings, weddings and funerals, and these eventually create a breeding ground for corruption. All of these factors combine to make it possible for these people to have direct access to the local state in its different forms and to be acknowledged in this brokering role by both the defendants and the local civil servants.

- *Lobbyists or unofficial agents in Senegal*   These actors, referred to as *agent d'affaires* (lobbyists), offer to sort out problems with the authorities for people who have hired them. Blundo's description of these intermediaries is eloquent: 'equipped with a briefcase and a rubber stamp of dubious origin', they take up position in front of the court building, an area that they know well. There, the lobbyist 'observes the entrances to the courthouse and the registrar's office in order to intercept clients who arrive there. He offers either to facilitate obtaining, say, a birth or marriage certificate, to speed up a procedure or even to give advice in a lawsuit. He may also pretend to be a lawyer, assuring the person facing trial that he will be able to "sort out his case for him" because he is on good terms with the judge.' Furthermore, these people are capable of 'demonstrating detailed knowledge of the main procedures required for obtaining various administrative documents. They acquire this skill due to their close acquaintance and connections with administrative employees in the courts.' (Blundo 2001a: 82)

To my knowledge their status is not recognized in law.... These are actors who have experienced the legal system, who have worked in the courts or in the administrative departments of the courts, they have retired, you know these people have a certain profile ... they have a human capital, that is to say, they know lots of people, they are extremely resourceful individuals, they have developed a familiarity with the courts over the years, so they now come along to their colleagues, to employees who they trained themselves, people with whom they used to work all the time. So if they ask a favour of them, those people cannot refuse and generally they have most success with people who are unaware of how the legal procedures work.... Requesting a copy of a police record, for example, is something every citizen is authorized to do, but sometimes someone who is out of town may find this difficult to do, he doesn't know, he gives his papers to someone and if that person turns up, he is, of course, received by the staff, his papers are dealt with in the same way as the others. These are procedures which are not tricky or difficult, but it's due to ignorance that people turn to the lobbyist. (Clerk of the court, Kaolack)

Thus, these lobbyists exploit the fact that the client is in a hurry or is unaware of how the procedures work so as to make him pay for the provision of documents which are normally issued free of charge. Thus, a lot of commercial transactions, of which these people are the most visible purveyors, take place within the courts, and all of these transactions are carried out on a completely unofficial basis.

- *Informal intermediaries in Niger* These people virtually monopolize the courts. They are there every day and hang out in the corridors, going from office to office to chat with people. Sometimes their presence is noisy and conspicuous. Everyone knows them. With recession and unemployment, there are even more of them around. Some judges at Niamey district court are highly critical of this state of affairs. However, they are powerless to do anything about it:

Well, you see, in order to deal with these intermediaries we have closed all of the main entrances to the court apart from one so that we can monitor people entering and leaving the building. But this doesn't prevent dishonest people, people with nothing to do ... when they see a defendant arriving at or leaving a judge's office, they ask him what he's doing in the courts. He tells them that he's come to see the judge; then the intermediary may say 'but he's my cousin, I know him, if you give me 100,000 CFA francs, I'll go and see him'. Nothing can be done. If the client is naive, he gives his money to the intermediary. The latter then goes to the judge's office, greets him, comes out again and then goes back to the client who is waiting and tells him that there's no problem, he will sort out the situation and after that the so-called intermediary disappears. Is it the judge's fault? You see, the guy who paid the 100,000 CFA francs thinks that he has bribed the judge.

These intermediaries have actually acquired useful skills which make them indispensable in the courts. Referring to a well-known intermediary at Niamey district court, a lawyer employed there explains the reasons for his continued presence, despite the criticism that surrounds him, thus:

He speaks several languages, which is useful for interpreting.... And then, that's not the only reason either, he is often used to go and cash cheques, because some judges and lawyers don't want anything on paper to bear their names, so he takes the risk. Indeed he's not the only one, but he's the most well known. He's just one among many others. (Lawyer, District Court of Niamey)

In fact, it is also possible to observe the existence of other types of unofficial intermediary:

There are elderly people aged sixty plus who are there, waiting. As soon as they see people from the countryside arriving, they rush up to greet them. Listen to this, a person can be charged as much as 50,000 CFA francs for a birth certificate, something to which they are actually entitled free of charge. Whether the court is in session or not, both old and young people can be found hanging around the precincts of the courthouse and that's all that they do. (Lawyer, District Court of Niamey)

In the case of the District Court of Niamey, this situation is probably the result of a rather lax state of affairs which has fostered the growth of a highly diverse auxiliary staff who engage in these sidelines to earn extra money. They were initially assigned various duties, for example sweeping, cleaning, shopping and other services, and comprise messengers, unskilled workers, ex-prisoners, voluntary clerks in the bailiff's office and general layabouts. Some of them, for example the interpreters, clerks, messengers and unskilled workers, earn very modest wages. They live off the various gifts given to them by the judges, lawyers, bailiffs, solicitors and so on. They manage, over time, to establish familiar relations with the court authorities and this enables them to compile a solid 'database' on each individual. Thus they sometimes intervene with the prosecutor or the examining magistrate on behalf of a prisoner or a defendant. The common denominator they share is to ensure that the defendant gets access to the 'right judge' or the 'right lawyer' in return for remuneration. They are indispensable in the court because of the myriad services they provide for both the legal system and its clients. They maintain a regular presence in the halls of the court. They take people who come to court under their wing and guide them as to what to do. They know which judges are honest and which ones accept bribes. They also know which lawyers are most successful. They have unofficial lists of judges and lawyers, which they make available to their clients. Some attain such a level of skill and visibility that they manage to pass themselves off to the clients as judges or clerks of the court. They acquire a certain reputation both in the courthouse and beyond in their neighbourhoods, where their efficiency in working the court system is recognized. They live off this brokerage activity. The existence of these intermediaries, who do not receive any fixed or official wage within the legal system, encourages all kinds of corrupt practices. Their remuneration may be financial or symbolic and depends on their skill and on the degree of satisfaction of their numerous clients, who can be simultaneously the corrupt judge, the satisfied defendant and the dishonest lawyer. It must also be said, however, that the institutional weakness of the courts also contributes to the development of corrupt practices.

Corruption and the institutional weaknesses of legal systems

Like those of most francophone African countries in sub-Saharan Africa, the legal systems of Benin, Niger and Senegal are hampered in their everyday operation by a number of structural characteristics – effectively constraints – that have an impact on the normal workings of the legal system. Corrupt practices thrive in the context of this highly dysfunctional situation. The dysfunctionality is connected to both the actual structure of the legal institutions and to the working conditions, under which justice is usually delivered in these countries.

Limitations related to the structure of the legal systems

At least four different types of limitation can be identified, each of which impacts on the functioning of the legal systems in their own way.

The impenetrability and complexity of rules: the remoteness of the legal systems   The everyday trappings of the judge and his court-room are always intimidating for the uninitiated. Few defendants are able to distinguish between judges, lawyers, bailiffs and solicitors. So far as they are concerned, they all wear the trademark black gown which symbolizes the power of the legal establishment. Furthermore, the language of the courts is not merely French, another mystifying symbol, it is a technical French littered with archaisms inherited from the French legal tradition. The solemnity of court hearings, with their semi-theatrical rituals, parades and performances, also intimidates defendants and triggers in them feelings of fear and distrust. All of these factors combine to invest the court with an aura of mystery and to create an incomprehension and a distance between the judges and the judged. To all this must be added the disordered combination of judicial practices of varied origins (i.e. French, Muslim, indigenous African), which further emphasizes the impenetrability and complexity of proceedings. Although some re-forms or attempts at reform have been implemented,[4] these countries have essentially retained legislation originating from colonial times and in the aftermath of independence set up a legal establishment largely modelled on that of the former metropolitan power. Some laws are inapplicable and in many cases have failed to evolve to adapt to contemporary reality (Chaïbou 1997: 67–73; Blundo and Olivier de Sardan 2001a: 80).

Thus, in the exercise of their duties, the judges are obliged to follow civil, commercial and penal procedures that are totally out-dated, the product of a different culture and a different era. The rules of procedure and their subtleties are totally baffling to the vast majority of people (Sidibé Soumana 1998: 20–21). The judges also have to implement laws which are totally alien to the people who use the courts. Their power derives precisely from their mastery and manipulation of this complexity, and their ability to navigate the labyrinths of the legal system. These are the factors that oblige the users of the courts to avail themselves of the services of a lawyer if they can afford it. If they cannot afford the services of a lawyer, they are forced to seek out other methods, such as magic and bribery, of dealing with these mysterious and obscure rules.

The plurality of legal regulations: confusion in the identification of the applicable law The fact that colonial laws remain on the statute books does not preclude the vitality of common law, which, in spite of everything, remains, in its diversity and evolving forms, a framework of reference for the great majority of people in the countries in question. Such a situation leads to all kinds of conflicting interpretations of legislation and, due to the different regulatory systems in force, always creates much confusion when it comes to deciding the law to apply in the settlement of cases. This state of affairs leads to the emergence of unofficial and negotiable structures which make the public sphere permeable to a variety of influences (Chauveau, Le Pape and Olivier de Sardan 2001: 150–51)

Weak legal infrastructure: inequality of access In all of the countries under consideration, access to justice is unequal because citizens do not have an equal relationship to the law. This leads us to consider not just the familiar problem of access to justice, but the more specific question of why court facilities are unequally distributed around each country. The courts are concentrated in the capital and in secondary urban centres.[5] Furthermore, the full range of courts is found only in the capital cities, towards which the other legal structures based in the interior of the country tend to converge. Indeed, in many areas, the power of the Justice of the Peace, or *juge délégué* (delegate judge), to use the new term used in some countries, is reinforced because of the inadequacy of the legal infrastructure in relation to the number of inhabitants.[6] The same situation also holds true for lawyers, who are found mainly in the capital cities, thus excluding a large proportion of the population from exercising their right to a defence in court. The inadequacy of judicial facilities is today forcing governments to speed up the training of judges and to establish new courts outside of the capital. In the meantime, many people who come to trial are marginalized outside the legal system.

Congestion in the legal system: waiting lists and the slowness of the legal process   Congestion in the legal system is reflected in the number of cases waiting to be dealt with and the extent to which judges are constantly overworked.[7] The processing of cases at the courts results in extremely long waiting lists, which oblige judges to select cases to be dealt with as a priority. Hence, having one's case prioritized is a real privilege, to which few defendants can hope to aspire. The consequence of this situation is overcrowded prisons containing large numbers of prisoners awaiting trial.

Poor working conditions

Analyses of the economic causes of corruption often draw attention to the low level of salaries and budgetary resources in government departments. This also applies to the legal system, which, in addition to experiencing the difficulties faced by other state institutions, also faces a number of specific problems.

Low salaries: a factor in the temptation to accept bribes   Despite the considerable powers with which the law invests judges, as is the case with civil servants in general, their salaries are not very high. It is true of course that compared to other state employees they enjoy a special status, which is accompanied by substantial perks. Nevertheless, some judges are all too conscious of the low level of their salaries not just in relation to the cost of living, but also in relation to the earnings of auxiliary staff within the legal system – for example, lawyers and solicitors – and in view of the heavy responsibilities associated with their role. Hence 'the larger the discrepancies between pay in the civil service and the private sector, the greater the temptation to make up for these discrepancies illegally ... and the opportunities for corruption then become the main motive for joining the civil service' (Cartier-Bresson 2000: 15–16).

Inadequacy of budgetary allocations to legal institutions   Once salaries have been paid, little remains in the legal system's budget for the funding or remuneration of the most basic administrative duties and services necessary for its efficient functioning. This results in inadequate or a total lack of communication and travel facilities, equipment shortages, inadequate court facilities, and so on. It is a constant battle for offices in the legal system to function normally: they have limited funding for basic stationery and supplies – paper, pencils, ink, telephone, photocopies, fuel, and so on – and also lack essential equipment such as computers and vehicles. This has consequences for the provision of services to the public by the legal system, which is often stalled, handicapped or diverted from its essential tasks due to this lack of resources. The fact is that the legal system has never been allocated substantial budgetary resources. Structural adjustment programmes, which drastically reduced the budgets allocated to government departments, have exacerbated a situation which was already far from perfect.

Lack of a public judicial arena   The work of the courts is rarely enriched by sustained information on case law and doctrine. Indeed, the question as to how the cases dealt with by the courts are subsequently documented is one that needs to be addressed urgently. Rulings delivered by the judges are not systematically recorded and statistical information is not always available. With the exception of important decisions in the higher courts (i.e. the Court of Appeal, Court of Final Appeal and Supreme Court), which are sometimes published when the availability of external funding makes this possible, case law is rarely published and circulated. The speeches made by the prosecution and by lawyers for the defence are rarely recorded and are, therefore, rarely made available beyond the context of a given trial. It would undoubtedly be useful if they were circulated and debated by specialists. Thus, even the most basic sources of legal doctrine are virtually non-existent. Public debate on matters of legal doctrine is totally lacking in the profession which needs it most. Thus, judges can only improve their professional skills by doing such work in a personal and voluntary capacity and without the support of their departments. In such a context, training courses continue to be highly coveted: numerous applications are submitted for places on such courses, but few are successful. Consequently, in formulating their conviction that they are satisfied beyond reasonable doubt as to the guilt or innocence of a defendant and in the use of their discretionary powers, judges have only their own common sense to fall back on for guidance. If we also consider the increasingly special- ized nature of litigation and the small number of specialist judges, judges can only feel helpless in the face of the quantity, complexity and diversity of the cases they have to deal with. In such situations, young judges are inevitably left to fend for themselves in a context where socialization in their given milieu plays a determining role in the formation of their professional ethics.

Conclusion: corruption and the transformation of the legal system

At this stage in our analysis, we can provide a broad outline of the transformations that have occurred in the legal system. What we see first and foremost is a legal system that is being used by the government and key actors within it for their own ends. Moreover, the corruption that has developed within this system has resulted in the development of extensive dysfunctionalities, which have forced the public authorities to instigate programmes of reform.

The exploitation of the legal system

There are two dimensions to this exploitation of the legal system. The first goes back to the history of legal institutions as they have become established in francophone Africa. The legal system was first used as an instrument in the service of colonization (Clauzel 2003: 649–729) before being used to shore up the political forces that took over the running of the post-colonial state. As Le Roy remarks:

> From the perspective of the combined experiences of the various states, the main trend of legal policy in Africa has been characterized by its relationship with authoritarianism, despite the manifold reforms which constitute a kind of 'smokescreen' and give the impression of a concern for the provision of a satisfactory legal system with general (and generous) proclaimed objectives, while at the same time ensuring the base designs of the government of the day, whether voluntarily or under duress. (Le Roy 2004: 146)

Thus the legal system is tainted with the stigma of this controversial history in the context of a democratization process which ascribes new roles to it. The exploitation of the legal system is here connected to the question of the autonomization of the established judicial power, which, as we know, always has many close links with the government: the power to appoint judges, the power to impose penalties, the control of careers, the allocation of funding. Given this state of affairs, 'the judge is more akin to an official whose role is to guarantee an established social order' (Le Roy 2004: 191).

The second dimension of this exploitation concerns the key actors in the judicial institutions. We are well aware of all of the strategies employed by these actors for the purpose of reinforcing both their professional and their social positions. Here, the law is analysed in terms of its least visible aspects, whereby the established actors engage in illegal practices that make a mockery of their office while they are actually carrying out their official duties. It is at this point that a whole range of corrupt practices, some aspects of which we have already outlined in this chapter, emerge and develop. These contribute to the gradual disintegration of the institution as a consequence of the new operational rules that come into play. Such results might be described as 'judicial disarray'.

Judicial disarray

This disarray is connected to the multiple facets assumed by the legal system when an attempt is made to give it a coherent profile. In the capital cities, the legal system gives the appearance of being a normal legal system, perfectly structured and endowed with all of the conventional formal attributes. However, our research has shown that it is actually highly deregulated. Some of its most significant traits in this regard can be summarized as follows:

- Traditional formal hierarchies are increasingly eclipsed by internal divisions stemming from the professional backgrounds of the judges, the different generations of people working together who don't always share the same points of reference or ambitions, their diverse political allegiances and their moral probity. Obviously,

some actors in the legal system combine all or some of these
characteristics to varying degrees.

- The transformation of an accused person's right to a defence,
whereby there is now little scope for ethics or fairness due to the
increase in bargaining activities.
- The unofficial establishment of an alternative legal system controlled by the criminal investigation department, which sometimes makes decisions on cases unbeknown to the judges.

In rural areas, the legal system is far less rigidly structured.
Common law is very much to the fore and constitutes the first stage
of legal proceedings. Hence a variety of rules predominate. In such
a context the role of the judge, which encompasses a relatively large
area of competencies, changes and he acquires additional powers
which counterparts in the capital do not possess. As the incontestable
focus of power in the locality, in most cases, the judge's decisions are
autonomous. He has control over the police. He is rarely restricted
by the presence of a lawyer. Human rights associations are thin on
the ground and the local press is virtually non-existent. The judge
combines the powers of indictment, preliminary investigation and
sentencing, and sometimes even controls the implementation of his
own rulings. Hence, he becomes a key actor in the penal system. The
dominant position enjoyed by judges in rural areas is the outcome
of a range of factors – for example, poor legal infrastructure and
inadequate numbers of auxiliary legal staff, who are concentrated in
the capitals. In these circumstances, the judge is frequently answer-
able only to himself, and country people who have to deal with the
courts are, therefore, exposed to the arbitrariness and the vagaries
of an unpredictable legal system.

From light grey to dark grey

As a result of all this, the corruption that has taken root in the legal
systems of Niger, Benin and Senegal is characterized by the variety
of forms it has assumed. Of course, petty corruption accounts for
part of it and has become quite commonplace. It allows a large group
of minor officials and other auxiliary staff to earn a supplementary

income by unjustifiable methods. Users of the legal system condemn it at every opportunity, but they put up with it since they continue to pay fees that they know to be totally illegal. This corruption can be categorized in an area which, to reformulate Heidenheimer's (1990: 160–61) distinction slightly, we could describe as 'light grey'.

Grand corruption is also in evidence, but it depends on the nature of the cases involved. Some of these can be very lucrative, when large sums of money exchange hands or when it is a matter of protecting the interests of certain public figures who are in trouble with the law and attempt to bribe the judge dealing with their case. This is the murkiest area of corruption in the legal system. Transactions are clandestine and usually conducted via networks. Their financial repercussions can only be inferred from the lifestyles of certain judges, the very ones who are presumed to be corrupt and who are stigmatized by their peers as a result. Adopting Heidenheimer's classification again, we can say that this form of corruption verges on the 'dark grey' and has become entrenched in the system. We know that it exists. It is widely condemned, but nobody can prove its existence.

The legal system in the dock

The legal system is the subject of lively debate in the countries under consideration in our study. We know that for a long time this debate mainly focused on the question of the independence of the judiciary in relation to the government. More recently it has extended to the question of corruption in the legal system. The reform of the legal system is a major issue in all three countries and, like the health and education systems, it has become a priority area for the governments. All of the aid providers want to fund it, arguing that reform of the legal system is a prerequisite for the emergence of good governance. This new trend will open up the way for development projects in this sector, which has been neglected by the government for a long time. Public investment will probably increase dramatically. In terms of the practical impact of such projects, we cannot help wondering whether they will not, in fact, have the effect of increasing corruption in a sector in which it is already rife.

Thus the legal system has all the appearance of an institution in crisis. In its everyday modus operandi, it is characterized by activities and procedures that are often far-removed from the ideals and standards on which it is founded. Furthermore, it is faced with major structural constraints, which foster the emergence within it of new pragmatic rules and the proliferation of informal circuits of information and action that substantially alter the nature of the work it is supposed to carry out. In these circumstances, an exploration of how the legal system really works brings us face to face with the problematics of government and democracy. The crisis of the legal system is one of the many manifestations of the crisis of the state in Africa, of which the legal system merely constitutes a single segment. Its structural weaknesses, the propensity of the social actors who work within and around it to manipulate its rules for personal gain, the incapacity of its institutional framework to deal with certain reprehensible situations, the increasing politicization of judges and their strong involvement in various social networks based on contacts and influence – all of these factors make the idea of the primacy of an established impersonal regulatory system appear entirely illusory. This 'real', and largely unofficial, dynamic within legal institutions imposes serious constraints on the process of democratization that is currently under way, as we know that this process needs a healthy justice system if it is to be strengthened. In the same way, it jeopardizes the attempts at reform under consideration in the sector.

6

'We don't eat the papers': corruption in transport, customs and the civil forces

Nassirou Bako Arifari

From Malanville to Cotonou with a flock of sheep

Malanville, 4 p.m. on a June day in the year 2000: a truck loaded with around a hundred sheep sets off. Its destination is Cotonou.

At the exit from Malanville there is a sign indicating 'STOP POLICE'. The driver gets out of the truck with his documents and moves towards the officers: 'It's sheep, boss', he says while handing over the vehicle logbook, beneath which are two 1,000-franc notes. The police officer moves towards the back of the vehicle and removes the two banknotes. Without even taking a look inside the logbook to see whether the documents are in order, he returns them to the driver and wishes him 'a good trip'.

A few minutes later, the driver is forced to stop at a customs sign. The owner of the sheep dismounts and heads over to one of the customs officers. He stretches out his hand pretending to salute the customs officer and slides a 1,000 franc note into his hand. Some 100 km later, at around 6 p.m., the driver arrives at another control post near Kandi. The driver stops the truck and gets out with his documents. One of the police officers asks, 'What are you carrying?' 'It's sheep, boss', the driver responds eagerly while handing him something. Before accepting the 'gift' the officer asks the driver:

'How much have you got?' '2,000 francs,' says the driver. The officer retorts: 'No, no no, if it is not 4,000 francs I won't accept it.' The driver pleads: 'Boss, I only have 2,000 francs and that's what we're giving you.' After negotiating for a few minutes, the driver slides the 2,000 francs into the officer's hand, who in turn slides it tactfully into his pocket. 'Thanks boss', says the driver, concluding the exchange.

It is around 8.30 p.m., the gendarmes are on security patrol at Bembereke. Their control post is situated in a bend on a downward slope. Parked vehicles prevent the driver from stopping in front of the sign. He decides to stop a short distance beyond the sign, when one of gendarmes puts up a barrier, no doubt thinking that the driver intended to ignore the sign. Having stopped his truck and established that the officer is wearing an armband indicating that they are there for security rather than control purposes, the driver turns to him and reproaches him furiously for his behaviour. A heated exchange ensues. The passengers and the research assistant, in particular, have to intervene and mediate. The second gendarme, who is more officious, orders the driver to leave. The driver has not given the officers anything.

Half an hour later, a lamp inside a red plastic bucket signals another control point, this time manned by the gendarmes who patrol the roads who are otherwise known as *les éperviers au bec crochu* ('the hook-beaked sparrow hawks'). The driver stops the truck and disembarks empty-handed – without the documents. 'Good evening boss!' he shouts to the officer, who merely replies 'What is it?' The driver answers: 'It's sheep, boss', while giving him 5,000 francs, which the latter grabs as though entirely his by right and does not say a word. There is not much chit-chat with the road police. They have a reputation for severity, and the illegal payment made to them is inevitably higher than that paid to the other road officers.

Again, barely half an hour later, there is another control post manned by gendarmes. The same scenario unfolds and the fee paid is the same, 5,000 francs.

Police and customs officers are on duty at the entrance to Parakou, 317 km from the departure location. The driver stops his truck and heads towards the police officers to conform to tradition and pay them 'their' 2,000 francs. Meanwhile, the owner of the sheep goes to pay 1,000 francs to the customs officers.

After a stop at Parakou, the vehicle takes off again at around 12.30 a.m. Two signs at the exit from Parakou announce again the simultaneous presence of the police and customs. The same routine ensues: 2,000 francs to the police and 1,000 francs to the customs officers.

A few minutes later at Tchatchou the presence of another security patrol is indicated by means of a large BMW motorcycle with a helmet on top of it, the purpose of which is to suggest the threat of pursuit if a driver fails to stop. The same formalities apply and a payment of 5,000 francs is expected. However, despite the presence of gendarmes with armbands, the driver did not stop at Tchaourou. When the researcher asks why he did not stop this time, he responds: 'It's because they are on a security mission. They only succeed in catching new drivers and Nigerians because they don't know this.' The gendarmes do not have the right to check vehicles when they are on security patrol. In the 1990s, the unions representing drivers and road hauliers had to fight to obtain the imposition of a regulation whereby officers of the civil forces must wear distinctive insignia when on security missions so as to prevent them from fleecing road users under the guise of checking documents. This explains the driver's rather daring attitude towards the gendarmes, both here and in Bembereke.

At the entrance to Savè, there is another control post manned by gendarmes and customs officers. Before getting out of the truck, the driver confides in the anthropologist:

> The gendarmes you see here are from Abomey. Unlike their Parakou colleagues, they are honest: if their colleagues are out at another control post, they tell you and only take 2,500 francs instead of 5,000 so that you can pay the other 2,500 francs to their colleagues at the next control post. But if they are on their own and there are no other gendarmes in their area, they tell you and charge the full 5,000 francs. The Parakou road police charge 5,000 francs every time you meet them. They are greedy.

Having reached the place they are standing, he stops and turns to them with a 2,500 franc note prepared in advance. 'Good evening boss!', he says to the gendarme, who in turn asks. 'What are you carrying?' 'It's sheep, boss.' The driver hands him the 2,500 franc note. Having checked it, the officer says: 'We are alone, there is no one else on the road.' The driver says carefully: 'Boss, if I see the gendarmes I will say that you took everything.' The gendarme reassures him, saying 'I am the one talking to you, no? We came out on our own today.' 'Of course, boss', the driver acquiesces, adding another 2,500 francs.

A while later, at around 2.45 a.m., there is a sign indicating the presence of customs officers at a control post. The driver stops the truck and the owner goes over to the customs officers to give them 'their' 1,000 francs. More and more police and customs controls follow and by the time we reach Cotonou we have passed a total of sixteen control – or, to be more precise, extortion – points along the 750 km route from Malanville to Cotonou.

Both the officers patrolling the bascule bridge and the CRS (Compagnie Républicaine de Sécurité) are present at the entrance to Cotonou. The officer whose job it is to weigh the vehicles charges the driver 700 francs, without actually weighing the vehicle, and then heads off to pay 500 francs to the CRS officer.

There is nothing at all unusual about this obstacle course. This is what daily life on the roads in Benin, Niger and Senegal is all about. It would appear that the customs, gendarmerie and police forces in West Africa are all dens of routine and highly visible institutionalized corruption, of which the widespread practice of extortion on the roads is but one manifestation. Moreover, in terms of the volume of the financial resources involved, the customs authority enjoys a significant lead ahead of the public procurement and tax authorities. A study recently carried out on the transport chain in Benin shows that the customs authority is identified in 70 per cent of the research sample on the subject as the authority with the highest level of corruption (see Lalèyè 2001). In Niger and Senegal customs officers are perceived as being so corrupt that they are undoubtedly destined for hell in the next world.

Almost all of the services provided by these public authorities are privatized to a greater or lesser extent. This interstitial privatiz-

ation of the state consists of the involvement of a series of parasitic
actors and 'informal' auxiliary agents in state tasks by customs and
police officers through segmental alliance-type relationships that
contribute to the perpetuation of corruption.

Sociological studies carried out on the police highlight in particular the phenomena of 'discretionary power' and 'hierarchical
inversion': the officers on the ground enjoy significant freedom
in terms of the selection of situations to crack down on, and, as a
result, any initiatives taken by more senior officers are extremely
dependent on the action of their subordinates (Monjardet 1996).
This discretionary power constitutes a key resource that puts the
police in a position of power vis-à-vis the users of the state's services.
However, the studies in question were often primarily concerned
with the corruption in criminal investigation departments and only
secondarily with the practice of extortion by police officers on the
roads (see Gupta 1995; Klitgaard 1988). Thus, while the image of
the corrupt policeman is a commonplace one in the international
context and constitutes one of the more perennial topics in the local
press, the internal logics of police corruption and their links with
the functioning and malfunctioning of police administrations and
state administrations, in general, do not often feature among the
analysts' main preoccupations.

With regard to the customs authorities, most studies concentrate on fraud, its scope and the losses it entails for state budgets,
as well as the methods that need to be implemented to eradicate
it (Stasavage and Daubrée 1997; Johnston 1997; Klitgaard 1988).
Customs fraud has frequently been linked to the phenomenon of
the informal (Usinier and Verna 1994) and has been perceived as
a reaction of excluded or marginalized groups – including women
– to the reduction in opportunities in the wage economy. According
to Niger-Thomas (2000: 58), the majority of businesswomen do not
believe that they have a moral obligation to pay tax to the state;
they are simply trying to obtain their 'share' in a society in which
everyone else seeks to obtain theirs. However, these studies focus
on a single group of corrupt actors, the smugglers, without showing
any interest in the public officials involved in the daily corrupt
interaction. If it is known that cross-border smuggling is carried

out on a vast scale and acts as a means of accumulating wealth for groups within the state which tend already to be privileged, it is possible to confirm that smuggling is not a phenomenon limited to marginalized groups, but a systemic activity that is often controlled by extremely influential actors.

In this chapter, we present the various actors involved in the everyday practices of corruption observed in the customs and transport sectors. The contexts, practices, mechanisms and logics of this institutional and structural corruption are described and analysed along with the networks and operating modes through which it manifests itself, and all of these phenomena are examined in relation to the structural constraints imposed by their circumstances. Finally, the changes triggered by corruption at both the social and the political level are explored. We show that corruption in the transport sector and in the civil forces responds simultaneously to an array of logics: the logic of economic competition, the logic of ordinary sociability, the logic of social exchange and, in some cases also, the logic of professional competency and even the attempt to provide public services.

Corrupt practices in the transport and customs sectors involve three main areas: (a) the identification of road users – the checking of identity cards and driving licences; (b) the technical and administrative status of vehicles – vehicle registration, technical inspection, insurance, general external appearance and so on; and (c) transported goods and customs duty. The roads, water courses, ports and airports – and the administrative services responsible for their management – provide the physical settings within which the corrupt everyday activities analysed in this chapter take place. Our research focused on all of the administrative services involved in the provision of documents relating to transport (e.g. the port system, the authorities responsible for inland transportation, driving schools, road safety centres, traffic police and gendarmerie, the forwarding and shipment companies, customs administrations, various trade unions representing drivers and hauliers, traders' associations etc.) and their many actors, both official and unofficial.

The context of corrupt practices

In the three countries, the elevation of political clientelism to a systemic phenomenon basically expresses the relationship between public services and their clients. The reduction of fines for traffic offences in Senegal under the PS (Socialist Party) regime – a measure introduced to win over the electorate in the transport sector – was a typical institutional manifestation of this political clientelism. A degree of continuity in relation to such practices can also be observed under the PDS (Senegalese Democratic Party) regime. The leader of the taxi-drivers' union of the town of Kaolack refers to one of the party's election slogans in the following comment: 'There are 3,228 unlicensed bikes on the road in Kaolack, but that also means 3,228 votes for the PDS.' The individuals involved here – the owners of the unlicensed bicycles – were generally former PS supporters who have been poached by the PDS.

A Nigerien policeman to whom I complained about the astonishing overloading of the taxi I hired to take me from Gaya to Niamey in 1998 responded as follows: 'Sir, we can do nothing now, it's the unions that decide.' This comment clearly demonstrates the shift in the power relationship between the officers of the law and private actors in the transport sector as a result of both the corrupt activities and electoral strategies of the current regime. Private actors and members of associations in the transport sector no longer fear the forces of law and order and this enables them to violate the legislation in force with greater ease and with impunity.

However, the war against corruption in the transport sector has been under way for some time now in all three countries. In the Beninese administration, for example, it started under the revolution (1972–89), in particular with the dismissal in the early 1980s of officers of the civil forces caught in the act of extorting money from road users. This process was not interrupted by the period of Democratic Renewal; indeed it was enshrined in two decrees passed in 1995. Before setting up SOS-Corruption, a body to which the victims of corruption could complain, the Committee of the War against Inflation (Comité de lutte contre l'inflation), which was created under Decree 95–171 of 9 June 1995, tried to establish a link between the cost of living and the practices of extortion on the road. Despite these efforts, however, the phenomenon is still on the increase. A study on road transport in Benin carried out by the World Bank noted that the existence of over twenty control points on the road linking Cotonou and the border with Niger raises the annual cost of transport on this route by 20 to 30 per cent, or two billion CFA francs (World Bank 1996).

Benin and Niger both share extensive borders with Nigeria, an outright champion in the field of corruption (according to the classification of Transparency International in 2003), which are crucial to their economic survival. The control of these borders represents a permanent challenge to the public authorities of the two countries, which have never really succeeded in gaining control over cross-border transactions that are deeply embedded in profound historical and ethnical relationships. The pull of Nigeria for Benin and Niger is replicated in Senegal by its relationship with Gambia. The latter represents a veritable free zone right in the middle of Senegal and a nucleus from which numerous branches of corruption and fraud develop, which are relayed to the country's interior through marabout networks. These networks provide impunity and inviolability for the transit zones as well as warehouse storage for the products of fraudulent activities (an example is Touba, the holy city of the Mouride brotherhood).

The budgets of these three countries are essentially tax-based and customs revenue is the main source of contributions. Having reached 52 per cent in 1999 immediately before the implementation of the West Africa Economic and Monetary Union (UEMOA) customs reform, which came into force on 1 January 2000, customs revenue in Senegal represented 40 per cent of budgetary resources in 2000. The corresponding figure for Benin in 2000 was 46 per cent and exceeded 60 per cent for Niger for the same period. This budgetary dependence on customs revenue is an indicator of the importance of business, transit and transport activities in these countries. This dependence is heightened by the reforms inspired by various structural adjustment programmes, which have put the governments in a vulnerable position vis-à-vis their customs authorities. A threat of strike by the customs authority is always a major cause for concern. And customs officers do not hesitate to resort to blackmail every time an action or inquiry is launched that targets corrupt practices in their sector. In 1999, the Beninese government quashed the results of a commission of inquiry on fraud and corruption in the customs sector following a strike by customs officers that resulted in a reduction of over two-thirds in customs revenue for the month of November. In Niger, the government was obliged to dissolve the National Union of Customs Officers (Syndicat National des Douaniers/SNAD) in 1997, having removed its members from the customs corps for striking in 1994 when the entire country was in severe crisis and customs revenue was almost the only source of income available to the government. More specifically, while Niger is a landlocked country whose economic survival is dependent on transport, Benin and Senegal both have ports which act as free ports for the neighbouring landlocked states, and for which transit activity and re-exportation is a key source of revenue (see on Benin Igué and Soulé 1992; Igué 1998).[1]

The actors involved in transport-sector corruption

Public-sector employees

The provision of services in the transport sector often requires the simultaneous involvement of several administrations. The obtaining of driving licences, for example, involves the transport service (in Benin only), the gendarmerie (more in the case of Niger) and private service providers such as driving schools. In all cases the registration of vehicles involves the services responsible for terrestrial, inland waterway and maritime transport, and, in the area of road safety, vehicles must undergo technical inspection by road safety centres, which may also carry out certain technical controls, such as the testing of blood alcohol levels and environmental pollutants in vehicle emissions, directly on the road (Benin). Finally, the police and gendarmerie are responsible for the monitoring of compliance with the rules of the road and the checking of the conformity of vehicles with technical and fiscal regulations in all three countries. Thus, these two bodies are involved in the checking of both people and transported goods. While identity checks within the territories of the three countries are becoming less frequent, with the recent intervention of the emigration and immigration police, they are assuming a whole new dimension at the various borders. In areas located at a considerable distance from customs posts, the gendarmerie assumes the role of the customs authorities by checking goods. However, this is more often done for the purpose of collecting money than for granting actual customs clearance. Various organizations are also simultaneously involved in the checking of transported objects (merchandise etc.). Thus, water and forestry officials check primary products originating from the bush, such as game and, above all, construction timber, fuelwood and charcoal. Agricultural officials check the transport of live animals on the roads, while fish and fishing equipment are checked by the officials from the fisheries services.

Of these civil forces involved in the transport sector, the customs authorities enjoy a monopoly position when it comes to the main source of budgetary revenue in the three countries – that is, from the customs clearance of transported goods and collection of taxes. Nowadays, the other services that are part of the work carried out by the customs authorities are mainly provided by private companies: those involved in transit, delivery and maintenance activities, on the one hand, and that check the value of imported products and monitor customs-clearance procedures, and the efficiency and accuracy of the collection of customs duty, on the other (i.e. Bivac in Benin, Cotecna in Niger, and SGS in Senegal).

From 'amateur' actors and intermediaries...

A range of different actors are involved in each of the stages in the transport chain referred to above, including driving-licence applicants, drivers, road hauliers (owners), trade unions representing drivers and hauliers, and passengers. Along with these we have the road transport intermediaries, who include groups of actors such as brokers or touts, known as *coxeurs* in Benin, Niger and Senegal, and the bus station 'bosses'. The last act as intermediaries between both the passengers and drivers and between the drivers and the civil forces based at the bus stations. Moreover, the bus stations have an entire floating population of informal brokers and touts, referred to everywhere as *racoleurs*. The gendarmes and police officers at all of the control points have accredited 'intermediaries' at their disposal who very often manage the 'rope' or 'road block'. In the three countries studied – and in particular in Benin and Niger – it is possible to observe the emergence of a new kind of road check which is being implemented by the unions representing drivers and hauliers and whose purpose is to ensure that the 'order of loading system' is observed. They have their own road blocks, which are different to those used by the police and gendarmes and are used to check for *mass* (abuse of the taxi drivers' queuing system) and to extort money from the people who 'elected' them.

In addition to the private actors mentioned above, various other actors gravitate around the customs posts: traders, driver-smugglers, 'professional' smugglers (*julo* and *njogaan* in Senegal, *fayawo* in Bénin, *smogalyze* in Niger),[2] 'escorts' of goods who specialize in obtaining reductions in customs duties, various other kinds of smugglers (such as the women smugglers in Benin and the 'customs smugglers' [*passeurs en douane*] found at the port of Cotonou, at the customs post in Niamey airport in Niger and throughout Senegal), the licensed customs brokers and, in particular, the ambulant customs brokers who operate unofficially in all three countries.

...to the corruption professionals

The customs brokers are merely the main facilitators of more vast networks of parasitic actors who live from the proceeds of customs-related corruption. These include auxiliary customs agents and intermediaries whose skills include expertise in the perpetration of corrupt transactions. In reality, the customs officers often avail of the input of these auxiliary brokers to support them in their work. The customs officers, who are themselves intermediaries in the chain of customs corruption, refer to them as 'customs assistants'; however, they are known as *klébés* ('note lifters') in the jargon of the smugglers of south Benin, as *karen dwan* ('customs dog') in the Hausa language in Niger, and as 'civil customs personnel' in Senegal. These generic auxiliaries are joined by various trackers, drivers and informers. Almost every customs officer has at least one or two and sometimes more of these actors at his service, and, more often than not, they are involved in duplicitous activities, as one of their number, M.A.D., a 51-year-old Senegalese informer, clearly explains:

> No Director of Customs can carry out his activities successfully without collaborating with the civil personnel. For example, if you wanted to risk getting rid of the civil personnel, the [customs] revenue would quickly fall by between 10 and 20 per cent as they would go and offer their services to the smugglers and give them all of the information about the customs officers. If the *civils* did not find favour with the customs officers, they would end up changing over to the side of the Touba smugglers. (Interview held on 18 June 2000)

This is confirmed by a Nigerien customs broker:

> Every customs officer has his *karen dwan*. His *karen dwan* monitors the high-level wheeling and dealing [that goes on] in the customs authority on his behalf. He comes and tells him about it and his boss gets involved in the business. In reality, the customs officers have *karen dwan* so that no deals take place without their knowledge. If, for example, a boss is informed of a deal, he will block it. He will say no, that he has to be involved or he will tell. Some customs officers have become *karen dwan* for their bosses; they report everything they see.

In certain border regions, in particular those bordering Nigeria such as Kraké (in Benin), the *klébés* are organized in 'local security civil brigades', which are created by the administrative authorities and the local development associations for the purpose of helping customs officers to control the numerous smuggling trails. In Kraké alone, the *klébés* number around 400 – over four times the number of security officers posted on this border. These auxiliary agents are not, however, paid a salary. They are paid on the basis of the seizure of goods – they receive 10 per cent of the value of seized goods – and also on the basis of the extortion they are tacitly authorized to practise among the users of the customs service. This practice is known in Kraké as the *clear* and is a kind of informally instituted 'toll'. Clients have to pay to 'clear' the way for their passage and the *klébés* are responsible for the collection of the fee for this right of passage. The same practices involving the delegation of customs functions can be observed in the port of Cotonou, where the *klébés* act as secretaries for the customs inspectors, whom they replace at several checkpoints. In addition to acting as informers, they also play the role of intermediaries in corruption transactions and collect money on behalf of the customs officers when the latter do not want to be seen. Thus they act as the interface between the corrupters and corrupted and collect payments from both sides. They sometimes even collect corrupt payments on behalf of their patrons, the customs officers, as described here by a Nigerien informant:

> In order to evade the various fines and the confiscation of his merchandise, a trader offered 500,000 CFA francs to the customs officer in exchange for his freedom. The deal was done and the customs officer had to go to the trader's house to get his money. Instead his informer turned up at the trader's house to collect the money on behalf, he said, of his boss. He [the informer] disappeared with the money, and as it was a secret and illegal operation the customs officer was not able to pursue his informer.

In addition to the *klébés*, the informal auxiliaries include the 'ambulant customs brokers', who are described as such because they act as customs brokers despite not being officially licensed. The ambulant customs brokers represent a central link in the chain of corruption in the transport sector and can be found in the ports – Cotonou and Dakar – and at both aerial and terrestrial border points. In general, the ambulant customs brokers handle cash, with which they pay the customs bills immediately, while the licensed customs brokers conduct customs transactions whose payments are deferred. As a result, the customs officers and the ambulant customs brokers have formed a kind of alliance against the licensed customs brokers. Due to their direct monetary relationships with the customs officers, the ambulant customs brokers have acquired a reputation for flexibility and rapidity in their processing of customs clearance operations, in particular those involving small quantities of goods. Indeed, the presence of these actors in the port and customs landscape in Benin has prompted the licensed customs brokers to start using the ambulant brokers as subcontractors by 'selling [them] their stamps' and hence making them their indirect representatives.

Thus the licensed customs brokers attempt to compensate for what they consider to be a loss of income arising from the interaction of several different levels of corruption by themselves engaging in a corrupt practice. Therefore the ambulant customs brokers act under the cover of the licensed customs brokers, who agree symbolically to shelter the former's operations in their own businesses symbolically without, however, recording their earnings in their turnover for taxation purposes. The ambulant customs brokers in Benin have even managed to legitimize themselves by forming trade unions and associations for the defence of their interests which are recognized by the Ministry of the Interior. Thus these actors, who are clearly involved in illegal activities and do not pay any tax to the state, have managed to obtain official recognition.

The ambulant customs brokers have also assumed the role of regulators of corruption in port-related transactions. They know the rates for corruption applied at the different checkpoints and this knowledge has become one of the elements of their professional expertise. At the port of Cotonou and in the Nigerien customs services, this knowledge of the topography of the locations of corruption and familiarity with the obscure system of rates is the guarantee of their effectiveness. For example, having a second-hand car released from the port of Cotonou involves passing through seventeen successive points of corruption, ten of which are located within the customs system. The procedure involved in the release of a container is the same; however, the payments are higher. Obtaining the release of goods from the customs post for *moyens de transport* – that is, vehicles – in Niamey involves passing through seven points of corruption which are under the control of the ambulant customs brokers.

As demonstrated by the following comments by a Nigerien customs broker at Niamey airport, corruption is becoming more and more common as a matter of professional competency, even within licensed customs brokerages:

> With regard to their company, CET, a budget was approved for these customs officers, which was distributed at the end of each year in the form of a New Year's gift along with the almost free use of the telephone by the customs officers. At Nitra [a Nigerien customs brokerage], for example, the customs officers are given petrol vouchers. The good

customs broker is the one who maintains a good relationship with the customs officers. The latter can see problems in the processing of files and turn a blind eye. Look, by maintaining these good relationships, the customs brokers can avoid the heavy fines issued by the customs.

The various actors described above can be classified in three main categories: (a) the public-sector employees; (b) economic operators; and (c) institutional or informal intermediaries involved in corrupt transactions. In reality, the boundaries between these three major groups are quite fluid: a policeman, a gendarme or a customs officer may act as an intermediary in a corrupt transaction between a customs user and a customs colleague, and so forth. Thus the blurring of the boundaries between these categories of actors involves practices such as the *cher collègue*[3] in the Senegalese customs, bogus customs escorts to cover up smuggling in both Niger and Senegal, and the import of goods through the port of Cotonou by customs officials who are also registered as traders under their wives' names.

The quest to accelerate procedures and the wilful pursuit of delays

The users of transport and customs services – private individuals thwarted by bureaucratic red tape, importers, exporters, taxi and truck drivers, hauliers – are all social and economic actors for whom time represents an important success factor, and any gain they make in terms of time enhances the competitiveness of their activities. Thus, these actors are on a permanent quest to accelerate official procedures and constantly need to find ways to achieve this. They are often under a lot of pressure and are, therefore, vulnerable in their dealings with officials and other public-sector employees. Even if their affairs are in order, they are often forced to engage in corruption so as to obtain a faster service. For example, in Niger there is a 48–hour lapse between the introduction of a declaration into the customs processing chain and the release of the merchandise, while the same process takes 72 hours in Benin. Users of the customs service generally perceive this wait as excessive and prefer 'to speed up procedures'.

Situations in which the cost of corruption to the client is often lower than the losses they would expect to incur if the completion of the desired process is delayed offer public-sector employees very real opportunities for extortion. Such contexts create a need for a personalized service among clients, who often engage entirely willingly in corrupt practices and sometimes even take the initiative.

> The customs officers play on our impatience. They know we are in a hurry so they do it to make us look for an arrangement. It is rare for a customs officer to request an arrangement explicitly. If they know that your affairs are not in order, they start by making threats to put you under pressure. Then they show that they are willing to help you and this is when you have to understand their game and make a proposition to them. Then you bargain. If, on the other hand, the customs officer really doesn't find anything having checked, he says: 'give me the *cola* money' [i.e. bribe]. (Trader, 10 April 2000, Kaolack)

Thus the customs officers and the officers who carry out road checks exploit people's lack of time. This strategy ranges from the simple order to 'park and give me your documents!', which policemen shout at drivers so as to put them under pressure, to the threat that goods will have to be unloaded, which is used – and frequently abused – by customs officers, as demonstrated by the following account provided by a Nigerien driver:

> For example, when you drive to Zinder or Maradi with a loaded truck, every customs officer on the road, in particular those in the squads, asks us for something even though we have completed the necessary formalities at the outset. You are forced to give them something or they threaten to unload the truck for a so-called check. You see the set-up they create to get at us. Well, imagine them asking you to unload in the bush where there is no help on hand. What's more, the truck owner does not pay you for it. So you understand why we give into their pressure against our better judgement.

The customs officers at the port of Cotonou deliberately create queues of users, particularly on Friday afternoons, the last day of the week, known locally as *la finale*. On that day, the customs officers arrive late for work at around 4 p.m. and the counters close just one hour later. Thus a process of haggling and bargaining starts with the clients making offers or customs officers making corrupt requests in exchange for the immediate processing of the client's files so that they can obtain the release of their goods. The failure to obtain one's goods on Friday afternoon when all of the release formalities have already been completed is seen as a disaster by the clients as it means not only a lost weekend but additional charges for storage and having to start again from scratch with the formalities the following Monday. This time pressure results in inflationary increases in the rates of corruption of up to 500 per cent, and in some cases even 1,000 per cent – the range is perhaps between 1,500 and 15,000 CFA francs.

The chain of corruption and its mechanisms in the transport sector

From the issuing of driving licences and the manning of road checks to the processing of customs transactions, this sector presents a sequence of opportunities for corruption, the modes of operation of which are highly varied and visible.

Obtaining a driving licence

The driving test constitutes the first process in the context of which public-sector employees can exercise their power of control in the transport sector. It brings together public-sector employees (driving testers from the terrestrial transport service), clients (i.e. the candidates), and 'private' agents (the managers and instructors from the driving schools) who act as intermediaries between the first two categories of actor. In fact, the driving school directors and instructors collude with the testers to extort money from the candidates. In this case psychological pressure is used to force clients to engage in corruption. The tactic consists in convincing candidates that they will not pass the test if they do not pay a bribe. As part of the practical advice given to them by instructors, pupils are told: 'You must think of the testers.' The driving instructors and driving school managers collect the 'corruption charges' and give them to the testers involved. The instructors are always present during tests and often point out to the testers the candidates who have and haven't paid. Those who haven't paid usually fail unless they can bring other resources into play, such as family ties, political contacts or networks of 'relatives, friends and acquaintances' ('parents, amis et connaissances', or PAC as they are referred to in Niger). The rates for corruption in this instance range between 10,000 and 20,000 CFA francs, payable one or two weeks before the test in Benin, and as much as 150,000 CFA francs, for example, in Ziguinchor in Senegal.

In addition to this institutionalized racket involving the awarding of the Beninese driving licence, which is officially referred to as a *permis propre* – that is, a clean licence, as its possession does not arouse any suspicion during road checks – the clandestine sale of forged licences of varying origins (Nigeria, Niger, Ivory Coast etc.) is common practice, in particular in the notorious Zongo neighbourhood of Cotonou. This illicit trade in driving licences can even have international ramifications, as in the case of Senegalese driving licenses sold in Italy and other European countries.[4]

The technical inspection of vehicles

The mechanisms of the corrupt practices engaged in during the process of technical inspection of vehicles are also quite varied. They include the systematic payment of 'stamp fees' for the receipt of a certificate of technical inspection without actual presentation of the vehicle, as attested to by a Senegalese broker: 'To have the technical test, you are not obliged to present your car, you just present your wallet.' This practice is standard in all of the technical inspection centres in Benin and Senegal. However, some centres are more adept at it than others. In some cases, actual networks involving public-sector employees, hauliers and intermediaries are involved in its implementation. The networks that collect the logbooks of heavy road vehicles in north Benin and in Senegal are an example of this phenomenon. In this case, the logbooks are transmitted to the officials at the road safety centres by their 'authorized' intermediaries for the issuing of the necessary stamps and receipts without the actual vehicles being presented, not to mention inspected. Due to the way this system functions, the corrupters and the corrupted do not even know each other. They are dependent on the intermediary, who receives payments from both parties. Vehicles from one administrative region may even 'undergo' technical inspection in another region thanks to the simple intervention of intermediaries and the functioning of the network, which, however, necessitates a certain level of trust between the actors involved. As a result, vehicles circulate with up-to-date documents while failing to comply with the applicable technical standards; in many cases even the basic indicator lights do not work.

The trade in registration papers and number plates

This practice often takes place in the context of customs clearance operations when certain users, in collusion with the officials from the terrestrial transport service and the customs authority, substitute the normal registration papers of relatively new vehicles with pre-dated registration papers so as to reduce the fee charged for customs clearance. Thus there are a number of vehicles in circulation whose official registration numbers differ from those marked on their chassis. This racket necessitates the recycling of the registration papers of unused vehicles, the production of counterfeit registration papers or the recycling of number plates. Thus it is possible to find apparently new vehicles bearing the number plates of far older models. However, far from referring such cases to the courts, the officers who carry out road checks use them as another way of extorting illicit payments.

Roadside checking (gendarmerie and police)

'The driver is always wrong before the law'

When those who comply fully with the regulations applicable in a given sector of social or economic activity are few and far between, the power to check compliance with the regulations constitutes a potential power to collect money. In the transport sector, for example, few vehicles have up-to-date papers, in particular those used for commercial purposes. It is virtually impossible for the officers who carry out roadside checks to insist on the regulation of all vehicles on the road as such demands would risk paralysing economic activity. The hauliers' and drivers' unions are very much aware of this. Sometimes officers pretend to be sympathetic towards drivers whose papers are not in order and concede that their work is often the sole source of income for a large family. Furthermore, the officer and the driver often prefer to 'come to an arrangement', hence the 'road charges' that the owners of vehicles pay their drivers in Benin and Niger so that they can meet the demands of the officers, who often address the drivers with the question: 'Where is whatever you were given for me?' In any case, the driver will never have all of the documents demanded by the officer. They start by requesting the insurance certificate, registration papers, driving licence, certificate of technical inspection, logbook, and so forth. If all of these are in order, they may then ask to see the first-aid kit, the fire extinguisher, and so on. In the exceptional cases in which they fail to find fault, the officers may then give up or shift register from the demand for a corrupt payment to a simple request for a favour, such as 'I haven't had any lunch yet' or 'Do something!'. Thus the demand for payment assumes a form of normal sociability, the soliciting of a gift, which everyone recognizes as legitimate. In this instance, the driver may give the agent 'coffee money', '*cola* money' or 'beer money' as it is variously referred to in Niger, Senegal and Benin.

In some cases, the officer may raise the stakes by adopting the register of discretionary power, for example by accusing the driver of offending a serving officer. In effect, he is the only one who can say whether he has been offended or not, and, as they say in Senegal, any way of 'making the motive stick' is admissible – in other words, any means of finding or inventing an offence and forcing the road user to negotiate. Some officers are more direct in their corrupt demands and immediately make this known to the drivers when they present their papers by stating 'We don't eat the papers.' Furthermore, when officers are on a security mission, as is the case in Benin, and do not officially have the right to carry out simple checks on vehicles, the strategy consists in interpreting the security mission as broadly as possible and thus enforcing the systematic searching of vehicles. The loss of time and energy involved in this process prompts drivers to consent to paying up so as to be able to move on and avoid having their time wasted.

The options in terms of recourse that can be taken against this form of extortion are identical to those available in the case of legitimate penalties, and also involve corruption. They include nepotism, whereby the accused refers to a relative who is a member of the relevant civil force, the presentation of gifts and the direct approaching of the offending officer's superior through administrative or political channels. The latter course of action often results in the humiliation of the subordinate. Thus, the fear of intervention with a superior is one of the arguments used by some officers to justify their preference for reaching 'friendly arrangements' with road users who violate the regulations rather than reporting the offence.

Very often, road users anticipate the corrupt demands of officers. Everyone is familiar with the supposedly 'secret' charges that apply at the road checks and every driver knows how much to pay at each checkpoint depending on the civil force involved, be it the police, gendarmerie or customs. For example, the minimum paid to the 'the hook-beaked sparrow hawks', the gendarmes who patrol the roads in Benin, is 1,000 CFA francs. The prices charged by the other types of officers – that is, police and gendarmes from the territorial brigades on security missions – range from 200 to 500 CFA francs, hence the origin of the expression 'two hundred with your papers' (*deux cents avec tes pièces*) instead of 'get out with your papers' (*descend avec tes pièces*). In the jargon of the Beninese gendarmerie, the expression *faire delta* describes the gesture of taking the vehicle logbook to remove the note placed inside and quickly transferring it to one's pocket. The practice is recognized as a 'right' of the officers and is now standard practice on the road. Thus, there has been a shift from the illicit transaction and extortion to the 'toll' which is based on largely agreed charges.[5] The officers of the civil forces who patrol the roads often justify this practice by referring to their low standard of living, as demonstrated by the following comments by a Senegalese gendarme:

> A gendarme or low-ranking police officer who leaves his family in the morning without giving them a single franc and goes to work on traffic duty never hesitates when it comes to [deciding] what attitude to adopt

to a driver who commits an offence and offers him a 1,000 CFA-franc note. In the eyes of the officer, all that matters is finding a way to feed his family at lunch time and the banknote is a step in that direction.[6]

The forms of customs corruption

The logics of customs corruption

When it comes to customs corruption, there is a head-on clash between the strategies of the different actors involved. The clients and customs brokers would like to accelerate transactions as much as possible, while the customs officers aim to waste the users' time for their personal gain. According to one customs broker, in this power relationship 'the customs officer is always right'. As a result, clients develop strategies for anticipating the corrupt demands of customs officers. In the eyes of his clientele, for the ambulant customs broker engagement in corruption is a matter of competency, credibility and confidence. The speed of his operations also enable him to compete with other agents. The clients of the ambulant customs brokers are also under permanent pressure to pay what are known as 'standard bogus charges'. What is involved here is a set of penalties or supplementary fees that are added to the transaction costs payable by traders if the customs broker does not succeed in having the trader's goods released within the normal deadlines – that is, security costs, customs storage costs, demurrage[7] costs and so on. In some instances, these 'standard' – official – bogus charges will absorb the entire profit a trader stands to make on a consignment of goods. Thus the traders are involved in a race against the clock and the sooner they can have their goods cleared through customs the more profit they will make on them. Therefore they prefer to pay the 'abnormal' bogus charges so as to minimize the 'normal' bogus charges they would otherwise incur (see MTPT 1998). Hence, customs corruption is sustained by the ignorance of the users as well as – and above all – by a desire to gain time, which is based on a simple economic logic and clashes with the bureaucratic logic of organized delay for the purpose of forcing clients to pay.

Due to the widespread nature of corrupt practices, customs officers never hesitate to use their own vehicles when on duty. Thus they make a personal contribution to the operation of a public service. In their eyes, this fact of supplementing a legitimate state service in this way legitimizes the various practices they engage in involving the collection of payments, racketeering, extortion and imposition of false tolls. Thus the corruption becomes the driving force of the public service in question and guarantees its day-to-day operation.

Agreements between customs officers and smugglers

Thanks to covert agreements, professional smugglers enjoy the secret 'approval' of customs offices whereby they are left to carry out their fraudulent activities undisturbed in exchange for regular payments. As a result, vast networks become established around the 'author- ized' smugglers, who act as the sponsors of small-scale smugglers who are unknown at the customs centres. This practice is very well developed in the border regions of Benin[8] and Niger with Nigeria and involves, in particular, trafficking in petrol, spare parts, electrical and electronic goods. In the case of Senegal, the same applies at the borders with Gambia and Mauritania. Professional cross-border escorts, who are familiar with the customs network between two countries and have contacts in the customs authorities on both sides of the border to be crossed, can be found everywhere. In general, these escorts carry out all-inclusive customs clearance operations based on the significant reduction – that is, under-declaration – in the value and quantities of the goods involved.

This form of fraud may apply to goods in transit (wheat, rice, cars etc.) to neighbouring countries, which are then sold at a low price at the expense of the official importers.

The discharge system

This is a form of global customs clearing of different types of goods which is made available to certain users to prevent their exposure to *écor* procedures.[9] It allows the under-declaration of shipments of goods, as the shippers have already negotiated the charges with the customs officers. This system of discharges led to the development of irregular forms of freight known as 'overdimensional loads'. Based on the privileges granted under the discharge system, the (always nocturnal) transshipment of cargo can often be observed at the Benin–Togo border crossing at Hilla Condji whereby certain vehicles carry one and a half times their normal load with no effect on the customs clearance charges – although the same does not necessarily apply to the corrupt charges – as the clearance fee is based on a rate per vehicle and not based on the quantity or quality of the goods.

Hidden transit

The so-called 'transfer' system practised at the Benin–Niger border makes it possible to complete all of the customs formalities for goods that actually follow a different route. This phenomenon is explained below by an informant:

> You see, for example, if the cigarettes come to Gaya, you export them via Nigeria. Now, when the vehicle arrives it does not even go to the customs [post]; they will simply put 'seen at the Niger exit' on the paper while the truck has not even left Gaya.... You see, while dimity textiles are expensive in Cotonou they are not in Malanville for the simple reason that the owners of these goods do not pay the customs duty. The traders play their trick saying they are going to Niger and they stop at Malanville to unload; they come to an arrangement with the customs officers in Malanville and go to Niger to arrange and display the stamp for the discharge of the vehicle; they bring the discharge [papers] back to Malanville, [making it look] as though the vehicle has returned from Niger. However, it stayed in Benin. D.G., a trader, got rich in this way. You see, he goes to Asia to pay for the goods, the containers arrive, they are put in transit for Niger but they never leave Benin.

The escort of goods

In general, like other goods, discharged goods are subject to customs escort. In this instance, however, it is not the owner of the goods who distributes the corrupt payments at each post; the customs officers do it instead. Sometimes the customs brokers are responsible for escorting the goods. In this case, escorting the goods involves getting in front of lines of vehicles and distributing the necessary corrupt payments at each customs point while communicating the vehicle references to ensure that they are not bothered. These escort operations require a larger network of accomplices; the goods must pass through each customs post at the exact time when the colluding officers are on duty.

One particular form of escort activity involves second-hand cars, which are often, officially at least, in transit for Niger, but which mostly end up in Nigeria via the thousands of cross-border smuggling channels that exist between Benin and Nigeria. It is forbidden to import vehicles to Nigeria that are over ten years old. Once the customs charges have been paid, the smugglers come to an arrangement with the various customs officers, as well as with those carrying out road checks and those in charge of the escorts, to avoid having to go through the Benin–Niger border at Malanville.

While in Niger and Benin, the escorting of goods through customs is mainly a fraudulent strategy implemented with the complicity of customs officers, in Senegal customs officers appear to use the escort process as a threat to pressurize traders to negotiate with them. The threat is made, for example, when a customs post is unable to clear certain quantities of goods. Thus the goods would have to be sent to a post that can process the transaction. This would involve significant additional costs for the trader as it would be up to him to organize and pay for the additional transport, the escort agents, and the unloading and reloading of the goods. Thus traders do everything in their power to avoid this process. A trader from Kaolack reported:

> The traders are willing to do anything to avoid escort operations. They involve too much time, money and risk. For example, when you have a large quantity of goods, you rent a truck for a week at a cost of 150,000 CFA francs, you pay the costs of the escort which come to 25,000 CFA francs, not to mention the warehouse bill and other papers that can take weeks to find. If the procedure has not been completed by the end of the week, you have to pay another 150,000 CFA francs for the truck; if you unload the goods you have to pay the warehouse costs. A trader cannot allow himself all that. It is essential to find an arrangement.

Thus the escort procedure becomes a threat and covert demand for 'arrangements'. The customs officers propose to the traders that they divide the quantities of goods so that each batch is below the threshold value that would necessitate an escort. In such a case, the goods would be divided into several batches worth 100,000 CFA francs or less so that they could be cleared through customs under different identities. The trader borrows identity cards from his friends so that several different receipts for less than 100,000 CFA francs can be issued. Thus he shifts from a position of 'illegality' to one of 'legality' with the complicity of customs officers and escapes the costs of the escort process while gaining a lot of time.

The false classification of goods

There is an official table of customs clearance charges for all categories of merchandise. The false classification of goods involves placing them in a category that incurs a lower charge, thus minimizing the cost of their customs processing. In all cases, this practice, which is widespread in the customs authorities in all three countries, involves complicity with the customs brokers and customs agents, who are the only people who fully understand the complex system of customs charges. The companies that monitor imports (BIVAC in Benin, COTECNA in Niger, SGS in Senegal) may also engage in this practice. In Benin, for example, some BIVAC employees issue customs evaluation certificates for a different category of goods to that of the merchandise in question. False classification often involves a network of different actors comprising customs officers and other intermediaries, generally customs brokers. Sometimes the network does not work, however, when the customs officer who checks the customs evaluation certificate is not well rewarded enough and decides to forward the false certificate to the legal department for the potential reward of 25 per cent of the fine collected from the dishonest operator. The discovery of such a network in 1999–2000 in Benin resulted in the sanctioning of BIVAC employees, some of whom received prison sentences.

Sometimes, customs officers 'formally' contest the customs evaluation certificates provided by the import monitoring companies. These certificates are only required by the customs authorities for cross-border transactions between neighbouring countries. In principle, once a user has obtained such a certificate, the customs value of his goods is established beyond doubt. However, a practice known as the 'challenging in principle of the customs evaluation certificate' exists among customs officers for the purpose of forcing traders to pay parallel charges and is quite simply a demand for the traders to engage in corruption. Since the charging and punishment of BIVAC employees in Benin for corrupt practices, customs officers often accuse traders of negotiating certificates stating lower values and constantly threaten to reject the certificates presented to them.[10]

The reduction of the customs value of goods sometimes involves negotiation between customs brokers and customs officers, as evidenced by the following statement made by an ambulant customs broker at the port of Cotonou:

> For a vehicle with a value of 1.3 million CFA francs, I declared 900,000 CFA francs. I was forced to give the head of the checking department 100,000 CFA francs [to buy his silence]. The inspector himself did not spot this. So I earned 300,000 CFA francs on this vehicle.

The reduction of the customs value of goods may also involve negotiation between the traders and customs officers. The drivers of the trucks containing the goods act as intermediaries between customs officers belonging to the same corrupt networks. This is how the system works in Niger where the reduction is based on the weight of the goods being cleared:

> When a trader buys goods from Burkina Faso or comes from there, once he reaches Makalondi, which is the first border post in Niger when you come from Burkina, the customs officers from there take all the information concerning the truck and its load to give it to the driver so that he can pass it on to their colleagues in Torodi who are able to complete the customs clearance process. In Torodi, the corruption takes place at the level of the weight of the goods. If the customs officer reduces the weight of the goods, you, the client, are obliged to pay him something to buy some *cola*. If he comes from Cotonou, it all starts at Gaya bridge [Benin–Niger border]. Thus, the customs officers record the information about the truck and merchandise on the bridge to give it to the driver so that he can pass it on to the customs officers at Gaya. (Nigerien customs broker)

The fraudulent removal of goods

At the port of Cotonou, the stripping of containers and the removal of merchandise is prohibited after 7 p.m. In reality, however, a good proportion of goods leave the port after 7 p.m., which means that it is possible to get around the ban on the nocturnal stripping of containers. Thus, not only are containers stripped, but entire containers may also be removed fraudulently. In the course of our study, three networks for the fraudulent removal of goods from customs depots involving customs officers were dismantled in the port of Cotonou. For example, in 2000 a network of smugglers with stamped bills of lading from various European transit companies and other counterfeit customs clearance documents was dismantled at the port of Cotonou. However, other networks continue to operate in complicity with customs officers for the removal of containers of textiles and other goods. Using this system it costs 3 or 4 million CFA francs to obtain a container of printed textiles, the estimated customs clearance cost of which would be around 14 million CFA francs.

In some instances what is involved here is the abuse of certain regimes of privileges for the fraudulent removal of goods. Thus, for example, in Senegal, traders from the OCAS market in Touba and even from the Sandaga market in Dakar use the fiscal privileges granted to the General Caliph of the Mourides to import goods fraudulently through the port of Dakar with the complicity of both marabout networks and officers from the customs administration. Once they have been unloaded, containers belonging to these traders are stamped 'Property of the General Caliph of the Mourides' or 'Material for the Touba mosque' and are released free of charge and, to all appearances, entirely legally.

As observed in our study, corruption in the transport and customs sector is not an activity engaged in by exclusive groups for the purpose of winning the favour of a dominant group, as is the case with the Singapore Chinese analysed by Scott (1969). The actors involved in the corruption in the transport and customs sector of Benin, Niger and Senegal are among the most affluent and politically influential in those societies.

Rounding up to the next thousand

Coins are not used in customs transactions; thus the payment of round sums is the norm. The ambulant customs brokers of the port of Cotonou refer to this system as 'rounding up to the next thousand'.

If the charge to be paid is calculated as 1,005 CFA francs, the actual sum paid is 2,000 CFA francs and the customs officer pockets the difference. The customs brokers at the port cash desk even refer to 'rounding up to the next thousand plus 1,000 CFA francs', the extra 1,000 francs being the minimum 'bogus charge' payable for the simple right to pay one's bill.

The overtime system

The customs administration grants the officers stationed at very busy posts such as the ports, airports and border crossings the right to do overtime. However, instead of being billed per hour to users, overtime (*temps supplémentaire de travail*, or TS, in Benin and *travail extra-légal*, or TEL, in Niger) is billed on the basis of the activity involved. For example, instead of being paid an hour's overtime for the processing of six files, the customs officer receives six TS payments – one TS payment per activity. This practice has become systematic and is now also applied throughout the day. According to a customs broker at the port of Cotonou, 'the customs officer is on overtime, even at nine o'clock in the morning'. At the Nigerien customs, the hourly overtime or TEL rate is 5,000 CFA francs per hour. As is the case in Benin, its payment is based on the activity involved, and some clients may be exempted from this charge in exchange for a corrupt payment. One customs broker reports: 'If you have ten vehicles, you pay the TEL for five without any receipt and the five others with receipts.'

The official overtime or TS rate in Benin is 1,350 CFA francs. In reality, however, service users have to pay at least 2,000 CFA francs per file processed.

> At the port of Cotonou, the TS rate is always higher after 4 p.m. in the afternoons and on Fridays, known as *la finale* in the jargon of corruption at the port, as this is the last day of the week and everyone wants to get their goods cleared to avoid having to pay additional weekend expenses.

A proportion of the overtime charges (15 per cent of the TEL in Niger) is sent to the general directorate of customs to provide – together with the fees collected by the legal service – the resources used to motivate officers stationed at posts with low volumes of commercial traffic and to provide the customs officers' second salary. The existence of a slush fund that acts as a corporate solidarity fund for the customs authority tends to be used as an excuse for legitimizing various collection operations carried out for the purpose of supplying this fund, which ultimately benefits everyone in the service. The existence of an overtime system that is paid for by the users facilitates this abuse, both in Benin[11] and in Niger.

Corruption as a professional imperative

Corruption has frequently been analysed on the basis of its mechanisms and processes, and in terms that focus on trust and the betrayal of the commission, as demonstrated by the 'agency model': the principal entrusts the agent with a task and by committing a corrupt act the latter betrays the former and his trust (Rose-Ackerman 1978). While it is undoubtedly relevant, this kind of analysis is very normative because it presupposes a functional context in which the principal provides the agent with the means necessary to carry out the appointed task. In a context characterized by the extreme dysfunctionality of public services, whereby the minimum level of resources necessary to provide the services in question is lacking, this analysis of the corrupt relationship requires significant relativization. In some instances, corruption becomes a professional imperative in the transport and customs sector; that is, it becomes an element of the strategies necessary to maintain the functioning of the public service in question or a channel for the indirect venalization of public costs and expenditure.

In effect, the officers of the civil forces are driven by a twofold logic: that of maintaining the functioning of their services and that of maintaining good relationships with their superiors to ensure their professional advancement. Thus they levy parallel charges on the standard services provided to users. For example, in Benin the two parties involved in a traffic accident each have to pay 5,000 CFA francs to the police and 7,000 CFA francs to the gendarmerie to obtain an accident report. Needless to say, no receipt is issued for the payment of these 'report charges'. These charges would be used to fund the compilation of reports and the purchase of paper for producing copies. In both Niger and Benin, police stations and gendarmeries have petty cash for miscellaneous expenses which are funded by their 'extraordinary revenue', such as on-the-spot fines paid by parties involved in conflicts whose resolution involves the services of the police and gendarmerie. Thus, it is said that these resources are used to supplement the incapacity of the state to provide the necessary resources for the operation of its public services.

Furthermore, on completion of every control mission, officers of the civil forces in Benin have to provide what they refer to as the 'CR', *compte rendu*, an account or report. This does not, however, involve an account of the assignment itself, but the presentation to their superiors of the money collected from road users. Failure to comply with this rule may result in an officer no longer 'seeing the tar' (working on the road), or being put 'into the garage' (assigned to a post that does not involve contact with road users). These 'dry posts', as they are referred to in Senegal, or 'red tape' posts, as described by Nigerien customs officers, often involve posts in the head offices of the police, gendarmerie and customs services and other roles that do not entail any major movement of people or goods. Apart from the systematic CR described above, the officers also have to give annual 'gifts' to their superior and other occasional gifts on important occasions in the latter's family life, such as marriages, baptisms, funerals. These 'gifts' account for the redistribution of tens of millions of francs within the Benin hierarchy.

Finally, like their victims on the road, the subordinate officers of the civil forces are in a vulnerable position vis-à-vis their superiors during their professional competitions and examinations. In order to succeed, they are all forced to pay a 'dowry' through parallel corruption networks supported by senior members of the hierarchy. In Benin's national gendarmerie, the officers are obliged to form a *bureau de promotion* and to make monthly contributions, which are collected by the members of the *bureau*.[12] Thus the latter reluctantly assume the role of intermediaries between their colleagues and the hierarchy of the gendarmerie, to whom the contributions are paid and, as a result, adopt the attitude that someone else must then pay these parallel costs, this 'someone else' being the road user.

One understands the entire sense of the suggestion made by a Nigerien police officer encountered in Niamey when he reflects that corruption is a phenomenon that operates on different levels: 'Everyone "eats" on his level. If you are on the second level, you eat on your level and don't watch what goes on the first and third levels.'

The allocation of assignments also offers real opportunities for every kind of corruption. An informal scale exists among customs officers, policemen and gendarmes for the evaluation of the different postings, which are classified on the basis of their potential for corruption as 'lucrative' and 'less lucrative' postings.

B is a customs officer formerly assigned to the port of Cotonou. In reference to Benin's forty-five head offices, squads, offices and customs posts, he comments: 'You see, all of these postings are ones that offer opportunities. Everything depends on the density of the traffic. With the exception of head office, any posting that puts you into contact with clients is lucrative. How lucrative a posting is depends on the volume of the traffic. Now, the volume of traffic depends on the times and facilities the clients have to complete the customs formalities.' (Cotonou, June 2000)

The lucrative postings also reflect the opportunities available for corruption and their mechanisms, as illustrated by the following statement by a Nigerien ambulant customs broker:

You see, it's good if you are head clerk and you are assigned to the service for the checking of merchandise, you will have opportunities for corruption. If the customs officer wants to do something for you, if you give [him] something, he does not have to check, he can reduce the number of packages as he deems fit. ... The warehouse bosses also do well. The warehousemen in the customs corps always have money on them. In reality, only the 'whites' are above board with the warehouse-man, because if a service sends them goods a receipt must be issued. ... The head clerks in Niamey also do deals with the traders involving the checking process. For example, if a trader brings 1,000 bales of fabric and the customs clearance fee totals, say, 5 million CFA francs or 8 million, the trader can do a deal with the head clerk whereby he will issue an order to have only half of them checked. The trader then shows us – the ambulant customs brokers – the paper signed by the head clerk and we work with that. You see, the trader unloads 1,000 bales but only 500 are declared; they will do a deal on the other 500. It's the same story with the head office of the customs service: that's where you have to go to feast on the 'big business' as it's called. (Ambulant customs broker, Niamey)

The main characteristic of a lucrative posting is the high density of transactions and their frequency, on the one hand, and the multiplicity of opportunities for both normal and illegal gain, on the other. The top position in the geographical pecking order of these postings is held by the customs offices at border crossings, followed by those at the ports (Benin and Senegal), the airports, the border postings located on busy road intersections, and, finally, the consumer protection postings (mobile squads and anti-smuggling squads). The less lucrative postings, or 'dry posts', are generally those with almost no contact with service users. The customs officers employed at head office have no extra sources of income on top of their salaries.

> The posting of an officer to head office is considered a punishment. For someone who earned between 200,000 and 300,000 CFA francs per day, to send him to a place where he does not see a trader, you see it's a punishment. No customs officer wants to leave here for head office. (A *karen dwan*, Niamey)

Assignment to postings considered 'lucrative' is the object of competition between officers and leads to corrupt practices among those higher up in the hierarchy. This is confirmed by the general secretary of the union of customs authorities of Niger:

> Do you know which job is the most lucrative in the customs? OK, I'll tell you, it's the battle for posting; it's the battle to influence assignments. The prevention of smuggling is a false game. The coveted services in the customs and for which prefects [chiefs of police], directors general of the customs and ministers intervene are the customs enforcement services. It's because they are places where you can get rich quickly. The people pretend to fight customs fraud and corruption, but they sell out in the face of their interests.

Another executive from the Nigerien customs condemns the clientelism and interventionism in the assignment of posts:

> One of the directors general of customs said when in office 'it is easier to form a government in Niger than to assign customs postings because, from the office boy to the most senior officer, everyone has his safety

belt.' Unfortunately, everyone wants their relatives or friends to go to an office where there is plenty of activity and where you can get rich. Some officers have done the tour of all of the lucrative postings, while others have worked since their recruitment to the customs in the same offices where there is nothing. There is not even the hope of seizures or opportunities to do illegal work.

The customs authority in Niger went through five directors general between 1995 and 1999. In Benin, the customs officers went as far as regulating the duration of different postings so as to enable more frequent rotation of personnel. Thus, at the port of Cotonou, the 'country's most lucrative' customs service, the average duration of a posting is two years.

The 'buyers of postings' are considered by the other officers as being most actively involved in corrupt practices because they need to recover the resources invested or promised in exchange for their lucrative assignments. Thus they operate on the basis of a commercial profit-oriented logic and not according to a logic based on the provision of efficient public services.

Corruption as a response to structural conditions and the availing of opportunities

The corruption in the transport sector and among the civil forces occurs at the point of convergence of several facilitating factors.

The rejection of legality

One of these factors can be clearly identified as the systematic rejection of legality or the overexploitation of the weaknesses of the legal system by various actors. In fact, it is generally reported that in the three countries studied almost all of the vehicles used in public transport are not fully compliant with the relevant legal requirements. A Senegalese policeman in Koalack made the following comment on 'Bongré taxis':

> Of one hundred taxis, only around twenty are in order. So if you take them off the road, you do wrong to an entire family. If you act legally, you put the lives of an entire family at risk. For example, there are vehicles that come from villages every day to go to the market at

Kaolack. If you impound these cars, you will prevent families from eating and the people who live there are our relatives. (Police officer, Kaolack)

Observation of road transport practices in all three countries highlights one particularly striking and constant practice: the number of passengers and volumes of luggage carried by all of the public transport vehicles in service exceed the capacity of the vehicles in question. In Benin and Niger, this situation is based on a degree of complicity between drivers and the traffic police and is an integral component of the daily exchange of corrupt services. As opposed to this, in Senegal this irregularity appears to be the result of far more complex political negotiations between the state and the transport-sector unions for the purpose of invalidating the relevant legislation. This is the case with the overloading of the so-called *drëm-drëm* taxis that carry six passengers instead of five, or minibuses that carry three to five extra passengers. Article 115 of the highway code, which threatens violations of this kind with the halting of the vehicle until any excess passengers disembark and the payment of an on-the-spot fine of 6,000 CFA francs, was invalidated when the fine was reduced by the authority to 3,000 or 1,500 CFA francs, depending on the category of vehicle involved, although the law that imposes the fine was not actually modified.[13] As a result, this 'goodwill gesture' is now being abused through the widespread practice of anticipated violation by drivers, who voluntarily pay the 3,000 CFA-franc fine with the intention of 'legally' overloading their vehicles. The receipt given to them as proof 'that they have already paid for their infraction' legitimizes their violation of the rules for twenty-four hours.

The tendency to engage in corrupt transactions

The structural opportunities for corruption are also more numerous in the customs sector due both to the powers at the disposal of public-sector employees with the responsibility for the regulation of this sector and to the widespread tendency among users not to conform to the rules in force. The strategies of both the corrupted and the corrupt involve obliging the opposite party to accept the necessity of resorting to the corrupt transaction. Such transactions take place

in a context characterized by the spread of smuggling and concealment activities on the part of traders involved in import–export
and their representatives. Making false declarations, usually in the
form of underdeclaration, is a sign of professional competency on
the part of the trader or businessman. The import–export business
involves the quest for profit through the minimization of costs. Thus
customs officers are under constant pressure to bend the rules. This
demand for corrupt transactions can extend right up to the level of
the ministry of finance, the supervisory authority of the customs
service. The customs reform of the West African Economic and
Monetary Union (UEMOA), incorporating the implementation in the
Union's member states since 1 January 2000 of a common external
tariff, the Tarif Extérieur Commun (TEC), which resulted in the
levying of a 20 per cent tax on products that were not previously
subject to taxation (e.g. sugar, rice, printed cotton textiles) and are
mainly intended for re-export, increases the opportunities for corruption through smuggling. According to the head of the Chamber
of Industry and Commerce of Benin (CCIB), this tax reduced importers' profits per container of printed textiles by almost two-thirds.
Following negotiations with the minister of finance, traders will
henceforth benefit from an informal provision whereby the TEC
is only applied to one-third of the content of each container, with
the other two-thirds cleared through customs based on the former
less draconian system. As a result, a system of double charges was
created for certain products.

Large-scale fraud as a matter of competency

Transport, transit and trade are among the activities most exposed
to corruption. The police, gendarmerie and customs have regular
contact with clients who have engaged in all kinds of fraud and are
responsible for the rooting of an actual entrepreneurial ethic in the
informal economy in Benin, Niger and Senegal (see N'Diaye 1998
on Senegal's *moodu moodu*). Evading tax is an essential factor for
professional success. Thus, in Niger, for example, the banks refuse to
communicate the balances of traders to the fiscal authority because
the traders threaten to take their custom elsewhere if they do.

Furthermore, this widespread informalization of transactions is a source of reassurance for the various parties involved in corrupt transactions: 'without paper there is no proof for the official, without paper the businessman can avoid tax', or, in the words of the ambulant customs brokers of Benin, 'the receipt compromises'.

In Niger, goods imported from Jeddah and Dubai arrive at the airport of Niamey without invoices. It is up to the head of the customs office to define their value after engaging in corrupt transactions with importers. Thus it is easy to understand why Nigerien traders and customs officers positively despise COTECNA, the import monitoring company:

> In reality, if you complete the customs clearance procedures correctly, you will not be able to buy the goods at the market. This is why when COTECNA came, no one wanted to order goods because COTECNA knew the prices from the outset, so the figure provided by COTECNA is used by the customs brokers when making the declarations. The customs brokers no longer work with the invoices provided by the traders. Therefore no declaration is processed at customs level without the COTECNA paper. (Customs broker)

The second-hand car sector is one of the most profitable in Benin today; however, it is also one of the sectors most active in the area of large-scale fraud and smuggling. According to the customs authority, in two years (2000–2001) 445,000 vehicles passed through the port of Cotonou, of which only around 15,000 were sold in Benin. Thus, over 430,000 passed though Benin, 50,000 of which were destined for Nigeria and almost 380,000 for Niger. However, in this two-year period, only 26,600 vehicles actually went through the customs post at Malanville (Benin–Niger border) in the direction of Niger. It has been observed that over 400,000 vehicles passed through Benin to enter Nigeria without reaching their official destination, Niger. Thus, transit to Niger is nothing more than a quasi-official strategy for the perpetration of customs fraud. In effect, the difference between the S110 customs tariff applicable for goods in transit to the hinterland countries (more flexible) and the S114 tariff applicable to coastal countries is of the order of 12,500 CFA francs. In the aforementioned two-year period, the loss in customs receipts for Benin arising from vehicles declared as being in transit for Niger, but actually destined for Nigeria, was in excess of 5 billion CFA francs. The losses incurred by Niger are even greater as the transit charge per light vehicle there is over 100,000 CFA francs. Moreover, the different mechanisms for the perpetration of customs fraud and application of bogus charges exploited by the ambulant customs brokers make it possible for them to make an average profit of around 30,000 CFA francs per vehicle at the port of Cotonou. It is estimated that the informal (undeclared) profits earned by the ambulant customs brokers on the 250,000 second-hand vehicles imported through the port of Cotonou in 2001 exceeded 6.5 billion CFA francs.[14] The widespread and pervasive nature of fraud and smuggling is a strong indicator of the systemic nature of corruption.

The informalization of the cross-border economy

The widespread informalization of cross-border transactions between the different countries is also a major source of corrupt practices. The situation concerning cross-border transactions between Benin and Nigeria, which is still difficult to evaluate, is typical of this phenomenon. In effect, the official imports recorded by INSAE[15] in Benin in 1997 totalled 5.21 billion CFA francs as opposed to a total of 50.65 billion for the imports processed through the informal sector. For the same period, the Federal Office of Statistics of Nigeria recorded 109.3 billion CFA francs worth of products exported to Benin (Igué 1998), while Benin merely controlled the entry of products from Nigeria to a value of 5 billion CFA francs. The remainder entered Benin through smuggling channels or via the various systems used to reduce the declared value of imported goods. Another study observed that in the re-export sector, INSAE recorded the official re-export of 298 million CFA francs worth of goods to Nigeria in the year 2000 as opposed to 120.7 billion CFA francs worth re-exported through informal channels.

These figures alone demonstrate the scope of the informal activities that more often than not are synonymous with fraudulent practices. Even if all of these transactions are not identified by INSAE, this does not mean that the customs services have no knowledge of most of them, in particular those involving re-export activities.

Based on an internal survey carried out by the Public Audit Office, Benin's minister of finance confirms that the sum involved in the direct corruption perpetrated by customs officers and officials, and the secondary corruption arising from it, would increase to between 50 and 60 billion CFA francs per year (i.e. one-fifth of the state's budget, most of which is raised from the customs charges levied at the port of Cotonou; see Bio Tchané 2000). The parallel annual revenue collected on a daily basis by a lowly customs broker at the port of Cotonou is estimated as totalling almost 800,000 CFA francs (see Adjovi 1999).

The vast scale of the informal transactions enacted within the economies of the three countries studied reflects the scale of fraudulent practices, which in turn supply the various channels and networks of corruption. These are also important indicators of the scale of the activities in the transport and business sectors which also feed these corruption channels.

Weakness in controlling national territory

The above-described fraudulent activity also thrives on the in-efficiency of the systems in the various states for controlling their national territories. In fact, one of the characteristics of the weak-ness of the African state lies in its inability to assert its authority throughout its territory. This incapacity may result from a lack of administrative resources, from political–clientelistic phenomena or from the strategies adopted by certain actors for the purpose of excluding entire zones from the state's authority and rule. This is the case in Senegal where customs officers are banned from enter-ing areas strongly influenced by the Mouride brotherhood, such as Touba. This type of territory or zone which is not subject to customs control constitutes an ideal area for all kinds of fraudulent transactions. Furthermore, the fraudsters and smugglers generally enjoy the complicity of the local populations in Benin, Niger and Senegal, who applaud them every time they succeed in evading the customs officers. Indeed, the population sides with the smugglers against the customs administration and actively protects them when they are pursued, to the point where the perpetration of acts of violence against imprudent customs officers are not uncommon in such situations. In the case of Senegal, the Mouride villages, which are dispersed throughout the area between the Gambian border and Touba, act as safe havens for the smugglers and their illegal activities, while in south Benin it is the secret societies (e.g. the *zangbeto*) that provide protection for the smugglers under cover of their ritual nocturnal outings. In all three countries studied locations exist that are inaccessible to the customs authority due to the threats and hostility of the population – for example, the Touba region in Senegal, the town of Birnin Konni in Niger and the city of Parakou in Benin.

'Border effects'

The frequency and intensity of corrupt practices in the transport and customs sectors appears to be directly related to the existence of or proximity to a border area. The border generates a particular attraction that results in the proliferation of all types of corruption in the transport and customs sectors. In a context in which freedom of movement from one country to another is not yet acknowledged and in which the users of border services rarely possess the necessary identity documents, officers of the civil forces create rules which they apply in parallel to the official regulations. Thus the lack of an identity card or vaccination record is replaced by a 'one-off fine', for which, as a rule, no receipt is issued. On both sides of the Benin–Niger border, the fine for the lack of an identity card is 500 CFA francs (for nationals) and 1,500 CFA francs (for non-nationals departing from the other country).

The border is also the location where nationalism and sovereignty tend to manifest themselves. When a national from a border country informs the officers of the civil forces of his own country of the harassment he was subjected to by their counterparts across the border, the automatic reaction is to reciprocate. Thus, corruption and its regulation become subject to a process of 'informal diplomacy'. On the Benin–Niger border at Malanville, the rates for corruption fluctuate on the basis of the micro-local relationships between the two countries. When decisions are taken by the central governments in relation to border policy, micro-local negotiations are often held which tend to result in the organization of the informal easing of these measures. Thus the closure of borders or banning of the export of live products originating from Benin to Niger resulted in the opening of corridors of which the officers of the civil forces of both countries were aware. According to a cross-border smuggler in Malanville, the greater the level of prohibition, the more profitable corruption becomes because the obligation to contribute something to the state coffers no longer exists.

Furthermore, customs officers often set up cross-border corruption and smuggling networks which generally operate on the basis of the disguised transit of goods, the discharge system, or the conversion of customs officers, police officers and gendarmes into quasi-professional couriers, as they enjoy the privilege of not being subject to any controls on either side of the border. This privilege is often extended to the administrative authorities of border areas, who along with their protégés are exonerated from control at border crossings. The opportunities for corruption are most numerous at the busiest borders. This explains why border postings are described as 'lucrative postings' in the terminology of the officers of the civil forces.

The obligation to provide services without resources and the exchange of services

Some facilitators of corruption can be found at the heart of the administration. The customs authority works like a private company and is obliged to produce results. In a context characterized by a lack of control over trade flows, the annual setting of the sum to be contributed by customs to the state's annual budget represents a factor that triggers corrupt activities as these predictions are generally exceeded every year. Using this imposed quota as justification, the directors of the customs offices develop strategies 'to attract clients' which are characterized by a certain 'flexibility' towards the clientele, and this is very often a source of corrupt interaction.

> This is why in order to attract clients to their customs units, the directors of the units facilitate them in fulfilling customs formalities.... For example, in the case of a wholesale trader who is used to dealing with

customs, the director of the unit may ask the officers to reduce the weight of the goods or, indeed, do it himself, i.e. underestimate the value so that the client will come back again. There are these little favours granted to clients simply to attract them.... In order to be able to meet your quota, you have to make your unit attractive to clients, i.e. make your unit easy to access and get through for clients. The state gains and you are also compensated [for your efforts] because you will gain little by little. When the client is happy with the way that customs formalities are fulfilled, he will give you gifts. (Customs officer, Cotonou)

Thus, even though it does not provide the necessary resources to the customs authority to carry out its work, the state sets targets for the revenue it must generate. This administrative malfunction creates areas of negotiation between customs officers and some of their clients, in particular the traders who provide petrol and vehicles to the customs officers – in exchange for certain favours – to enable them to provide the public service. In most cases, customs officers in Benin, Niger and Senegal use their own vehicles to provide services on behalf of the state authority they serve.

Under these circumstances, engaging in corruption becomes a professional imperative. Moreover, the decentralization of customs services in one and the same administration, which forces clients to attend different offices for the customs clearance of just one item, is a source of minor irritation that many try to overcome by taking short cuts. Due to the fact of the significant discretionary power enjoyed by the customs authority, and that in cases of customs fraud it is up to the perpetrator to prove his innocence, the general public views the customs officer as a much-dreaded official with whom it is better to try to reach agreement.

In all three countries studied, there was a failure to pay the motivational reimbursement of 25 per cent of fines collected by officers of the civil forces – police officers and gendarmes – for contravention of the highway code. As a result, these officers give priority to 'arrangements' with road users who are in breach of the regulations.

The malfunction of the state administrative apparatus is widely exploited by the different parties who interact in the transport sector. In this context, corruption can cover an entire generalized system of exchange of services between the actors of the transport sector and the officers of the civil forces. In effect, in the majority of the locations studied, the drivers' trade unions and associations provide vehicles and petrol for the police and gendarmerie for use in security operations and other missions. Thus it is possible to observe the existence of an extensive exchange of services and system of reciprocal indebtedness between drivers and officers of the civil forces. These exchanges affect, for example, the distribution of administrative mail in Senegal. The driver of a vehicle transporting mail becomes someone 'privileged' on the road.

Thus the gendarmes and police officers are under obligation to the drivers' and hauliers' unions, who refer to them pejoratively in Benin as 'our friends of the road'. In return, they can intervene in the resolution of conflicts between officers of the civil forces and road users. In fact, the leaders of the unions assume the role of negotiators and bring about the reduction of fines and other corrupt charges. In certain places, such as Malanville (Benin), Kaolack (Senegal) and Gaya (Niger), actual secret contracts have been established between the civil forces and the representatives of road users whereby lax control practices are exchanged for weekly payments.

Insufficient manpower is one of the arguments most often used by the hierarchy of the civil forces to justify their inability to provide adequate security for people and material assets and to provide urgent intervention when needed. While it is not entirely unfounded, in practice this argument is used in support of the internal privatization of the public security services. Thus, any intervention by the police or gendarmerie is 'billed' indirectly to the beneficiary under the form of 'beer money', 'petrol money' or 'travel costs'. In the port of Cotonou, in particular, both the gendarmerie and police sign 'security contracts' for the surveillance of warehouses containing goods being processed by customs and the fleets of vehicles managed by private companies. The public service is 'leased' on the basis of negotiated tariffs. This form of privatization of the public services is quite widespread; for example, a private company can be billed for the simple act of a gendarme directing road traffic so as to facilitate the exit of vehicles from the port.

> For every gendarme or police officer who helps us provide security during the transfer of vehicles from the port to the external fleets, we

pay between 5,000 and 10,000 CFA francs. (M, operating manager of a parking area for second-hand cars)

At the port of Cotonou, certain officers of the civil forces do not hesitate to act as receivers of stolen goods, taking advantage of the privilege of not being checked at the exit to the port to move goods outside of the port area in exchange for corrupt payments.

The malfunction of customs administrations prompts the adoption of 'survival strategies' on the part of the state on the initiative of its officers, who, by their own account, act out of professional necessity. In Niger, the customs authority has around one hundred vehicles to cover a vast territory. In Benin, each customs officer has to use his own private vehicle and provide the necessary petrol in the fulfilment of his professional tasks. The following comments by a Senegalese customs officer illustrate clearly the situation in the three countries investigated:

> We sometimes have to spend our own money or club together to buy petrol. Sometimes we even spend the money we have received from other people. People may give us 30,000 or 50,000 CFA francs, but we use this money for work. When the traders lend us money, we reimburse them from the seizures. (7 May 2000, Kaffrine)

Thus, due to the establishment of permanent relationships between customs officers and the private suppliers of operating resources, chains of corruption are created which tend to become structural in nature. These private suppliers usually benefit from special privileges in the form of priority access to goods impounded in the customs warehouse, as occurs at the port of Cotonou, or to goods seized and sold at targeted 'auctions', as is the case at the Kaolack customs post in Senegal.

Artificial sociability and conformist civil society

With regard to the police and gendarmerie, simple sociological phenomena may also contribute to the emergence of corrupt practices between officers and drivers. Habitual and repeated contact fosters lasting ties between drivers and police officers and between traders and customs officers, which lead to exchanges of services that penetrate beyond the professional setting into the realm of the familial. Ultimately, the boundary between public and private spheres becomes blurred.

The emerging civil society in the different countries studied (trade unions, professional associations, NGOs etc.) is highly embedded in the political administration and system, and it very often resorts to administrative and political interventionism as a means of exerting political pressure. Its representatives put pressure on low-ranking officers by approaching their superiors or politicians. As a result, for many police officers and gendarmes it is better to negotiate with a lawbreaker than apply the relevant sanction, as demonstrated by this Nigerien police officer:

> The officers often come to an arrangement with the drivers, we close our eyes. There are fewer contraventions because it is democracy, the unions are strong and you hesitate because interventionism is widespread.

Conclusion

Despite the widespread nature of corruption in the customs and transport sectors in the three countries studied, it is possible to observe a certain time-lag in this process of generalization. In Benin, the 1970s represented a major turning point marking the beginning of a crackdown on this phenomenon; in Niger, ordinary corruption on the road appears to be a more recent and contemporary phenomenon, which emerged in the early days of the decline of the state, around the late 1980s; and in Senegal the phenomenon would appear to go back to an even earlier period, having no obvious links to any crisis of state, and being observable as early as the 1960s.

However, it is possible to confirm that the strong similarities between the forms, actors, mechanisms, chains and networks of corruption in the three countries arise from a common situation which forms the basis of the vicious circle of corruption that exists in the transport and customs sectors.

On the one hand, we have the dilapidated state of the vehicles; widespread lack of respect for the highway code; the existence of powerful unions of hauliers, which are involved in clientelistic relationships with politicians and, thus, represent pressure groups capable of imposing extra-legal regulations in their favour, either by means of negotiation (informal financing of the public service) or threat (strikes); the prominence of private-sector actors who have made fraud into an ethic of success (rejection of legality, fondness for deals, refusal to provide fiscal proof, preference for direct financial transactions in the customs sector); societies that afford protection to the illegal, illicit and informal, sometimes on the basis of emic norms (based on the fact of the illegitimacy of state rules from the perspective of the majority of social actors) and sometimes in accordance with relationships based on political clientelism (alliances between the powers that be and their social support, as in the case of the Mourides in Senegal); the existence in all three countries of informal 'free zones' or 'non-state' pockets in which all state regulations governing commercial transactions are outlawed or undermined.

On the other hand, we have public-sector employees (security and customs forces) who are at once the victims of the gap between their statutory responsibilities and the actual resources at their disposal, but who also benefit from these malfunctions to develop an ethic of abuse of position as a means of rent-seeking and therefore tend to 'legitimize' the practice of collecting money from their clients. Thus it is possible to observe among the customs officers, police officers and gendarmes a certain awareness of their privileges and a certain team spirit, which produce and sustain the internal protection networks in relation to corrupt practices, in particular.

As a result of all this, it is possible to observe a normalization of corrupt practices and the emergence of increasingly detailed nomenclatures ('customs clearance charges', 'miscellaneous', 'bogus charges', 'dowry', *compte rendu*'). These practices are associated with tariffs that are recognized and regulated on the basis of a logic of supply and demand, whereby corrupt transactions are based on 'negotiated thresholds' between the corrupt and corrupted. Hence, when an officer 'exaggerates' – that is, exceeds an agreed threshold – he can be accused of 'greed' and may be 'reportable' through the activation of standard regulatory procedures, such as strikes by hauliers and drivers in protest against police activities or strikes by customs brokers in protest against the activities of customs officers.

This entire system, which produces an infra-state normality and functions with the help of its own actors, who only engage in petty corruption, would appear to be more professionalized in the transport sector and among the civil forces in the three countries studied. This high level of professionalization is based on the extensive presence of large numbers of auxiliary agents, formal and informal intermediaries (ambulant customs brokers, various intermediaries and customs agents), whose remuneration depends, above all, on the 'parallel revenue' generated by various corrupt practices.

Thanks to the widespread corruption in these sectors and tax avoidance, it is possible to observe today the emergence of new success models: the rent model and the extortion model have supplanted the production model in the processes of accumulation. Based on today's models of social success, those who have accumulated wealth by means of corruption are most esteemed. Thus the ambulant customs brokers and the fraudulent traders enjoy a positive image in all three countries.

However, it is possible to observe differences in the phenomenon of corruption arising from certain specific elements of the three countries. If the corruption in the transport and customs sectors would appear to be a constituent element of the structure of the state in all three countries, and the financing of politics by traders (who are often beneficiaries of corrupt practices) is also widespread, in Senegal the phenomenon of Mouridism has a strong influence on the structure of the political support networks (alliance between the political regime and the brotherhood), and a good proportion of corrupt practices in the customs and transport sectors would appear to result from regimes of privileges, from which this religious movement benefits. In both Niger and Benin, in contrast, the informal 'free zones' are more manifestations of 'bottom-up politics': the dominance of society over the state through guile, the delegitimization of state norms, the refusal to inform on the perpetrators of illegal acts, the recourse to magical-religious practices, and so on.

In Senegal, the corruption in the transport sector is strongly characterized by the phenomenon of electoral clientelism, which results in the official authorization of the 'violation' of the legislation in force, rendering the civil forces powerless vis-à-vis road users; for example, prior payment of fines for authorized overloading of vehicles and the transport of administrative mail by taxi drivers for the purpose of obtaining legal exonerations. In Benin and Niger, the practices of corruption are structured by the direct segmental alliances that exist between public-sector employees and road users (customs officers/customs brokers and traders; gendarmes and police officers/hauliers and drivers), thus lending corrupt interaction on the road a transactional character.

7

An ordered corruption?
The social world of public procurement

Giorgio Blundo

'You're interested in public procurement contracting? Then go and have a look at the new bus station!', a technician from the Senegalese commune of Kaolack, obviously irritated by my questions, flung at me in a semi-allusive, semi-ironic tone. Ignored by the city transport companies since its completion in 1998, this station was constantly at the heart of rumours concerning the bad habits of municipal management. Intrigued, I went to the place several times during the rainy season of 2000. There was no need to be an experienced technician to understand why the station had been abandoned even before its inauguration: a part of the esplanade, whose poor-quality cement had begun to degenerate, was flooded because of bad levelling. The shed, of shoddy design, was obviously not conceived to accommodate coaches or minibuses, as the distance between the pillars supporting the roof was too narrow. No site had been anticipated for taxis. The public toilets, deprived of running water, had no waste-disposal system. Clearly, no one could have used them, not least because the septic tanks were flush with underground water, a sign – a French technician commissioned by the town hall to assess the work explained to me later – that the waterproofing had been done in a slapdash manner. The small buildings surrounding the station, destined to accommodate shopkeepers and restaurant owners – despite the fact that the drivers' trade union had demanded in vain that the town hall reserve some of them for offices – were temporarily occupied by populations having fled neighbourhoods affected by the recent floods. Decrepit-looking lamps supplied the feeble lighting. I later learnt that they were 'a bargain'.

Work on the bus station had officially been started in 1994 on the basis of the commune's own funds, following a formal tendering process. The real processes of procurement contracting and completion of the work, however, remained a mystery – the key to which, according to rumour, was held by the former mayor, his road surveyor and the contractor. First contacts with the firm and the municipal authorities were deceptive, punctuated by embarrassed silences and a cunning handling of platitudes: 'I am part of the system, that's it; I know how it works, but I'm not saying anything', the road surveyor had told me, not beating about the bush, while dismissing me at the end of an interview given only reluctantly. But as I unravelled the whole affair of the bus station, I came to penetrate an underground world of small contractors who had subcontracted some of the work; of local deputies who had gone over to the opposition and were keen on unmasking the shady side of the former municipal management; of employees of the regional committee of public procurement contracts holding different contracts that had been agreed upon between the municipality and the local firm.

Unable to raise the funds necessary for the completion of the project in his electoral constituency, the former mayor, Ablaye Diack, had asked the owner of the biggest public works firm in the region to put up the money for the cost of the work. S.S. could not refuse him this favour: a small blacksmith until the end of the 1970s, he had been projected into the world of business by the mayor by becoming his privileged supplier of false bills. Having reached a high economic status, achieved at the cost of constant elimination of competitors though rigged contracts, this ardent Mouride had occupied positions of responsibility at the highest levels, becoming first the regional then the national president of the chamber of trade. As the head of the biggest firm in the city, which he had expanded by buying up the tools and material of the public works department when it was privatized, he was feared by his rivals, whom he had removed one by one, but at the same time respected by the small contractors to whom he regularly subcontracted some of the work.

The importance of this public project – according to the town hall's report of the 1997 budget, the total cost of the bus station would be as high as 572 million CFA francs – presented a dilemma: the rules required an open tendering process, whereas in fact the contract was destined for S.S. – in other words, a direct negotiated agreement had to be struck. In order to give the appearance of legality to the process, the contract was split up into several parts, all worth less than 20 million CFA. This allowed them to avoid the need for approval by the administration's national contracts committee, and to obtain the guaranteed consent of the regional committee, prepared to close its eyes before this semblance of public bidding for the contract: indeed, S.S. could count on a network of grateful subcontractors who put in false tenders in order that he be allocated each part, whom he later rewarded by giving them work on the construction site. It was thus that the canalization, the public toilets, the 'restaurants' and the shed came to be the work of small contractors who preferred to be underpaid rather than not work: 'it's interesting to say "yes" only when one has the option of saying "no"' (in Wolof: *waaw defa am njëriñ su fekke mën nga waax dédet*), one of them told me. The signatory of the contract only did the asphalting of the walkway and the electrification. To judge by the final modest result, approved by the accommodating inspection of the accomplice client, a part of the investments swallowed up by the bus station would have, according to the subcontractors involved in its construction, served to finance the political activities of the retiring municipal council and reward, through corruption, this modern variant of classic forms of evergetism. One example will suffice: the ten 'restaurants', which supposedly cost 23 million CFA francs according to the communal budget, in reality would have cost 8 million francs to construct, according to the subcontractor who had worked on them. And he would have been paid only 2.5 million francs for the manpower.

Compared to the inquiries carried out within the administrations of control (customs, police) and service provision (health, justice and registry office), the field of public procurement confronted us with forms of corruption of a slightly different nature. Although, in a schematic way, the customs officer cashes in on his power to sanction and the commercial clerk extracts a high price for the juridical act he is supposed to deliver free, here it is the public administration that incurs expenses to gain access to goods and services provided by private individuals. Through the short-circuiting of norms of transparency, competition and impartiality, which are supposed to regulate public procurement, and by the payment of a price higher than that which could be accepted by the private individual, the decision-makers create an illegal revenue which they share with the contractor or the supplier through the means of payment of a commission given by the latter. It is, therefore, at this level that the most accomplished forms of transactional corruption can be observed.

We are here face to face with the most 'regulated', polite and stabilized form of corruption: indeed, one is far from the practice of constraint and dehumanization that characterizes relations between public agents and consumers in customs, justice or health. If, in the corrupting transactions that concern the world of customs or road traffic, agents 'take hostage' consumers' time, in the procurement contracts it is information that is the object of bargaining and manipulation, as well as the rules in force, which find themselves emptied of their content. As the case that opens this chapter shows, we are often faced with corruption that maintains an appearance of legality.

Rather, we are in the presence of negotiations between equals (and sometimes in a situation where the actors of the private sector have social and economic superiority): many contractors told us that they negotiate the sum of the commission fiercely, even if it entails giving up the work if they consider the price to pay too high. Besides, the practice of bargaining does not rule out relations characterized by a strong overpersonalization: each decision-maker has 'his' contractor, who can in turn count on a loyal 'friend' at the heart of the inspection committees and regularly visits ministries or town halls to see if they have a contract to propose to him. For the frequentation between public and private partners creates links and reciprocal favours. 'Those who draw water from the well together get their ropes entangled' (*ñuuy rotaando ñoy laxaso goj*), says a Wolof proverb. For the rest, this complex system of connivances explains why in the absence of victims (outside the firms excluded from the game but which hesitate to denounce these irregularities in the hope of being selected in their turn) public procurement remains the sector for which it is the most difficult to produce evidence.

This is also thereby a field that is governed by norms of functioning and its own ethic. 'Being straight' in this universe of the initiated implies respecting the given word, the oral contract, conforming to a code of behaviour with its own etiquette, its own taboos – that which is allowed and that which is forbidden.

> In their filthiness, in their corruption, there are still rules of behaviour. There is a line of conduct, a respect for the given word, for commitments and there are laws governing relations between them. I don't think that on this level there are blunders. (Y.F., Dakar, 16 January 2001)

He who sees himself given a contract and who 'forgets' those who have selected him at the time of payment will not benefit from help a second time, a contractor in the Kaolack building told us. Such an attitude would be equivalent to 'beating the tam-tam with an axe' (*tëgg dënd yi ak tel yi* in Wolof). To fail to respect the verbal contract of corruption 'is to close doors to future contracts', observed, in the same vein, a contractor from Parakou in Benin (Bako Arifari 2001: 89).

Finally, the study of concrete mechanisms of public procurement reveals a veritable continuity between petty and grand corruption. From the big contracts of transport infrastructure to the small contracts of supply to local collectivities, by way of construction of administrative buildings, the corrupting practices have become the norm in the three countries studied: they are set up in a system, in the sense that this latter can no longer function without them.[1]

The context of the study

Our comparative analysis is based on data collected in the three countries during field investigations spread out between 2000 and 2002. In Senegal, the locations chosen were the city of Kaolack and the small commune of Koungheul. A certain number of interviews (sixty-five in all) and documentary research were carried out at Dakar, among the principal authorities of allocation and examination, representatives of unions and professional organizations and some big firms vying for contracts on an international scale. On the other hand, examination of the Senegalese press since 1978, as well as analysis of annual reports of the court of budgetary discipline, published in the *Journal officiel*, have given us a broader view of the phenomenon and allowed us to consider mechanisms at work at the level of the central administration and public firms.[2] In Benin, investigations were carried out in the city of Parakou and more generally in the departments of Borgou and Alibori, adding up to a total of sixty-seven interviews. In particular we studied the contracts thrown open by the programme of public investment (PIP), financed by the national budget and whose full cycle is controlled at departmental level. For Niger, where, to begin with, the theme of public procurement was not retained for the inquiry, we are dependent on a more restrained corpus of twenty-six interviews, carried out for the most part in Niamey.

Our research has thus principally concerned public procurement concluded by the decentralized administration and local collectivities, given the fact that in the three countries the reforms of decentralization have granted a greater financial autonomy to local governments, albeit in different degrees.

The field inquiries were carried out during a period of profound questioning of the system of public contracting in the three countries, following international pressures in favour of 'good governance' and reflection within the UEMOA (Economic and Monetary Union of West Africa), which in June 2000 resulted in the launching of a project of reform of public contracting among its member states. In Senegal, Abdou Diouf's appeal, a few months before his departure from the political scene in 2000 ('In the public markets, corruption leads to distortions of competition: it is not healthy that the firm that wins is the firm that cheats'[3]), was being echoed a year later in the demand of Abdoulaye Wade to be informed personally of all public tenders, in order to 'survey the transparency of contracts.'[4] It is in the context of public display of the quest for good governance, but, equally, of the political use of audits of thirty-odd national firms (whose most

obvious result has been to accelerate the process of political migra-
tion from the Socialist Party towards Abdoulaye Wade's PDS), that
Senegalese public opinion was informed of certain files concerning
irregularities in public contracting by the central administration.
The Senegalese code, which dated from 1982,[5] has henceforth been
regulated by decree no. 2002–550 of July 2002. Niger, criticized
in 1998 by the World Bank for restricted consultation and unclear
evaluation of tenders, immediately began a programme to improve
the rules of public contracting, which led to the replacement of the
1989 decree[6] by statute no. 2002–0072 of 18 September 2002 and
the creation of a Permanent Secretariat of the Central Committee
of Contracts, intended to improve the transparency of budgetary
implementation and the effectiveness of public expenditure. Similar
pressures, both internal and at international level, led Benin, alone
among the countries of the subregion, to equip itself with a Code
of Ethics and Moralization of Public Procurement[7] in 1999, and to
reform public contracting, with law no. 2004–18 of 27 August 2004,
which rendered the Beninois code of 1996 obsolete.[8]

The new contracting codes inaugurated important modifications
to the rules: to cite only the case of Senegal, the new law reaffirmed
the need to respect the contracting rules governing public expenditure and to verify the existence of sufficient budgetary credit before
concluding a contract; in order to ease the process, it raised the
thresholds of contracts; to avoid contracts being granted to fictitious
firms (see below), it imposed the need for preliminary approval for
tenders in the building sector and for public works; it deprived
the Administration's National Committee of Contracts (CNCA) of
the prerogative to permit deviation from contracts, which opened
the path to forms of 'legal' corruption (see below), and abolished
the National Committee of Examination (CND) and regional committees, even though their replacement by contracts committees
internal to each organization could compromise the requirement of
transparency (M.A. Sow 2000: 12). Finally, it reduced the possibility
of future recourse to the process of direct negotiated agreement and
extended the time period of the tendering process, in order to make
it easier for firms to prepare their bids. However, the decree did not
regulate the controversial question of the sale of tender documents

(*dossier d'appel d'offres*, DAO), which often represents, as we shall see, a dissuasive factor for small firms due to their cost.

Although our analysis refers to the situation before the reforms came into effect, in our view it remains valid. Despite advances made, the implementation of the reforms is a struggle: in Niger, the new Authority of the Regulation of Public Contracts (ARMP) 'is not yet operational and the central Committee of Contracts that plays the role of regulator and inspection is not involved in the application of public procurement' (Doe et al. 2004: 23). Furthermore, several supplementary clauses, such as those relating to systems of concessions, to the delegation of superintendence work and to the system of recourse, have not yet been finalised (Doe et al. 2004: 23). As for Senegal, the new code is not yet operational, in the absence of implementation decrees, and yet is already in trouble; on the one hand, some of its arrangements contravene the 1965 Code of Obligations (*Code des obligations*) still in force; on the other hand, systems of derogation (provided by Article 264) were not abrogated as planned; finally, the new monitoring organs remain for the moment empty shells, their personnel having not been appointed and their internal rules still to be drawn up.[9]

In this chapter, we address ourselves to the different phases of the process of public procurement. If the preparation of the consultation files and the choice of the firm and the contracting party are evidently in the most 'corrupt prone' steps and those where corruption is dressed up in a certain 'legality', the phases of execution and reception, a veritable 'combatant's run' for the contractor, takes us back to the universe of petty banalized corruption, made up of traps, falsifications, of small extortions and favours.

'Legal' corruption in public procurement

The Senegalese are very good in matters of procedure, they know how to respect them while emptying them of their content. (State general inspector, Dakar)

The practices that we are going to examine can be defined, following A. Heidenheimer (1990), as 'grey' corruption: an object of criticism and stigmatization by citizens, they have been able to flourish under the protective wing of the different regimes that have succeeded each other in the three countries examined. This apparently legal corruption has been possible through the means of two mechanisms: the permissive interpretation of regulatory texts and the creation of mechanisms waiving decrees in force. In practice, exceptional processes have become the norm, and normal ones have ended up becoming the exception.

Abuse of the direct negotiated agreement

The first deviation consists of the generalized abuse of contracts by a direct negotiated agreement (in French *entente directe* or *gré à gré*, 'private agreement') in which the administration discusses and deals directly with a supplier or contractor. Given that recourse to a private agreement allows the minimal requirements to be avoided in the choice of the firm and permits the establishment of a contract on the basis of vague or inexistent lists of rules, this process was strictly regulated by national legislations. According to the terms of Article 39 of the Senegalese decree of 1982, for example, a contract can be finalized by a direct understanding only when a single supplier of the object or service required by the administration exists; when, after two appeals for competition, no tender had been presented; or when, for imperative reasons linked to national defence, the administration is obliged to choose its contractor directly.[10] In Benin, the mutual agreement contract is allowed in the case where the invitation to tender would have proved abortive or in the case where the contractor possessed letters of patent. But it does not exclude the opening up of competition between candidates. As for Niger, it applies only to expenditure of less than 5 million CFA francs.

Despite the existence of these barriers, private agreement contracts have assumed such great proportions that in Senegal they already represented in 1993 a total of 51 per cent of the project contracts submitted to the administration's National Committee of Contracts (CNCA) and 59 per cent of their global cost (World Bank 1993). Frequent recourse to this kind of contract was at the root of an erroneous conviction firmly held by certain decision-makers that 'up to 10 million CFA francs, one does a mutual agreement'.[11]

Besides, given that the texts provide that 'contracts finalized according to the procedure of direct negotiated agreement need a preliminary authorization from the administration's National Committee of Contracts' (Article 39 of the 1982 decree, paragraph 2), this arrangement was interpreted as granting the CNCA the power to authorize contracts by direct agreement outside the three conditions cited above, on the basis of a simple request on the part of ministries, motivated – wrongly – by the urgency of the provision or the service:

> To my knowledge, according to reports I have from different architects, it is the mutual agreement contracts that have practically become the common practice. You tell people: 'I have a budget to spend before the end of the year, but I don't have time to organize an invitation to tender.' And one asks for authorization to effect contracting by mutual agreement. (architect, Dakar, September 2000)

In Niger, if contracts by mutual agreement represent 4.4 per cent of the public procurements approved by the Central Committee of Contracts (CCM) in 2002 and 12.7 per cent in 2003, their global cost was still 762 million and 1.8 billion CFA francs respectively (Doe et al. 2004: 24). But most of the small contracts escape this calculation, because the CCM only has jurisdiction on tenders above 100 million CFA francs. Between 1996 and 1999, clients attached to the Bare regime greatly benefited from the mutual agreement system, especially in contracts linked to the privatization of certain state-owned firms (Issa Abdourhamane 1999: 92). In 2005, the national press denounced massive frauds involving mutual agreements where orders were greatly inflated: 1.2 billion CFA francs for the purchase of 12,000 tonnes of fertilizer, and 3.7 billion CFA francs for a contract dating from 1996 with Niger's New Printing House.[12]

Yet it is above all at regional and local levels that, in the three countries, mutual agreement has become the most common form of public contracting. On the one hand, most of the contracts involving local collectivities are of very little economic value. And even when the overshooting of the regulatory threshold (5 or 10 million FCFA, according to the old laws in force in the three countries) would trigger the process of invitation to tender, 'one can divide [the contract], and then it becomes a mutual agreement' (A.S., supplier,

Niamey, 10 April 2002). According to a former secretary general of the University of Niamey (M.M., 20 April 2002) the practice of segmenting would also seem to characterize the contracts of the National Centre of University Works. On the other hand, the mutual agreement is a common occurrence in supply contracts (fuel, tyres, phytosanitary products, office articles), 'where those in charge no longer take the trouble of calling for tenders. Each institution today has a supplier, who is often a brother, a friend. Thus he carries out all the orders' (G., contractor of Parakou).

Systematic recourse to this process is sometimes justified by the absence of tenders when the contract is launched. This is the case with the Kaolack prison, which, since 1995, has been unsuccessful in finding contractors for its annual food supplies. The reasons are to be found in issues of solvency and the shortage of funds experienced by administrations. These contractors who agree to work with the state specialize in mutual agreement and charge very high prices to compensate for the inevitable delays in payment.[13]

Besides mutual agreement, those responsible for Senegalese public procurement contracts have perfected a 'new find',[14] the direct order. Unlike the mutual agreement, this does not lead to the concluding of a written contract, but limits itself to a letter carrying authorization to place orders with one or more suppliers listed in the annex. In the view of the payments officer of the Senegalese Treasury, 'the adoption of this procedure in the enforcement of budgetary credits has known a dizzy acceleration in the last five years to the extent of becoming a rule for some big ministerial departments (Ministry of the Interior, Ministry of Health, Ministry of the Armed Forces, etc.)',[15] with some 70 per cent of the market allocated by direct order.

Indeed, although Articles 2, 3 and 4 of the Senegalese code of responsibilities state that 'it is compulsory to conclude a contract for services whose value equals or exceeds 10,000,000 francs', a subsequent clause allows the CNCA to waive the preceding stipulation.[16] The National Committee, which interpreted these arrangements in such a way as to institute an autonomous system of public procurement contracts, widened the breach even further, regardless of the scale of the service provided, the only requirement being to obtain the committee's authorization. Such deviations thus create the conditions that permit violation of the principles embodied in the decree, while maintaining the appearance of regularity.

The system of derogations

In the manner of the exceptional regimes that waived the common law under colonial administration (see Chapter 2), public powers have appropriated the means to evade the objective of transparency sought by the codes governing public procurement. In Senegal, nearly all the plum sectors are submitted to regimes of derogation, such as roadworks[17] and petrol markets.[18] One could also cite the contracts of the autonomous port of Dakar and those of the Cayor canal, authorized outside the systems applicable to each public firm. The aim of the different derogations, as their text makes clear, is to soften the rules of contract laid down in decree no. 82–690 of 7 September 1982.

The most flagrant example is that of decree no. 97–632 of 18 June 1997, concerning the regulation of contracts for the project of construction of administrative buildings and the renovation of Senegalese state buildings (PCRPE), an initiative closely linked to the priorities of political financing, according to several sources. This decree authorizes the procedure of direct agreement up to the sum of 100 million CFA francs for planning and supplies and up to 150 million CFA francs for new works. In addition, it imposes mutual agreement for all work of cleaning, renovation and maintenance. It leaves one wondering what could be the reasons for derogation of the 1982 decree, which, among other things, aims to encourage the emergence of local industries, economic expansion and job creation, and simplification of contract procedures; for the projects in question (the construction of the Palace of Justice and an Olympic pool, to cite only the most important examples) do not appear to justify recourse to a specific system.[19]

The case of the Palace of Justice is representative of the deviations that the legalized abuse of derogations can engender.

In June 2000, work was stopped on the order of Wade's new political regime. In fact, enquiries revealed that the contractor, the Consortium of Firms (CDE), had not been selected following regular invitation to tender, but on the simple basis of a purchase order in which the estimated cost of the project was not even quantified.[20] Moreover, there was no contract between the firm and the PCRPE.

According to one architect who followed this case closely:

> It became clear when there was a change in the direction of the state that the firm that was working on the Palace of Justice did not yet have the contract. Worse, of all the PCRPE projects whose construction had begun or which had been constructed, not a single one had been authorized for construction.... The leaders of the project had been given the possibility of approving contracts by mutual agreement up to 100 million francs, including the planning contracts.... Or a planning contract worth 100 million francs for the state corresponds to works worth 2 billion francs, so that means that the budget of 500 million francs for the architecture competition was largely exceeded. Moreover, one found oneself in a situation where the Republic's presidency executed projects, so it was transformed into an agent of execution. Or it is the presidency that controls the body of state inspectors. How was it going to control itself?... Another deviation: ... the general secretary of the presidency of the Republic was the director of the project; when he was appointed Budget Minister and then Minister of Finance, he remained director of the project.... A Minister of Finance who was the executor of an operational project on the field – that was in complete contradiction to the intentions of the Senegalese state regime (J.C.T., 18 September 2000, Dakar).

It also seems that the cost of the work was largely underestimated: at the time of the architecture competition for the design of the Palace of Justice, the contract was calculated at 2.7 billion CFA francs, which was lower than the price per square metre charged for the low-cost housing of the Housing Bank. Today, it is estimated that between 5 and 6 billion CFA francs would be required to complete the Palace.

There is also the recent case of Niger, where the minister of finance, the prime minister's office (*Primature*) and the presidency would have deviated from the rules of public accounting by registering in 2003, on temporary account no. 47013 (called by agents of the Treasury 'the account I devour'), 4.6 billion CFA francs in payments without a preliminary order (*Paiement sans ordonnancement préal-*

able, PSOP).[21] A subsequent audit showed that the PSOP represented 31 per cent of the total expenditure of the Nigerien state, excluding foreign financing, in 2003. The same study also revealed that the

> expenditure of the president's special programme [for the reduction of poverty], rising to 5.8 billion FCFA and to 2.2 billion at the beginning of the years 2003 and 2004 respectively, did not follow the customary procedure of payments but rather the exceptional procedure of payment without preliminary order (PSOP). The authorities justified recourse to this procedure by their desire not to delay the execution of projects (Doe et al. 2004: 34, 36).

Systemic corruption: complicity between decision-makers and contractors

Outside 'legal' avoidance of the rules (abuse of authorizations of mutual agreement and regimes of derogation), it is possible to direct the choice of contractor through a multitude of strategies:[22] by skewing the information regarding the call for tenders (by minimizing advertising, by not disclosing essential elements of files, by delivering privileged information, etc.), by abuse of the broad discretionary powers vested in the different examination committees, or, again, by simulating an open and fair competition (especially through the means of prior agreements between firms or the creation of fictitious firms).

The preliminary exclusion of bidders

In order to reduce the number of potential tenderers and thus eliminate competition, several strategies are applied. Their common denominator is the manipulation of information.

Opacity

The first strategy is that of opacity. In this case, it is a question of limiting publicity for the call for tenders. The texts recommend a wide diffusion of the tender invitation by means of the written press, radio, and information bulletins of the chamber of commerce. But testimonies of contractors and state agents describe the problems encountered by the advertising of calls to tender, particularly concerning medium-size contracts at regional and local levels, for which information is supposedly confidential and is generally given by word of mouth. If the big contracts benefit from advertisements in national newspapers, smaller-scale contracts come to the attention of contractors and economic players through the practice of canvassing: one visits the head of the purchasing department and one knocks on the door of the director of administrative and financial affairs of a ministry (*Directeur des affaires administratives et financières*, DAAF). As a general rule, contractors based in secondary urban centres find it difficult to access information and prepare their bids:

> Those of Cotonou have the advantage of information. Chances are not equal in accessing information concerning a new call for tenders.... There are administrative papers that can be obtained only at Cotonou; for example only the Ministry can sign the certificate of classification. (D.S., Parakou)

The waiting rooms of town halls are thus crawling with a multitudinous microcosm composed of subcontractors, artisans and canvassers seeking to see the mayor, his assistants or the technicians of urban planning, in the hope of obtaining a small construction contract or an order for supplies. For these small contractors, the simple fact of walking the corridors, reminding the authorities of their existence and 'showing oneself' represents the chance of being called one day or, failing that, of meeting big contractors likely to offer them a subcontract. 'This simple coming and going can result in them giving you small sums to test your capacity to redistribute', confirms this Nigerian supplier (A.S., Niamey, 10 April 2002).

Dissuasion

A second strategy consists of the application of mechanisms of dissuasion: access to regularly published information is rendered difficult, or interested contractors are urged to desist. An example is the practice of unfairly reducing the time given to potential bidders to place their tenders. A simple consultation of the *Bulletin d'information économique* of the Senegal Chamber of Commerce shows that the time limit for receiving tenders is often less than the regulatiion twenty days: for example, an invitation to tender is published in the 31 January issue, with a closing date of 13 February. In these conditions no firm is able to prepare its tender properly – unless, that is, it has been informed of the schedule by other channels beforehand. According to several directors of Senegalese firms, the prescribed time is generally respected only in the case of international bids.

Another means used to discourage small firms consists of fixing a high sum for the acquisition of tender documents (*dossier d'appel d'offre*, DAO). Even though it is not a legal requirement, the administration demands amounts (or payment in kind to the same value: reams of paper or office supplies) ranging from 10,000 to 5,000,000 CFA francs, which are not reimbursed in case of non-allocation of the contract. This practice also constitutes, according to the secretary of the Kaolack Chamber of Commerce, an encouragement to corruption, inasmuch as firms with little capacity to finance their activities up front, and thus unable to guarantee repeated payment for DAOs, will be encouraged to ensure the success of their tender by resorting to illicit agreement.

Dissuasion can thus function through strategies of pretend scarcity, with the aim of creating an artificial 'tailback'.

> [The call for tenders] was made public on time, but I couldn't get them on time. Because it can be stated in a journal: 'the invitation to tender is open, you can collect the files in such a place at such a price' but when one calls to ask 'are the files available?' the answer is 'No, they are finished'.... But in fact they aren't. The response 'No, they are finished' means that they are trying to delay as long as the particular firm they want has not yet shown up. So they say: 'they are finished' until ten or fifteen days before the end of the process, and at that moment the files are released. (R.B., Kaolack, 2 January 2001)

When DAOs must be collected at Dakar, Niamey or Cotonou, the fictional disruption of stocks can represent a major obstacle to firms located deep in the countryside, which will have to make several visits – costly in time and money – to the administrative offices to procure the necessary documentation. The victims of this organized dysfunction – mainly those contractors left outside the illegal understandings with the committees that grant public contracts – will be heavily penalized, for they will lack the necessary time to prepare their tender properly.

Shattering the confidentiality of bids

In this context, no one risks submitting a tender without knowing the technical and financial details of the project in advance (this explains the small differences between the prices quoted). Sometimes the contractor will have a foothold within the administration; sometimes the information will go through canvassers, or by way of retired officers who hover around the contract offices of different ministries. For a discreet diffusion of information concerning new tenders, the profile of the perfect intermediary is the

> small politician, businessman, and deputy of a place or a party, commission agent. Finally, one can dress it up in all possible and imaginable kinds of ways, but it's always the guy who'll say 'good morning' to the minister who will be at the cocktails; in short it's the guy who knows his way in and out. (Y.F., Dakar, 16 January 2001)

With regard to the more technical questions and to finding one's way around in the labyrinths of the administration, in turn, this intermediary

> will always need junior officers to supply a small piece of information, to know where such and such a file can be found, to follow it and so on.... And if this person is pleasant and allows me to have access to information regularly and normally, I will call upon him regularly. Eventually, when I'm travelling, I'll give him his little *sëricaa*.[23] (Y.F., Dakar, 16 January 2001)

Yet one is generally suspicious of intermediaries, who 'may blackmail you one day', one Dakar contractor told us. Thus each economic player counts on his personal experience and on the contacts he has gradually accumulated within the administration and which he owes to himself to maintain by well-thought-out strategies of redistribution:

> I always count on the relations I have at the level of Sonitel. You know, already before even going to fulfil the first [contract] I got there, friends informed me that there would be a contract of 15 million. All the agents

in the field are friends; they already informed me how it would work....
You understand now why I hadn't been wrong to maintain this entire
tissue of friends there.... To make my tender, I was already informed
by an inspector of the office, he gave me a little idea of the price I
should propose to have a good chance of winning the contract.... It's in
everyone's interest. He knows very well that when I have the contract,
he'll get his share. (A.K.B., former agent of the SNCCT, 31 January
2002, Niamey)

You work with them every day. You are introduced in one, two, three
ministries, ... you see them in meetings, they are your friends, you'll
eat at their home, you're in the plane, in the hotel together: 'What
perspective do you have?' It has an official aspect, because, in any case,
before obtaining the financing of a hospital by the World Bank, there
has already been financing for the study. That day, you know who's who
and what's what. But all this is official, you have mixed committees,
you know everything. (P.L., Dakar, 16 January 2001)

The files thus circulate well before the contract is advertised,
for, as one Beninois contractor put it: 'information, that's half the
war. When you have the right information, you're sure that you
are on the same track as the others. Otherwise you pay the cost of
your ignorance' (D.N., Parakou). Therefore it is crucial to have the
information in advance: 'you don't enter a tender at the moment you
buy the file, it's too late.... The one who does that, he's lost all the
battles, so he'll lose the war' (P.L., Dakar, 16 January 2001). The
stake is also economic:

For a firm like mine, it's important in the sense that I already have to
give 3 or 4 million FCFA, because I'm obliged to call upon a private engineering and design department to prepare that very tender. Already,
it's dangerous for me, because financially it's heavy, it's very heavy,
and I'm not sure of winning that call for tender. A firm that's had the
information in advance doesn't need to spend these 3 or 4 million to
prepare the tender. From that moment, I don't put in a tender because
it would work out too expensive for me. In the case of the other firm,
which has the same capacities but received the information in advance,
it will put in the tender anyway. And that's where it makes a difference.
(R.B., Kaolack, 2 January 2001)

Putting in a tender for a contract demands a heavy investment in time
and energy. For a contract of 590 million ..., the expenditure of putting
in a tender can rise to 20–30 million, and take between three and four

months of preparation. And one enters in the invitation to tender one year before the DAO is even rendered public. I never won a bid by luck. (P.L., Dakar, January 2001)

Competition is sometimes so sharp that in Benin some firms, to be sure of winning, don't hesitate to have in their pay owners of photocopying centres so that they can discreetly pass them the files that other firms submitting tenders have deposited for copying.

The files of tenders can, finally, be 'made to order' so that there is only one competitor capable of presenting himself: one plays with the necessary figures, on the amount of the bank deposit or again on previous experience. For example: 'In a file of calls for tenders, the applicant firms were asked to provide proof of having constructed a minimum number of twenty-five water towers. It was clear that the firm capable of meeting this condition was known in advance' (B.D., general director of a business firm, Dakar).

The role of discretionary power in the commissioning process

The different inspection and verification committees at national and regional levels clearly constitute a strategic place to the extent that they benefit from wide discretionary powers; this is especially true of committees responsible for the technical evaluation of tenders. After the opening of envelopes containing the tenders and before their submission to the committee of technicians, it is possible to find fault with a contractor's calculations. That is, a rival's submission may be queried on the basis of sometimes questionable technical motivations, by taking advantage of the vague or imprecise specifications,[24] and thus grant poor technical marks to good files, just as one can 'redraft' a technically flawed bid, or one too high in relation to the target price:

> The guy who is on your side, when he's examining your offer, he'll tell you 'he's made a mistake, I've calculated, I've done ten times four, that's 40 million, and he has added 20 million'; or then he'll say, 'he's made a mistake in the column of unit prices' and he'll correct your figure 2. It's only 2,000 because he's put 20 million. Who's right, who's wrong?

> And if at the moment of giving in your tender, you are 20 million too
> expensive, he'll change the 2 and at the end he'll say 'He made a mistake
> in the calculation' (P.L., Dakar, 16 January 2001)

Indeed, according to contractors, committee members rarely
oppose the opinion of technicians, because they often ignore the
terms of the regulations, given that they are not schooled in contracting. It must be noted that regional services, as much in Benin
as in Niger and in Senegal, are not always kept informed of the new
decrees, legislative texts and statutes that modify the rules. It is
therefore the technicians who must be 'kept in one's pocket'.

> So the main thing is to have the technicians who discuss and also have
> a kind of majority; that is to say you find out if there are six, seven or
> eight members. There are also an enormous number of inspecting
> committees, which are not represented at the meetings. Those who
> are in the Ministry of Health, for example, are invited but they don't
> come. If you know someone, or if you know two or three members of
> the ministry and if you have approval or have got yourself placed first
> – because its often a matter of 'getting oneself placed' by the inspection
> committee – these friends have to be called in the different ministries
> – 'don't forget to attend because it's for me'. Otherwise, they risk
> being in the minority. So, you ask them to strengthen your majority.
> All these small services also have to be paid. If you ask someone in
> the ministry, 'go to the inspection, it's for me', it's certain that on
> coming out of the committee, on the day I get the contract, I'll give
> him 200,000 or 300,000 because he's done me a favour. (P.L., Dakar,
> 16 January 2001)

Studies conducted in Benin by our investigators at the time of the
assessing of tenders have shown that some contractors do not attend
because they know their file is being monitored and 'sponsored' by
a member of the examination committee and that therefore they are
sure to obtain the contract.[25]

The work of a committee can also be affected by political pressure,
as attested by the case of a contract for supplies tendered by Niamey's
National centre of University Works (CNOU). The value of the order
exceeded 200 million CFA francs. Rather than assessing each and
choosing between the two candidates, the committee appointed the
firm that quoted less and whose tender was lower than its rival's by
100 million CFA francs. The file of the chosen firm was incomplete,

however. As the supplier was reputed to be a serious supplier, having already worked with the university administration (not to mention the fact that the state owed him money for earlier supplies), the decision was upheld, on condition that he produce the missing information – the national social security fund papers – within forty-eight hours. However, some members of the committee, who had received promises from the rejected rival, urged the latter to question the committee's decision. On the basis of his influential position within the CDS, at the time the party in power, he duly threatened to get the secretary general sacked from the university. The matter was referred up to the president of the time, Mahamane Ousmane, who put the decision in the hands of the ministers of commerce and higher education. The contract was finally awarded to the more expensive firm, taking advantage of the fact that the smaller offer had meanwhile been withdrawn (M.M., former secretary general of the university, Niamey, 20 April 2002).

Another factor that permits the creation of durable links both between members of committees and between members and contractors is the non-renewal of personnel. This feeds the networks of complicity and, in the absence of 'victims', makes control difficult:

> Personally, I don't believe in committees, unless they are committees whose members are rotated and don't stay in place too long.... If their coexistence lasts too long..., I don't think there is efficiency at that level. People know each other in Senegal, you know, relations between people are very cordial, very intimate, very familiar. Sometimes, it is not even in the office that the problems will be resolved, but in the house, because one has entry into their homes and that's where problems will be resolved. (L.L., Inspector of Finances, Dakar)

> The national assessment committee must be suppressed, for one sees the same people there all the time, for whom the stake is to make money. The proof: they ask to be registered as present even if they are absent! (K.S., expert in public procurement)

'Public procurement tontines' and fictitious firms

Another common device is to fix the outcome of the tendering process while giving the appearance of a regulated competition between different bids. A prior understanding between firms serves to create a veritable 'public procurement tontine', where it is agreed that each will win in turn. For example, in a tender for road repairs in the Senegalese city of Kaolack, one of the only two firms able to fulfil such public works knowingly submitted a tender pitched too high in order to favour their rival, with whom they had made a non-competition agreement. Questioned on the affair, the contractor admitted having estimated his costs at 300 million CFA francs in the knowledge that the commune only had 50 million. As for the other details, according to another contractor on the spot, 'the road could not have cost more than 25 million, because instead of making a bilayer surface as anticipated, they only filled in and watered the laterite, put on hot tar, passed the gravel spreader, threw on the gravel and it was done. I didn't even see the laterite stabilized.'

At a higher level, the system is so well oiled and tacitly accepted by the contractors that, cognizant of the fact that the contract for which they are putting in a tender is reserved for a rival, they readily accept the rules of the game by asking the decision-maker for advice on the best way of presenting a bid so that it is rejected:

> There is also the kind who say 'No, this one isn't for you'.... The guy has an agreement with my rival and the agreement is concluded, and he's straight to the point of telling me that it's not for me. But I ask him, 'how much do I have to put in?' If it's a billion, I put in a billion + 100. But he strengthens his position. I'm not going to fight against him, he's straight with me, but then we discuss the following case. (P.L., Dakar, 16 January 2001)

In Benin, the 'co-contract' is also widely practised. According to several interlocutors, this has the merit of preventing unfair competition practices and discouraging contractors from 'price breaking'. The urban constituency of Parakou even decided to regulate the 'public procurement tontine' by introducing innovations in the system of restrained tenders[26] applied in this commune. By basing itself on a list of some sixty recognized firms, this system prohibits the recipient of a public contract from putting in a tender, as long as other firms have not been selected in their turn (M.B., Parakou, 18 December 1999).

Another variation on this strategy – common in the case of demands for information and prices and in the case of restrained tenders – is the creation of fictitious firms that submit tenders with bogus bids. In order to retain the semblance of normality, the contractor who is illicitly preselected is asked to provide other estimates, under the guise of other firms' tenders; the latter will be represented either by 'actors' from the circle of the chosen contractor, who will have corrupted the committees of contracts, or by freelance individuals who, for a reward, will do the bidding of contractor or work for him on a subcontracted basis. These testimonies of Nigerien contractors are eloquent:

> In restrained consultations there are too many intrigues. A shopkeeper who wants to bid comes to an agreement with the DAAF [Direction des Affaires Administratives et Financières] to contact other shopkeepers, who quote fantastic prices to allow their man to get through. A shopkeeper can himself fill in the forms using the names of fictitious shopkeepers, to give his tender the maximum chance. And this is done with the knowledge of the DAAF – that is, the DAAF tells them the price they should propose. (J.A., contractor, Arlit)

> If someone tells you to fix prices, in addition to my quote, I can add fictitious names of shopkeepers with prices higher than mine. This is in complicity with the DAAF sometimes; as it is he who asked for it, he gives you the contract without any problem. As for me, I can go see the shopkeepers with whom I get along to fix the prices. In this case, the DAAF has to be given its share. (A.I., supplier, Niamey)

So far as Senegal is concerned, a recent example comes to us from the audit report concerning the National Society of Low-cost Housing (SN HLM), deposited at the beginning of February 2001 before the president of the Republic. Investigating an obvious case of overbilling (a luminous sign which cost 740,000 CFA francs, billed to the SN HLM at 7.18 million francs), the auditors examined the procedure of restrained consultation leading to the granting of the contract to the company Décor & Art. The latter, which turned out to be a fictitious supplier, was supposedly contacted by HLM, along with two other firms, CESP (Consortium d'entreprises de services et de production) and SOBATP (Société de bâtiment et de travaux publics), whose respective tenders were 8,092,975 CFA francs and 8,627,520 CFA francs. It was discovered that cheques made out to Décor & Art were in fact cashed by the director of SOBATP, despite the fact that it was a rival in the tender. 'It thus appears [according to the audit report] that the other two firms [SOBATP and CESP] served only as a means to justify the choice of Décor & Art.'[27]

Firms that 'fit into a briefcase'

This context of systematic corruption encourages the proliferation of fictitious or improvised contractors, either used to supply bills and estimates, or specialized in the resale of public procurement and other 'purchase bills'.

> Today, there are nearly 300 Nigerien operations that call themselves firms but don't even have an office, and it is they that win the contracts. These firms sometimes aren't even registered, don't have a letterhead, or facilities, or accreditation, or Chamber of Commerce endorsement. Nor do they pay a professional tax. (J.A., contractor, Arlit)

Their means are varied: some may exploit contacts established during a previous round of activity, as with A.K.B., former employee of the Nigerien Society of Telephone Lines (Société nigérienne de canalisation et de conduite téléphonique, SNCCT), a partner firm of the Nigerien Society of Telecommunications (Société nigérienne de télécommunications, Sonitel). When his firm went bankrupt, he set himself up on his own. An inspector of Sonitel proposed him for a 5 million FCFA contract as a mutual agreement. Not having the technical and financial means to honour the contract, he resold the purchase order to a local shopkeeper. In Niger, high officers and retired cabinet ministers turn to suppliers of ministries. Benefiting from the contacts and acquaintances built up during their career in political administration, they manage to secure small mutually agreed contracts, or orders that they can then subcontract: 'What's certain is that if I have a purchase order, I will be able to sell it on to a contractor who has the means to do the work. Then I can take 50 per cent and give 50 per cent to the contractor' (A.K.B., former agent of SNCCT, 31 January 2002, Niamey).

According to a Niamey supplier,

> Today, if a marabout or a carpenter has a relative who is highly placed, to help them the latter can give them a purchase order, which they then sell ... if they cannot themselves execute the contract. Some officers

make this into a commercial business; there are also false purchase orders, which can be sold several times. (A.S., supplier, Niamey, 10 April 2002)

It must be noted that the phenomenon of contractors who 'fit into a briefcase' came about and was consolidated, in the three countries studied, in the context of political clientelism and the informal privatization of the means and mechanisms of public contracts. Political activism is thus the major springboard in these types of career. At the bottom of the ladder can be found people like D.G., Social Party activist in his Kaolack neighbourhood and *bukki-man*,[28] who (before he was relegated to political oblivion on the victory of Wade's followers in the capital of the peanut basin) was able to obtain, as a reward for his activist work, a contract for maintenance of the city's graveyards – an operation costed at 7 million CFA francs, which he fulfilled by setting fire to the weeds with the help of his children. At a higher level, we could quote the case of M.B., a mason of Gossas who became a senator in the last parliament of Abdou Diouf, who, in conjunction with a network of seven municipal tax collectors, produced false bills for supplies and fictitious works undertaken. According to sources close to the inspector of finances, his part in the scam amounted to two-thirds of the total amount misappropriated, estimated at 3.4 billion CFA francs.

The ascension to power of a party often constitutes the awaited occasion to embark on a career of shopkeeper or contractor specializing in public orders:

I began with MNSD's arrival in power. I was in the cabinet of the Prime Minister Hama, I saw the protocol, and I told him: 'well, now we are in power'. I told him that I didn't need anyone to give me 10,000 F that one gives sometimes to activists, I told him I wanted to do business. So he told me that it was well thought out. He gave me visiting cards to produce for *Primature*, I went to see a printer, we made a sample and I went to show it to him, he told me it's good and then I delivered the rest, that's how I began. (A.I., supplier, Niamey)

This shopkeeper then enlarged the range of his activities: planning, health, defence, interior and justice, by targeting ministers controlled by his party. 'As soon as I arrive, I tell them that I'm in the MNSD, and they tell me to go make my price proposals'. Not being obliged to corrupt to obtain orders, he can then resell them to third persons who will carry them out:

> Me, I'm a politician, I'm from the MNSD, therefore I can find orders without even giving money, because I know people and it's often they who recommend me to the DAAF. Me, I'm different from other shop-keepers: if I have an order that I can't fulfil, there, nothing to be done, one will sell it to others.

In Niger, the general feeling is that 'every side that comes to power comes with its own businessmen. So, just as one changes officers, that's the way one changes businessmen' (A.R., businessman import-export). In Benin, it has been noted, 'the big tendency is towards partisan transfer among contractors and other businessmen, in order to ensure that their activities prosper' (Bako-Arifari 2001: 88).

The absence of an updated official classification of firms favours these drifts. In Senegal, a decree establishing a classification of firms was put in force in 2000 after long years of negotiations between the business world and the administration. According to the director of a big Dakar firm, this decree 'was greatly resisted by the administration, because the people had their own firms, they had their own list. And there everything could be found: informal, formal, anything one can imagine' (Y.F., Dakar, 16 January 2001). But the system is flawed to the extent that it remains relatively simple to set up a firm. The same problems arose with the classification done by Agetip (Agency of execution of works of public interest against underemployment), an agency created in 1989 in partnership with the World Bank: some people buy approvals of compliance, thanks to which they win construction contracts for buildings, which they then subcontract to a genuine firm. Thus one 'places agreements', as in the case of a restaurant owner from Kaolack who bought an approval from Agetip for 200,000 CFA francs for works in civil engineering and on the roads.[29] This situation aroused the anger of professional contractors:

> Yesterday I met a relative, he's a shopkeeper, he told me: if you like I'll sell you a contract for renovation.... He already has it! You see, he has his shop; he sells cement, iron, and rice. It's we who are in the profession ... he will have a contract with I don't know who, then he'll subcontract this or he'll sell it to other people. (I.G., Kaolack, 5 October 2000)

Now, at the level of Senegal, everyone wants to be a building contractor, even the mechanics, and the shopkeepers.... Out of ten firms, only five are legitimate, and even these five, in general, they have problems because firstly the people who created these firms are not... in the profession.... That is to say, a tailor, one bright day, he wakes up and creates his firm, so now he's a contractor. Of what? Of building. Through his good relations, advisers here and there, he gets hold of a contract. You think this guy is going to limit himself to respecting the norms? No, but to respect norms one has to know them!... We haven't learnt this profession to be humiliated, no. (C.S., Dakar, 13 September 2000)

The sale of contracts is already common in Benin: the subcontractor will realize the contract for a reduced amount, a part having been kept by the seller. But the final responsibility remains with the official subcontractor – with resulting problems that can be imagined in the case of bad work.

'The key word is to give': corruption costs in public procurement

Commission at the start of the contract

Illicit agreement between contractors and decision-makers gives rise to the practice of bribes – of the order of 10 per cent of the total contract, payable when work commences. In view of the oral nature of the contract, trust is crucial: 'The commission is given after being paid, that's my rule, and when you have concluded an agreement, if you have to give 100,500 F, you give 100,500 F, not 100,000 F' (P.L., Dakar, 16 January 2001).

Often, the cost of commissions is already included in the project's budget:

The town planning department, which does the preliminary study, will already overbill the estimate, in a way that the firm can find and give the bribe to that guy.... For a real contract of 10 million for example, the firm will tell him: 'you over-bill, go up to 12 or 13 million, and from there you'll get back one million or 500,000 etc.' The VAT is included in that – everything is included in that. (R.B., Kaolack, 2 January 2001)

> In the case of a contract for supplies, the commission can consist of a discount on the total amount of the order: it will not be accounted for but will be directly encashed by the administrative person responsible for the order. (H.M., former manager of Nigetip, Niamey, 13 April 2002)

But the 'form of what is given varies greatly. It goes from money in cash to construction materials by way of villas and cars. The three-piece boubou suits, sumptuous drawing rooms, computers and modern electronic gadgets form part of the desired products' (Bako Arifari 2001: 92). Beyond the commissions (in cash or in kind) a system of reciprocal obligation is also created: the contractors who work with communes say they can't refuse small favours to the mayor – such as extra work outside of the contract, or diverting some of the construction materials. For example, a contractor in public works at Kaolack told us of having recently 'offered' to the mayor of Gandiaye road kerbs worth 800,000 CFA francs.[30] In such cases, the payment of bribes is not necessary, for within the long-term relationship the subcontractor can benefit without breaking the rules. They 'help' the decision-makers with small discounts on the work done, and then they share the difference.[31] However, once a contractor plays the system, he risks being taken advantage of, 'for the administration sucks you till the end'. 'The key word is to give', confirms another contractor from Kaolack. 'When I was carrying out the works of the public place at Nioro, the mayor came to see me to inform me that he expected a big guest the next day. It was Abdou Diouf. I immediately understood and I slipped him 400,000 FCFA in cash.'

As the mechanisms of complicity and interest develop in relations between the private sector and administrators of regional services, the notion of bribes ceases to be relevant, in that distinction between public and private becomes obscured. Take the example of urban planning services in Senegal. Following the 1996 regionalization reform, they are no longer the executing services, but act in response to the demands of the local collectivities, who henceforth have the skills concerning the allocation of space, housing and construction. But the urban planning engineers also form part of the administration's regional committee of contracts (CRCA) and draw up the technical specifications of building projects and execute site visits.

Strengthened by this central position and increased scope, the urban planning engineers not only prepare tenders for the contractors but also create their own firms, which bid for the work, while continuing to draw up and award contracts. An accomplice contractor will put in technical files to order, in return for a part of the contract, which will be carried out by the technician's firm. Supervisors are therefore supervised at the same time.[32]

Unlike the situation in Niger and Senegal, it seems that in Benin illicit agreements between decision-makers and contractors can, in some conditions, be sanctioned by written contracts:

> This kind of contract comes up when the contractor is new in the world of public procurement, or if he enters into contact for the first time with a corrupt partner who doesn't trust him yet. This type of contract in writing is made in the form of a discharge, without specifying the object or the nature of the transaction. It is often discharges of loans in which the contractor recognizes having borrowed such a sum from the officer and consequently, commits himself to reimbursing him following a list of payable bills, which curiously roughly sets down the anticipated dates for the various payments during the duration of the contract's execution. (Bako Arifari 2001: 92)

From realization to final reception: the combatant's circuit

The 'supplementary costs' or 'supplementary charges' – euphemisms employed by contractors to designate bribes, which they account for minutely, even keeping lists of the beneficiaries and the sums distributed – are not confined to the initial phase of tendering. They also inform both the fulfilment of the contract and payment of fees: 'corruption in the beginning to win the contract installs the contractor in a machine of corruption, to "complete" or get the work accepted with all its insufficiencies' (Bako Arifari 2001: 90). The contractors meet with actors outside of the contract committees eager to receive their share in the various circuits of public order. The verification procedure differs according to the nature of the contract and the status of the partner organization, but three phases are universal: inspection during the execution of the contract; reception, during which the client makes sure that the works have been carried out correctly; and payment.

The controls

So far as controls are concerned, they range from accommodating absence in case of a preliminary corrupt agreement, and the meticulous verifications effected in order to invite the contractor's generosity. If tendering for the contract takes place at a central level, inspection fees amount to between 3.5 and 5 per cent of the total contract; at the local level the decentralized local services take over this role.[33] The contractor's responsibility is to cover 'the costs of travel, lodging and feeding the members of the inspection committees, not counting the "gifts"' (Bako Arifari 2001: 89–90).

At the local level, human and material resources are frequently insufficient to carry out this role with any success. Not only is it common practice to place, at this strategic level, political clients of the decision-makers, who do not possess the requisite competence. One also has to take into account the resources of the regional service of town planning of Kaolack, which only has 580 litres of petrol – or fifteen days' supply – per semester. In these conditions, officers are hardly able to survey works within the city, much less sites at the regional level. The chronic scarcity experienced by the inspection teams favours forms of corruption that ultimately have the effect of economic levelling from above. Thus, for a big building contractor in Dakar, corruption allows private and public partners to maintain egalitarian relations:

> It is as dangerous to have a relationship with corrupt officers as with straight officers. Or, an officer who encashes money is not necessarily corrupt. Ha, no ... Often, when I began a site and I had one or two inspectors who were there on the spot permanently, I used to call this fellow and tell him: 'Listen, my engineer who is at your level, in my place he has 700,000 F, you have 100,000 F per month. From now on and for the next three years, you do only my site or you do two sites. If you do my site, I'll pay you every month the difference between your salary and his. You are at the same level. When I go to the site and I go to the hotel, you come with me in my car or in my plane. You go to the hotel, I pay it and we are in the same conditions. Whether we fight or whether we don't. I give you this every month, but you do your work and I'll do my work. Don't make me false accounts, don't make a false paper, and when you have to come and approve my account, you come, and not in one month.' (P.L., Dakar, 16 January 2001)

Competent authorities obviously need to authorize the regimes of inspection. In the case of public works in Senegal, the statement forms which periodically review the works and expenditures incurred by the contractor have to be countersigned, by order of the inspection office, sent to ministry of public works, and thence to the partner ministry. These signatures are nearly always bought. In the case of market contracts of PIP in Benin, several contractors have recognized that the signature of the departmental director of environment and housing is worth around 300,000 FCFA.

Reception and the circuit of payment

The phase of reception marks the last stage in the process of completion. It is at the end of this stage – with the production of a certificate of services realized, or its attestation – that the contractor is paid. The certificate must state that the work has been well executed by the contractor, and that it is in conformity with all the requirements of the consultation file, and therefore of the contract. It is therefore interesting that this committee – generally a representative of the awarding body and a representative of the financial controller – 'lowers the bar' in the evaluation of the work done. It seems equally normal to pay its members the 'price of fuel' or *cola* for travel'.

The circuit of payment also demands a considerable investment in time and money, in order to accelerate payment or simply to avoid it being blocked: 'if you do your calculations and you wait, you can be sure you'll wait a year', deplores a Senegalese contractor in public works, forced to follow up his payment in its journey between the finance ministry's department of debt and investments, the Treasury and the computer processing department, to arrive finally in the office of the payments officer of the Treasury, who is responsible for issue. The local contracts also present complex procedures of payment, as the case of Benin shows: 'having "interested"' at district (*prefecture*) level 'from the [platoon] up to the head of the financial service' in order to obtain the draft for payment, the firm has to make sure it is well connectd in the Treasury department:

> In the Treasury, the contractor is subjected to three levels of control: the tax controller who ensures that the contractor is within the rules (which is rarely the case, therefore the money paid...) the receiver of

the Treasury who settles the file and finally the cashier who pays. At each step, the instrument of pressure in the hands of the public agents is the game, with and in the contractor's time. This pressure is even stronger at the Treasury, which the contractors often fear towards the end of the year, 'the principle of the exercise in camera' which drives them towards administrative difficulties and to the next year before getting their money. (Bako Arifari 2001: 90).

Thus, even the payment transforms itself into a veritable crusade for the contractor: the accountant can accelerate or slow down the procedure; the administrative head can sell the signature of the 'bill to pay'; the public Treasury can give proof of diligence, for in the case of insufficient funds the collector can establish a list of priority payments with the foreman, and there too favour the 'ones who give the most' – or who have contacts in the paying organizations. According to a testimony of a Nigerien supplier,

> if you don't know anyone in the Treasury, they'll tell you they don't have the money. They make you come and go, finally you are forced to find someone with whom you'll have an understanding there. You propose a sum to him and it's at that moment that he'll do everything to get your money out.... It's a place of high intrigues, otherwise, for a small bill of 2 to 3 million, if you're not careful you can easily spend two months waiting.

If, for large firms, 'the times one loses is much more important than the amounts one gives' (I.N., Dakar, 11 January 2001), for small-scale contractors these repeated and drawn-out payments can total half the value of the contract, as a Beninois interlocutor underlined: 'In certain PIP contracts the cost of corruption can [thus] reach up to 30 to 40 per cent of the total cost of the contract' (Bako Arifari 2001: 90). Hence the lack of interest of small contractors in contracts that come from the national budget, in favour of public procurement with external financing.[34]

'The contract is like a pregnant woman': strategies and representations of actors of public procurement

Because they are systemic, the corrupting practices in public procurement produce among the actors involved strategies of adaptation and ambivalence, torn between indignation, resigned acceptance and amused justification. It should be noted in advance that all our Beninois, Nigerian and Senegalese interlocutors judged that corruption is a generalized, necessary component, even commonplace in the universe of public procurement: 'Our profession does not leave us the space to refuse corruption, still less deal with it. For if you always refuse, others will take, whatever the price. Better to take yourself as well', affirmed a contractor from Parakou. Even if an individual is at the beginning of his career, determined not to give in to illicit practices, he realizes

> that there are things in which one is obliged; one doesn't have a choice. So one does the minimum, but one is always forced to go through with it.... From the moment you have a firm and the personnel and the overheads which cost a lot each day, so you have to make profits, you no longer have the choice', explained a French contractor based in Senegal. (R.B., Kaolack, 2 January 2001)

And he becomes persuaded of the inevitability of corrupt practices: 'many people can't bring themselves to believe that one can obtain a contract only on the basis of one's own value', exclaims a former manager of Nigetip in Niger, who found himself being offered envelopes by contractors, convinced that they owed the contract to him whereas he had simply pointed them towards the procedures to be followed (H.M., Niamey, 13 April 2002).

In order to survive this discrete universe of hidden transactions, the contractors develop and cultivate particular skills and learn to 'speak well', otherwise their papers 'will be put in the drawer' (A. A., Niamey, 9 April 2002). Many remember that it is important to show generosity to guarantee one's own success, on the example of this businessman in import–export from Niamey: 'He who keeps his hand closed can't do business [*mutin mai rike hannu shi mai tauri bai iya kasuwanci*]. If you have money, but you don't help anyone in the family, some even seek to kill you. It's the same thing in the administrations: if you don't give, you'll be stuck till death.' Here one finds the same strategies of 'corrupting investment' noted elsewhere (see Chapter 3).

According to this former Nigerien sub-prefect, 'as soon as you arrive in a neighbourhood, even before you're settled in, people arrive. One brings you chickens, sheep; people anticipate. So, sometimes, you are forced to decide who can supply you. Of necessity, there is a certain complicity' (R.O., former sub-prefect, Niamey, 11 April 2002).

It is a question of 'preparing one's path for tomorrow': 'when some economic operators learn that X has been appointed minister, they begin first by furnishing his drawing room, and already they are preparing the ground' (A.S., supplier, Niamey, 10 April 2002). These apparently disinterested generosities are aimed at indebting the decision-maker, who because of this will enter into the well-oiled machinery of obligation and reciprocity:

> I could not give at all, but as we say here, one needs two hands to wash one with the other [*kambe hinka non ga cer nyum*], so, if I want another contract, it is necessary to give something to these guys.... Everyone now knows that the world of contracts, it works like this: one has to give so that one can give to you [*bur ga no no, ima borno*]. These guys, one has known them for a very long time, but that's not enough, money is necessary to maintain relations [*nooro nonga bortara gaay*]. (A.K.B., ex-agent of SNCCT, Niamey, 31 January 2002)

For the rest, the maintenance of relations within the administration by means of liberality overrides the strict framework of public procurement. It is the protection of the firm that is at stake, as a building contractor based in Kaolack underlines:

> We have vehicles moving on the road. If one of the trucks has an accident and a person is killed, if one refuses something to the president of the court and there is a verdict subsequently, he'll be extremely severe. The truck will be seized, the driver imprisoned. There will be no possibility of calming things down, very simply. So one must always have these people on one's side. (R.B., Kaolack, 2 January 2001)

In many interviews, contractors in the beginning tend to denounce the shady behaviour of agents of the administration: 'It's the officer who pushes the businessman to corruption.... The comings and goings that officers impose on businessmen are to force them to give something' (A.S., supplier, Niamey, 10 April 2002). But, as the discussion deepens, the accusations are followed by a period of understanding, even justification. Thus the argument of corruption as a strategy of survival is evoked by the officers:

You ask someone to manage a project of 3 billion, while this person with his 150,000 francs CFA per month, he can't even manage his monthly expenditure. The woman at the hospital, the child whose school necessities he must provide, otherwise he won't get in ... he can't work. And the contractors are there to blackmail him. (K.S., expert, Dakar, 29 December 2000)

The contractors, for their part, argue:

If someone brings me a contract and tells me 'give your price and put in 2 million for me', I won't hesitate: I have the tax office behind me; the CNSS is there, I have a salaries bill of 4,000,000 CFA francs to pay.... And then I need to put food in my mouth. (A.A., company director, Niamey, 9 April 2002)

It must not be forgotten that public procurement is a closed world where a web of deep complicity is woven between the public and private sectors, in such a way that, as we have seen, corruption is dressed up in a transactional form perceived as mutually beneficial. Thus the awarding of a commission is assimilated into a gift given 'to people who have really given their skills to prepare your file' (I.T., company director, Niamey). Taking the side of the authorities who have appealed to a private partner, the bribe is more an expression of gratitude: 'Because this project which was a plan, perhaps it wouldn't have been done if these people hadn't put in their bit to find finances, the planning and all that is required to realize it. You know, here there is such a prejudice that everyone defends his own truth' (Y.F., Dakar, 16 January 2001).

Even if 'it is more certain than the papers', the generalization and ordinariness of corruption at all levels and all stages of public contracting leads contractors and suppliers to the conviction that the system is completely uncontrollable and unpredictable: 'the contract is like a pregnant woman [*kasuwa, mace mai ciki ce*]', an importer from Niamey told us. 'Today you have one, tomorrow you have nothing. That's how things are, you get along.' Confronted with a system that resembles 'a lottery where there are only two possibilities: winning or losing', in the words of a contractor from Parakou, knowing how to distribute, target, cultivate relations, fight in the right political camp, respect the given work, constitute skills as indispensable as technical or professional skills.

Conclusion

We can in conclusion recall the principal elements of this system, which Benin, Niger and Senegal share with an astonishing similitude. In the first place, it functions across alliances and networks, which tend to structure themselves and become permanent. Hence the collective nature of deviant behaviours: the corrupting facts require a triangle composed of corrupting contractors, corrupted officers and intermediaries, giving rise to real chains of complicities. This system produces forms of commonplace corruption, as proved by the absence of sentiment among contractors when committing an offence.

Second, public contracting is a field wherein one sees the coexistence of corrupt local state and the falsifying state. Verifications carried out in the field by the state general inspector or by the inspector of territorial and local administration have sometimes permitted flagrantly unfinished work, although all the receipts and the documents dealing with contracts are available. To do this, many signatures are necessary at very different levels.

Third, these practices are closely linked to the financing of politics – and here a comparison between Africa and Europe would be relevant. Far from being confined to the sphere of public works, corruption working in public procurement feeds other corruptive networks. For example, fictive or improvised firms manage without difficulty to procure the administrative documents which have to be attached to a tender: enrolment in the trade register, bank deposit, attestation from IPRES, social security branch, works inspection, fiscal receipt, attestations from the administration of previous works, and so on. The firms can produce administrative documents that are false or obtained quickly and questionably, and committees have no power of verifying the authenticity of the documents or the truth of their content.

The results of the widespread nature of these practices are diverse. On the one hand, the awarding of contracts according to the logic of corruption contributes to an increase in public expenditure, because of the common practice of over-billing, and gives rise to a decline in standards. The selection of substandard firms condemns to inactivity the numerous operators who are highly professional. Those who win the contracts often lack the requisite skills and are forced, in order to maintain their profit margins, to use poor-quality materials. And 'when a contractor can't play on the quality and quantity, because he gave himself up to 40 per cent or sometimes even 50 per cent of the global amount of the contract as costs of the contract with charges of corruption, he abandons the site' (Bako Arifari 2001: 88). The results of this state of affairs are well known: roads narrower than the norm, tarmac that will disintegrate within months, small or incomplete wells, sometimes even nonexistent works which are vouched for and paid for – such as the construction and equipping of a theatre and municipal library at Koungheul in Senegal, which was declared in the administrative accounts of the commune without ever having seen the light of day.

Moreover, the monopoly situation in which certain firms enjoy political support – having contacts among decision-makers or the means to interest them – produces bankruptcy among those rivals who have no such support, and favours the proliferation of subcontracts. For example, large private operators (both local and international) control 85 per cent of the contracts within BTP network in Senegal, which represents an annual public investment of 70 billion CFA francs (out of a total budget of 170 billion). The 1,300 local small and medium enterprises are left to share the rest of the meal.[35] The same system, based on a monopoly of contracts by large contractors close to elected assemblies and mayors, is reproduced at the local level. In Kaolack – where at the end of the year 2000 nearly seventy firms could be counted, four big firms shared the most interesting contracts and then subcontracted to smaller firms. Thus, the lack of resources and the imperative of sprinkling works with the objective of political clientelism led mayors to approve accords with rich economic operators who advance the necessary sums for the realization of infrastructures or agree to provide local collectivities on credit. The procedure of disguised mutual agreement and the division of contracts then becomes the rule. In this context, he who doesn't have 'a long arm' must, in order not to be left out, try to diversify the range of his activities, to the detriment of professionalism: 'Today you see me in the offices; tomorrow I'm in building; the day after

I'm in transport. I can come back to building because in between there was a lull somewhere. Well, I come back new. Because, as the English say, no condition is permanent' (D.S., Parakou).

This system reproduces itself in a context of generalized helplessness. The scandals exposed and/or sanctioned are rare and represent only punctual flushes of an underground river. If, as the Beninois minister of state responsible for planning and development proudly notes on his website, 'the attribution of public procurement contracts strictly obeys the principles elaborated by the World Bank',[36] a remark that can be heard in the two other countries examined, neither purely institutional reforms nor initiatives of struggle against corruption with whiffs of the witch-hunt could prevail over a system equipped with its logics, its processes of justification and ordinariness, its profound overlapping with politics.

Notes

Chapter 1

1. The European Commission and the Swiss Agency for Development and Cooperation (SDC) awarded funding for the study on the basis of a research proposal compiled and presented by the project team.
2. N. Bako Arifari, T. Bierschenk, G. Blundo, M. Mathieu, J.-P. Olivier de Sardan, M. Tidjani Alou.
3. A. Imorou, C. Nansounon, L. Adjahouhoué, A. Morat Lafia, R. Sariki and A. Badou for Benin; A. Moumouni (coordinator), H. Moussa, Y. Issa and A. Tidjani Alou for Niger; P. Monteil, C.T. Dieye, A. Ndao, Y. Bodian for Senegal. The documentary collection and analysis were carried out by C. Akpovo, A. Tomon, E. Adjovi and M. Boucari (Benin); A. Alborkirey and M. Boukar Maï Ali (Niger); Y. Bodian, C. Ba and M. Ndoye (Senegal). The institutes that provided the framework for the research were: SHADYC (EHESS–CNRS, Marseille, France); LASDEL (Niamey, Niger); and the Institute of Ethnology at the Johannes Gutenberg University (Mainz, Germany).
4. Blundo and Olivier de Sardan 2001b.
5. Blundo and Olivier de Sardan 2001b.
6. In French: *La corruption quotidienne en Afrique. Une approche socio-anthropologique (Bénin, Niger, Sénégal)*, Paris: Karthala.
7. See Bako Arifari 1995, 1999, 2000; Bierschenk 1988; Bierschenk, Chauveau and Olivier de Sardan 2000; Bierschenk and Olivier de Sardan 1997, 1998, 2003; Blundo 1994, 1995, 1996, 1998; Jaffré and Olivier de Sardan 2003; Mathieu 2002; Olivier de Sardan and Elhadji Dagobi 2000; Tidjani Alou 2000, 2001, 2002.
8. See Olivier de Sardan 2005.

9. See the title of the APAD conference held at Leyden in May 2002: 'Daily Governance. The Relationships between Public and Collective Services and Their Users', forthcoming. A selection of the papers presented at the conference have been published in Blundo 2004.
10. See Olivier de Sardan 1999.
11. See also Nye's (1967) frequently cited definition. Definitions and typologies of corruption are legion; on this topic, see Blundo 2000.
12. As opposed to this, the main aim of legal approaches to corruption is to identify as clear as possible a boundary between practices. For a stimulating comparison between the legal and sociological approaches in this regard, see Boltanski 1982.
13. Donors who sometimes insist on not 'seeing' corruption, despite all the evidence (see Bähre's 2005 study on South Africa).
14. See Jaffré 1999.
15. It should be noted that the African press is not primarily investigative in nature and rarely respects the principles of information-gathering and provision of proof. Indeed, a number of journalists are themselves reputed to be corrupt (see Adjovi 2003 on the case of the Beninese press).
16. Lambsdorff 1999.
17. Moreover, the president of TI himself, Peter Eigen, confirms that 'the index serves as a powerful tool for the people to hammer home the reality of endemic corruption, removing the possibility for governments to deny the problem' (TI, 'Corruption Perceptions Index Press Conference', 18 October 2005).
18. While the questionnaire-based approach is not a recent invention (see the study directed by Price [1975] on the perceptions of corruption among Ghanaian officials), it was first widely used in the 1990s, a development that coincided with the constitution of the phenomenon of corruption as a societal problem (see Razafindrakoto and Roubaud 1996 on Madagascar; Kpundeh 1994 on Sierra Leone; and Langseth and Michael 1998 on Tanzania). Various local branches of TI (for example, in Morocco, Senegal and Burkina Faso) regularly publish national surveys to legitimize their work in raising awareness of corruption among the general public.
19. A presentation of the methods we used in our study of corruption was published in Blundo and Olivier de Sardan 2000. For a more detailed presentation of the 'field policy' and its methods, see Olivier de Sardan 1995.
20. We know that many so-called collective research programmes content themselves with simply adding individual studies end to end.
21. The ECRIS procedure; for a presentation of this procedure, see Bierschenk and Olivier de Sardan 1997.
22. The corpus compiled contains 2,740 articles for Benin (for the years 1972–99), 448 articles for Niger (for the years 1960–99) and 1,575 articles for Senegal (for the years 1977–2000). This database has not been used extensively in the compilation of this book. It is intended to use it as the basis of another publication.
23. See Olivier de Sardan 2005.

Chapter 2

1. The map in question may be viewed on the Transparency International website, www.transparency.org/cpi/2005/images/world_map.pdf.

2. The same observation regarding the lack of anthropological reflection on corrupt practices is made by Kondos (1987: 15) and Sampson (1983: 63, 65).

3. On this question, see Olivier de Sardan 1990.

4. Curiously, and contrary to all expectation, this trend outlived the functionalist approach as it re-emerged in more recent works which focus on venality, materialism and the feeble morality of public servants (Sarassoro 1979; Brownsberger 1983; Nembot 2000).

5. The minor revolution in Africanist political science represented by the francophone trend of 'politics from below' (Bayart 1981), which prompted the search for politics beyond its institutional locations of expression, did not produce detailed empirical research and has, therefore, remained on an essentially programmatic level (Bierschenk and Olivier de Sardan 1998). Meanwhile, anthropology mainly studied and produced documentation on the precolonial political formations and their contemporary vestiges (for example, the chiefdoms).

6. Chabal and Daloz correctly note that both theories insist on the hybridization between a legal–rational bureaucratic model and native political registers (Chabal and Daloz 1999: 20).

7. For example, Tangie asserts peremptorily – and incorrectly – that 'since there is no African language word for it, it [corruption] did not exist in pre-colonial Africa' (Tangie 2005: 4).

8. In the words of Balandier (1951), as inspired by Gluckman.

9. In French West Africa of the 1930s, there were around 1,000 French colonial officials for an estimated population of 15 million Africans (Arnett 1933: 242).

10. In a comparative analysis of the administrations in francophone and anglophone Africa, Arnett refers to circulars published in 1932 by Brévié, the governor of French West Africa, in which he stated that due to repeated abuses in the area of taxation, neither the canton chiefs nor provincial chiefs should collect colonial taxes (Arnett 1933: 246–7).

11. See also the study by Njoku (2005) on the 'warrant chiefs' imposed by the English on the Igbo in south-west Nigeria.

12. A contemporary report suggests that the upheaval was caused by a rumour to the effect that a new tax on women was to be introduced in the region. The taxation of men, instituted in 1928, was marred by cases of extortion and corruption on the part of the members of the Native Courts, who were already infamous for their corruption (Anonymous 1930: 542–3).

13. The first, led by Bernard Storey, Mayor of Norwich, in 1953, prompted 'the first extended public discussion of widespread corrupt administrative practices in Nigeria' (Tignor 1993: 185) and became one of the most frequently quoted in studies of corruption in developing countries. In 1955–56, it was the turn of eastern Nigeria with the inquiry on the municipal council of the city of Port Harcourt. The report 'found considerable evidence of bribery in the letting of contracts, favouritism in the allocation of market stalls,

and illegal payments from junior members of staff to their seniors for large increases in their emoluments' (Tignor 1993: 189). The inquiry came to the same conclusions in the district of Onitsha. Inquiries were also expedited in western Nigeria, in particular in the district council of Ibadan in 1956, by Nicholson, the mayor of Abingdon.

14. According to Richard A. Joseph, a prebendary regime is characterized by: (1) the widespread appropriation of so-called 'public' resources for private ends; (2) the distribution of resources within ethnic patronage networks; (3) diffuse clientelist relations and a decentralized type of redistribution (quoted by Lewis 1996: 100).

15. On the 'Zongo affair', in particular, see Hagberg 2002.

16. On electoral clientelism in Benin, see Banégas 1998.

17. However, it must be acknowledged that despite the proclamation of the principle of aid conditionality (the requirement that African states implement 'good governance' measures), countries that have been the victims of a suspension of aid represent the exception rather than the rule, e.g. Kenya (Cooksey 1999: 3) in 1997, Equatorial Guinea (Malaquais 2001: 13) and Tanzania in 1994 (Fjeldstad 2003).

18. For a general overview of the practices of corruption that can develop within international cooperation programmes in Africa, see Berkman 1996; see also Chapter 9 for a case in Senegal.

19. See Maipose 2000 for the cases of Kenya and Tanzania; for an analysis of West Africa, see Olivier de Sardan 2004.

20. According to Cooksey, the World Bank is slave to two logics, 'approval culture' and 'disbursement culture', which compel it to concentrate its efforts on the identification and implementation of new projects instead of focusing on the evaluation of the results of operations already under way (Cooksey 1999: 5; Cooksey 2002: 49).

21. For general consideration of this topic, see Andreski 1968, 1970; and Mbaku 2000a. For a detailed case study, see Ouma's 1991 study on Uganda.

22. See Vaughan 1987, quoted in Anders 2005: 143.

Chapter 3

1. It goes without saying that we have not allowed ourselves to extrapolate judgements above and beyond our own study, which is limited to these three countries. However, our reading of the literature available on other African countries (see Chapter 2) and other studies we have carried out, in some cases for other programmes (Mali, Ivory Coast, Guinea, Burkina Faso, Central African Republic), would prompt us to believe that the situation revealed here largely extends beyond the three countries investigated. However, this observation should not obscure the differences that exist on the African continent. For example, certain geopolitical situations uniquely highlight the scope of certain phenomena (e.g. economies funded by diamond or petrol exports, not to mention the economies of war and pillage). Conversely, it should also be noted that some African countries have frequently been described as being relatively free of corruption, especially Botswana and to a lesser extent Burkina Faso, prior to the death of Sankara.

2. Of course certain features exist that are also specific to each: e.g. the political participation experienced by the citizens of the four municipalities (Quatre Communes de plein exercice) of Saint-Louis, Rufisque, Gorée and Dakar from the last decades of the nineteenth century; Dahomey was nicknamed the 'Quartier Latin of Africa'; Niger was described as the place where the English allowed the 'Gallic cock to scratch its spurs in the sand'. However, the three countries were subject to the same type of colonial administration and embarked on independence under similar conditions.

3. For an analysis of this very specific process of construction of the colonial and post-colonial bureaucracy, see Olivier de Sardan 2004. For specific analyses of corruption 'in the colonies', see Arditi 2000 (Chad); Smith 1964 (Nigeria); McMullan, 1961 (British colonies); Becker 2006 (Tanzania).

4. Although unrestricted multipartyism was officially re-established in Senegal from 1981 and the country enjoyed official freedom of the press, the hegemony of the Socialist Party (PS) up to 2000 meant that a quasi single-party system prevailed for an extended period. Conversely, the *coups d'état* in Niger of 1996 and 1999 did not cause any damage to either pluripartism or freedom of the press. Since the late 1980s (National Conference in Benin in 1990 and National Conference in Niger in 1991), the political situations in the three countries are more similar than they might seem, and today they can even be described as identical: beyond their very different post-colonial histories and the individual political vicissitudes that peppered the recent decades, the three countries have democratic regimes that emerged from true changeovers of power and three democratically elected presidents.

5. This is merely a simplified model which attempts to establish a minimum of order amid the complexity of the corrupt phenomena described in our study, and does not in any way claim to be representative of reality.

6. It is for this reason that the 'basic forms' of corruption presented here do not correspond to the standard legal categories or typologies of corruption.

7. Witness the requests *man ay baa?* (Zarma) and *ana suma wàll?* (Wolof): 'Where is my share?'

8. See in Jaffré and Olivier de Sardan 2003.

9. According to Paul Veyne (1976), this term refers to a contribution to a city's public expenses in the form of donations and other gifts.

10. See Olivier de Sardan and Alhadji Dagobi 2000.

11. The 'joking relationship' (*relation à plaisanterie*), which extends the teasing exchanges of cross cousins to entire social groups, represents a common way of 'personalizing' anonymous relationships.

12. For a definition of the practical rules associated with corruption and professional cultures in the case of custom officers and midwives, see Olivier de Sardan 2001.

13. A. Gupta was one of the first authors to stress the importance of the performative dimension of corrupt relationships. On the basis of a failed attempt at corruption – observed as part of a case study carried out in India – he suggests that when villagers complained about the corruption of the state officials, they were not only bemoaning their exclusion from state services due to their cost, they were above all expressing their frustration at their lack of cultural capital, which is indispensable to the skilled negotiation of these services (Gupta 1995: 381).

14. For examples of administrative brokerage in Senegal, see Blundo 2001a.
15. See Jaffré 1999: 5–6 for the case of the health services in Mali; and Olivier de Sardan 2004, for a more general analysis.
16. See Jaffré and Olivier de Sardan 2003 on the case of health.
17. In the words of Michael Hertzfeld 1992, all bureaucratic systems are based on the 'social production of indifference'. This indifference arises from the imperative of procedural rationality: each user is, in principle, a typical case for the official and should be treated in an impersonal way and according to the same procedures and regulations.
18. Needless to say, the military dictatorships and single-party systems also had their own less obvious and more factional forms of clientelism.
19. This is the case, for example, for the posts of Grade A officials and for management functions within the territorial command.
20. In the sense expressed by Bourdieu 1979.
21. An initial attempt at inventorying such 'logics' can be found in Olivier de Sardan 1999.
22. We were surprised to find ourselves accused of being 'culturalists' by Dahou (2002), who, in an article based largely on insinuation and caricature (that blithely ignores the vast 'culturalist controversy' that permeates the socio-anthropological literature on corruption), appears to have forgotten the lessons of 'de-culturalization' which he preaches to others, as, according to him, the 'normalization of corruption' in Senegal could be explained by the models of honour in the Waalo.
23. This theory developed by Berry (1993) has been frequently revisited, in particular in Lund 1998; Chauveau, Le Pape and Olivier de Sardan 2001. For the case of Mediterranean societies, see Lucchini 1995.
24. For an analysis of the relationship between official rules and practical rules in the health sector, see Olivier de Sardan 2001.
25. On the extensive and central use of the notion of 'shame' in Africa, see Ouattara 1999: 33.
26. For example, 5,000 CFA francs for someone with a monthly salary of 50,000 CFA francs.
27. In Olivier de Sardan and Ehadji Dagobi 2000.
28. Extract from Ouattara 2002 (interviews carried out by the author).
29. Certain forms of privatization actually end up affecting the sovereign functions of the state (the levying of taxes and monopoly on legitimate violence), as attested by the proliferation of private security and mercenary companies and the privatization of the tax system (see Hibou 1999).
30. See Blundo 1998.
31. The presence of intermediaries is not a new phenomenon; it goes back to the establishment of the colonial bureaucratic structures. However, both their number and the scope of their tasks have increased considerably since the implementation of structural adjustment programmes.
32. See on this topic Bayart, Ellis and Hibou 1999. Our observations refer to more localized and less violent criminal practices.
33. Based on the expression 'white-collar crime', this could be referred to as 'civil service crime'.
34. We are thinking mainly of Françafrique, described and analysed inter alia by Médard 1997; Verschave 1998.
35. To be brief and blunt, in our view the characterizations of the African

state based on the theories of extraneity (see Badie 1992, who refers to the 'imported' state) and on culturalism (see Chabal and Daloz 1999) are not productive. This is not the case, however, with, inter alia, the work of Médard (1982) and Bayart (1989), which is largely compatible with the data we produced, even if it concerns a different register.

36. Certainly, Hibou is thinking more of 'large-scale corruption' and its re-investment in business, which can give the impression of a functionality 'despite everything' at least in certain countries: things function differently but they work and the state continues to 'run'. Her own studies largely concern the countries of the Maghreb, where the large-scale corruption practised at the top levels of the state does not prevent the reproduction of despotic and hence, in this sense at least, 'strong' states. The situation in West Africa is very different. However, Hibou considers (incorrectly in our opinion) that her theory is applicable beyond the countries of the Maghreb and is valid for all southern countries.

Chapter 4

1. To recap, our team compiled a corpus of 920 interviews, some of which were held in French and others in different local languages (Fon and Dendi in Benin, Hausa and Zarma in Niger, and Wolof in Senegal); a large number of our interviews were recorded and transcribed. The role of rumour in the context of corruption should not be neglected. On the methodological motivation for the consideration of gossip and 'chit-chat' as data relevant to the study, see Blundo and Olivier de Sardan 2000: 32–3.

2. The term 'shared representations' is understood to mean a realm of ideas, conceptions, descriptions, perceptions and evaluations, which is sometimes described using the term 'emic', which encompasses not only the discourses actually uttered in the context of a study but also those that can be potentially uttered (see Olivier de Sardan 1998: 151–66).

3. Of course, semiologies exist that are specific to certain bodies or sectors, the use of which makes it possible to distinguish between the insider and the neophyte.

4. Our team carried out a systematic analysis of the press in the three countries studied; see our research report (Blundo and Olivier de Sardan 2001a).

5. Our use of the term 'symbolic' would be wary of the 'strong' meanings associated with it (i.e. religious, metaphysical, systemic, structuralist or psychoanalytical meanings), preferring instead the 'soft' or 'weak' meanings – that is, infra-ideological as opposed to meta-ideological meanings.

6. Of course, official rules and ideals may be inspired by different ideological registers. For example, in his analysis of 'The Dynamic between Critical and Legitimizing Discourses about Corruption in Indonesia' (forthcoming), Heinzpeter Znoj listed four main ideological registers: neoliberal, official statist, civic religious and that of Islamist mobilization. For recent anthropological analyses of the discourse on corruption, see also Hansen 1998; Gupta 1995.

7. For information on the relationship between practical and official rules and norms, and an example of corruption in the health and customs sectors, see Olivier de Sardan 2001.

8. See the formulation proposed by Peter Ekeh (1975), which expresses the moral obligation in Africa to work first for the 'primordial public' (to which the spheres of family, ethnic and promotional relationships correspond) at the cost of 'civic public' (the state, the administration).

9. During his long political career, Ablaye Diack was director of the Senegalese national transport company Régie des transports du Sénégal (RTS), minister for information, deputy mayor of Kaolack, first parliamentary administrator in the National Assembly, president of the Regional Council of Kaolack and, most recently, president of the Senate until its recent dissolution.

10. Extract from Babacar Dione, 'Abdoulaye Diack fait son entrée. "J'ai détourné de l'argent et je l'ai partagé avec les kaolackois"', *Sud Quotidien* 2411, 18 April 2001.

11. See also Blundo 2001b; Jean-Louis Rocca (1993: 73) had already proposed a distinction between 'redistributive' corruption and 'monopolizing' corruption.

12. See Olivier de Sardan 1996a.

13. See *Le Cafard Libéré* 250, Wednesday 18 November 1992: 5.

14. On the 'techniques of neutralization' studied in a European context, see Pizzorno 1992: 51.

15. All of the terms printed in italics are taken directly from our studies; in most cases the local African French version is followed in brackets by the English translation and the corresponding versions found in the local languages. Most of the examples from the local languages are in Wolof and Zarma, the two local languages we speak. The terms and expressions in Fon, Dendi and Hausa, which are often very similar, were collected by Nassirou Bako Arifari and Mahaman Tidjani Alou.

16. See, of course, Bayart 1993.

17. All of the examples concerning Benin quoted in this chapter are taken from studies coordinated by N. Bako Arifari in the north of the country and are translated from the Dendi language; like Zarma, which is spoken in Niger, Dendi is a dialect of Songhay.

18. In Wolof, the idea of mutual help is also expressed by the verbs *jappalante* and *neexalante*.

19. In the three countries studied and, indeed, in all of sub-Saharan Africa, magic and witchcraft play a major role in everyday life, in both the domestic sphere and social life as well as in the context of polical relations: this is evidenced by the vast body of anthropological literature on the subject.

20. See the 'grounded theory' of Glaser and Strauss 1973. Of course, it is possible to produce interpretations 'far removed from the data' on everything, including corruption; in other words, interpretations based on a speculative or 'essayist' register or even 'over-interpreting' (on the traps of over-interpretation, see Olivier de Sardan 1996b). We are only interested here in empirically based interpretations – that is, interpretations rooted in structured study data.

21. The economic and political science studies carried out on corruption, which are the most numerous, involve other interpretative areas linked to their disciplines, as, for example, studies concerning the agency model (see Cartier-Bresson 1998).

22. These last two metaphors are commonplace in the French spoken in Benin.

23. On the 'witchcraft of wealth', see Geschiere 2000.
24. Even if the author does not think that 'the politics of the belly' is the only form of expression of political imagination in Africa (see Bayart 1989: 325), nonetheless he attributes a real centrality to the notions of 'belly' and 'to eat' as a common factor in the areas of sorcery and politics. Thus it is this centrality that our data drive us to explore in more detail.
25. See Lakoff and Johnson 1980; Keesing 1985.
26. On this point, see Chibnall and Saunders 1977.

Chapter 5

1. See, for example, the speech delivered by Ms Marième Diop Guèye, a judge at the Superior Departmental Court of Dakar, on the occasion of the inauguration of the new session of the courts on 3 November 1999. It is interesting to note that in a speech on the subject of legal prevention and the judicial response to corruption, at no point was the issue of corruption in the legal system raised. The speech focused exclusively on corruption in other areas and on ways of dealing with it.
2. It is interesting to note that in Niger most ministers for justice who have come from the ranks of the judiciary have been recruited in the public prosecutor's office.
3. Copy of a court ruling or of a notarial deed containing the executory formula.
4. For example, the Nigerien penal code has just been reformed. The National Assembly approved a law to this effect on 5 May 2003 . See *Le Sahel*, 6 May 2003: 3. According to Bako Arifari, in Benin 'the Bouvenet code, promulgated in the colonies from 1877 on, is still in force in its version of 1958, whose provisions date from 1930 (with very severe sentences).'
5. Although variants exist according to their respective political histories, the court systems in the countries we have studied are based on relatively similar organizational structures. In Benin, there are eight different courts of first instance, a court of appeal and a final court of appeal (Blundo and Olivier de Sardan 2001a: 80). In Niger, the legal system is structured in terms of the supreme court, two courts of appeal, six district courts and twenty-five *délégations judiciaires* (Thalès, DGD 2002). In Senegal, the legal system comprises twenty-six departmental courts, ten district courts, eight courts of employment, four criminal courts, one court of appeal, one court of final appeal and one Council of State.
6. Eighty practising judges in Benin in 2000; 140 judges in Niger in 2000; 228 judges in Senegal in 1998.
7. In Benin, an examining magistrate constantly has to work on an average of 600 cases per year and the number of cases increases at a rate of 150 per year (Blundo and Olivier de Sardan 2001a: 80).

Chapter 6

The field studies that provided the basic material for this chapter were carried out in Benin, Niger and Senegal by the author and his research assistants, specifically Cheikh Dièye in Senegal, Cather O.Z. Nansounon and Moumouni Boucari in Benin, and A. Tidjani Alou and Younoussi I. in Niger.

1. For example, without taking customs revenue into account, the transport sector accounts for 8 per cent of Benin's GDP on average and also accounts for almost 25 per cent of public investment in the period 1995–96. It employs around 3 per cent of the active population (see World Bank 1996) and has a fleet of around 100,000 vehicles.

2. *Julo* refers to the category of peddlers who are generally referred to as *Dioula* in West Africa and who specialize in cross-border fraud. The term *njogaan* refers to women smugglers in Senegal, who are often in league with customs officers. However, like the *julo*, the activities merely involve small quantities of goods. The *fayawo* (in Yoruba) and *smogalize* (a term from the Nigerien language Zarma which is derived from the English verb 'to smuggle') refer to the same types of smugglers. However, these are more generic terms and do not specify the gender of the smuggler or take into account the quantity of goods involved.

3. This is the recommendation of a smuggler by a customs officer to his colleagues to ensure his exoneration from eventual levies. The message on a note of recommendation often starts with the expression *cher collègue*, 'Dear colleague'.

4. *Le Tract*, 8 January 2001.

5. A driver of a truck loaded with yams who travelled the 295 km between Gaya and Niamey in half a day passed eight checkpoints (in reality toll points) and confirms having spent a sum of 180,000 CFA francs in unreceipted corrupt payments. This is the equivalent of the monthly salary of a secondary-school teacher.

6. Reported in *Le Matin* of 21 June 2000.

7. This is the term used by shipping companies for the supplementary fees they charge for containers when they are left in their warehouses beyond the agreed date.

8. In Parakou in Benin, the agents who escort goods from Nigeria to Benin pay a lump sum of 600,000 CFA francs to the customs every week. The latter undertakes to process the dispatching of these goods for a combination of normal and corrupt charges.

9. The counting of parcels and rapid checking of goods by the customs service.

10. BIVAC (like its predecessor COTECNA) is a company that monitors imports. It is managed by European expatriates, whose presence has never been accepted by the customs authorities in Benin. Customs officers in Benin are often accused of infiltrating these companies through the intermediary of local agents whom they employ to discredit the monitoring companies.

11. The official rates in Benin are: 340 CFA francs per day and 350 CFA francs per night in the customs divisions and 350 CFA francs per day and 400 CFA francs per night in the customs offices.

12. The only gendarmerie trainees who avoid this monthly contribution are young recruits who are not yet paid a salary.

13. The transport actors obtained these 'favours' in relation to both the number of passengers carried and the cost of the fines imposed from the political and administrative authorities following a series of strikes. In effect, fol-

lowing an increase in the price of petrol, the drivers mobilized themselves to obtain an increase in the profit from road transport from the state. However, in order to avoid the social tension that would arise from such an increase, the state reached a compromise with the drivers which consists in the tolerance of one, two or three excess passengers, depending on the type of vehicle. See Dièye 2001.

14. For more information on these figures and the trade in second-hand vehicles at the port of Cotonou, see Perret 2002.

15. Institut national de statistique et d'analyse économique, Benin.

Chapter 7

This chapter is a very modified version of an article exclusively devoted to Senegal, enriched by a comparative analysis (Blundo 2001). The case study concerning the bus station of Kaolack has been published in a more succinct form in a methodological text (Blundo 2003).

1. On recent definitions of the notion of systemic corruption, see Robinson 1997; Langseth, Stapenhurs and Pope 1997: 15.

2. The information on the evolution and the details of the regulation were examined by M. Yaya Bodian, research assistant affiliated to Credila (University Cheikh Anta Diop de Dakar). See his research report, Bodian 2001.

3. Extract of a speech made by Abdou Diouf on the occasion of the reopening of courts and tribunals 1999–2000, *Le Soleil*, 4 November 1999: 3.

4. S.J. Diop, 'Wade veut veiller sur la transparence des marchés', *Walfadjri* 2564, 29 September 2000: 2.

5. Decree 82–690 of 7 Sepember 1982.

6. Decree 89–117 of 27 April 1989.

7. Decree 99–311 of 22 June 1999. This code obliges the parties involved in a public contract to sign a document that commits them to renouncing all practice of corruption. In case of their failing to do so, the law provides for severe sanctions, with, among others, the temporary or definite exclusion from the processes of public procurement.

8. Ordonnance 96–04 of 31 January 1996.

9. See the note of synthesis relating to the new code of public markets in Senegal, drawn up by the economic Mission of the French embassy at Dakar, www.izf.net/izf/EE/pro/senegal/7024.asp.

10. The new decree of 2002 added the following circumstances: the contract is restrained by the existence of letters of patent, it concerns the field of research-development or it is launched in an urgent situation.

11. According to the words of an inspector of the Ministry of Youth, Dakar, 14 September 2000.

12. See the press review of PNUD for the month of July 2005, www.pnud. ne/pnudfr/revues/rev_juilo5.htm.

13. See World Bank 1993: annex 2.

14. Expression borrowed from Diagne 2000: 1.

15. Diagne 2000: 2.

16. Decree 83–669 of 29 June 1983, modifying decree 82–690 of 7 September 1982.

17. Decrees 92–83 of 9 January 1992 and 97–1113 of 11 November 1997.
18. Decree 95–262 of 21 February 2001.
19. According to the presentation of the motifs of the decree concerning the creation of this project, 'the creation at the level of the General Secretariat of the presidential Services of the Presidency of the Republic, the PCRPE aims ... at permitting the realization of investments corresponding to the answers that the Head of State wishes to advance in response to the expectations of the Senegalese people. And this, while respecting deadlines and costs of realization, maintainance and upkeep.'
20. M. Diarra, 'La construction du Palais de justice n'a pas redémarré', *Sud Quotidien* 2248, 30 September 2000: 6.
21. See article by Maman Abou, *Le Républicain*, 17 July 2003.
22. For a general picture of these practices also see Hadjadj 2002: 135–8.
23. It is thus that the gifts given by the traveller to his circle are called in Wolof. In this context, the term indicates a small gift to express his gratitude for work well done.
24. In Senegal (though one could extend these observations to other countries), this scarcity can partly be attributed to the privatization of services of public works and the dismantling of their planning offices. It results in the absence of clear rules, a certain lack of specificity of criteria of evaluation of tenders by technical committees: 'One is not going to lead a football match, wait for the ball to come out becore deciding if it's a touch or a corner', deplores an expert of the regulation of public procurement in Senegal (K.S., Dakar, 29 December 2000).
25. Parakou, departmental committee of grants of MP, 21 June 2000.
26. See Act 2, chapter II, of decree 99–312 of 22 June 1999 dealing with the fixing of thresholds, the procedures of mutual agreement and consultation and rules applicable to Beninois market contracting.
27. Extracts of the audit report were published by *Le Populaire* 378, 13 February 2001: 3–7.
28. In the urban markets, the *bukki-men* ('hyena-men')are persons specialized in informal arrangements in credit or in cash. See Ebin 1992.
29. R.B., building engineer, interview, 2 January 2001, Kaolack.
30. M.E. contractor, interview, 3 January 2001, Kaolack.
31. E.M., contractor, interview, 6 January 2001, Kaolack.
32. This practice has also been documented for Benin: 'often it is the officers in charge of the conception of the tenders who are at the same time the contractor's advisers for the elaboration of his answer to the same tender' (Bako Arifari 2001: 88).
33. In Benin the inspections are guaranteed by the Ministry of Environment, Habitat and Town Planning, delegated foreman; in Senegal, they are given to the regional services of town planning.
34. These are contracts with a low cost of corruption, according to the contractors, because of the involvement of representatives of the financial backer in the entire chain of public procurement. Here the technical and professional competence of the contractors receives greater recognition.
35. M. Ndaw, 'Bâtiment. Un secteur exsangue pour les PME', *Walfadjri*, 5 July 2001.
36. www.gouv.bj/ministeres/mcppd/.

Bibliography

Abarchi, D., M. Rabo Mainassara and H.S. Gado (2003) *La corruption dans les secteurs de la justice, de la santé et de l'éducation (analyse du phénomène et propositions d'actions)*, Niamey.

Abélès, M. (1988) *Jours tranquilles en 89, ethnologie politique d'un département français*, Odile Jacob, Paris.

Abélès, M. (1990) *Anthropologie de l'État*, A. Colin, Paris.

Adamon, A.D. (1995) *Le renouveau démocratique au Bénin. La Conférence nationale des forces vives et la période de transition*, L'Harmattan, Paris.

Adebayo, A.G. (1995) 'Jangali: Fulani Pastoralists and Colonial Taxation in Northern Nigeria', *International Journal of African Historical Studies*, vol. 28, no. 1: 113–50.

Ades, A., and R. Di Tella (1996) 'The Causes and Consequences of Corruption: A Review of Recent Empirical Contributions', *IDS Bulletin*, vol. 27, no. 2: 6–11.

Adjovi, E.V. (1999) 'Port de Cotonou: les faux frais sont vrais!', in J. Badou (ed.), *Visages de la corruption au Bénin*, Agence Proximités, Cotonou.

Adjovi, E.V. (2003) 'Liberté de la presse et "affairisme" médiatique au Bénin', *Politique Africaine* 92: 157–72.

Amselle, J.-L. (1992) 'La corruption et le clientélisme au Mali et en Europe de l'Est: quelques points de comparaison', *Cahiers d'Etudes Africaines,* vol. 32–4, no. 128: 629–42.

Amuwo, K. (1986) 'Military-Inspired Anti-Bureaucratic Corruption Campaigns: An Appraisal of Niger's Experience', *Journal of Modern African Studies*, vol. 24, no. 2: 285–301.

Anders, G. (2004) 'Like Chameleons. Civil servants and Corruption in Malawi', *Bulletin de l'APAD* 23–4: 43–67.

Anders, G. (2005) *Civil Servants in Malawi: Cultural Dualism, Moonlighting and Corruption in the Shadow of Good Governance*, Law Faculty, Erasmus University, Rotterdam.

Andreski, S. (1968) *The African Predicament: A Study in the Pathology of Modernisation*, Michael Joseph, London.

Andreski, S. (1970) 'Kleptocracy as a System of Government in Africa', in A. Heidenheimer (ed.), *Political Corruption: Readings in Comparative Analysis*, Holt, Rinehart & Winston, New York: 346–57.

Anonymous (1930) 'Editorial Notes', *Journal of the Royal African Society*, vol. 29, no. 117: 535–52.

Apter, A. (2005) *The Pan-African Nation: Oil and the Spectacle of Culture in Nigeria*, Chicago University Press, Chicago.

Arditi, C. (2000) 'Du "prix de la kola" au détournement de l'aide internationale: clientélisme et corruption au Tchad (1900–1998)', in G. Blundo (ed.), *Monnayer les pouvoirs. Espaces, mécanismes et représentations de la corruption*, *Nouveaux Cahiers de l'IUED*, Genève, no. 9, Presses Universitaires de France, Paris: 249–67.

Arnett, E.J. (1933) 'Native Administration in West Africa: A Comparison of French and British Policy', *Journal of the Royal African Society*, vol. 32, no. 128: 240–51.

Asibuo, S.K. (1992) 'Inertia in African Public Administration: An Examination of Some Causes and Remedies', *Africa Development*, vol. 17, no. 4: 67–80.

Atouhun, M. (1998) 'Quelles stratégies pour éradiquer la corruption et la pratique des faux frais au port de Cotonou?', Communication à la journée de réflexion sur la corruption et les faux frais au port de Cotonou, 31 March 1998, Cotonou.

Awal, A.A. (1987) 'Anatomy of Corruption in the British Colonial Service in Nigeria', *Odu: A Journal of West African Studies* 31: 92–103.

Badie, B. (1992) *L'État importé. L'occidentalisation de l'ordre politique*, Fayard, Paris.

Bähre, E. (2005) 'How to Ignore Corruption: Reporting the Shortcomings of Development in South Africa', *Current Anthropology*, vol. 46, no. 1: 107–20.

Bako Arifari, N. (1995) 'Démocratie et "logique du terroir" au Bénin', *Politique Africaine* 59: 7–24.

Bako Arifari, N. (1999) *Dynamiques et formes du pouvoir politique en milieu rural ouest-africain: étude comparative au Bénin et au Niger*, doctoral thesis, EHESS, Marseilles.

Bako Arifari, N. (2000) 'Dans les insterstices de l'État: des courtiers en col blanc', in T.Bierschenk, J.-P. Chauveau and J.-P. Olivier de Sardan (eds), *Courtiers en développement. Les villages africains en quête de projets*, Karthala, Paris: 43–70.

Bako Arifari, N. (2001) 'La corruption quotidienne au Bénin', in G. Blundo and J.-P. Olivier de Sardan (eds), *La corruption au quotidien en Afrique de l'Ouest. Approche socio-anthropologique comparative: Bénin, Niger et Sénégal*, research report, EHESS–IUED–IRD, Marseilles: 51–95.

Balandier, G. (1951) 'La situation coloniale. Approche théorique', *Cahiers Internationaux de Sociologie* 9: 44–79.

Banégas, R. (1998) '"Bouffer l'argent", Politique du ventre, démocratie et clientélisme au Bénin', in J.-L. Briquet and F. Sawicki (eds), *Le clientélisme politique dans les sociétés contemporaines*, Presses Universitaires de France, Paris: 75–109.

Bayart, J.-F. (1981) 'Le politique par le bas en Afrique noire. Questions de méthode', *Politique Africaine* 1: 53–82.

Bayart, J.-F. (1989) *L'État en Afrique. La politique du ventre*, Fayard, Paris.

Bayart, J.-F. (1990) 'La corruption en Afrique', *Histoires de développement* 9: 36–40.

Bayart, J.-F. (1992) 'Argent et pouvoir en Afrique noire', *Projet* 232: 67–70.

Bayart, J.-F. (1993) *The State in Africa: The Politics of the Belly*, Longman, New York.

Bayart, J.-F. (2004) 'Le crime transational et la formation de l'état', *Politique Africaine* 93: 93–104.

Bayart, J.-F., S. Ellis and B. Hibou (1999) *The Criminalization of the State in Africa*, James Currey, Oxford.

Becker, F. (2006) '"Bad Governance" and the Persistence of Alternative Political Arenas: A Study of a Tanzanian Region', in G. Blundo and P.-Y. Le Meur (eds), *The Governance of Daily Life in Africa: Public and Collective Services and Their Users*, Brill, Leiden.

Berkman, S. (1996) 'The Impact of Corruption on Technical Cooperation Projects in Africa', *International Journal of Technical Cooperation*, vol. 2, no. 2: 67–82.

Berry, S. (1993) *No Condition is Permanent: The Social Dynamics of Agrarian Change in Sub-Saharan Africa*, University of Wisconsin Press, Madison.

Bertrand, J. (2003) 'Le "cas" Cardoso au Mozambique. La violence et la corruption en procès', *Lusotopie* 10: 453–63.

Bierschenk, T. (1988) 'Development Projects as an Arena Of Negotiation for Strategic Groups: A Case Study from Bénin', *Sociologia Ruralis*, vol. 28, no. 2–3: 146–60.

Bierschenk, T., and J.-P. Olivier de Sardan (1997) 'ECRIS: Rapid Collective Inquiry for the Identification of Conflicts and Strategic Groups', *Human Organization*, vol. 56, no. 2: 238–44.

Bierschenk, T., and J.-P. Olivier de Sardan (1998) 'Les arènes locales face à la décentralisation et à la démocratisation. Analyses comparatives en milieu rural béninois', in T. Bierschenk and J.-P. Olivier de Sardan, *Les pouvoirs au village: le Bénin rural entre démocratisation et décentralisation*, Karthala, Paris: 11–51.

Bierschenk, T., J.-P. Chauveau and J.-P. Olivier de Sardan (eds) (2000) *Courtiers en développement. Les villages africains en quête de projets*, Karthala, Paris.

Bigsten, A.M., and Karl Ove (1997) 'Growth and Rent Dissipation: The Case of Kenya', *Journal of African Economies*, vol. 5, no. 2: 177–98.

Bio Tchané, A. (with P. Montigny) (2000) *Lutter contre la corruption. Un impératif pour le développement du Bénin dans l'économie internationale*, Le Flamboyant/L'Harmattan, Cotonou/Paris.

Blancq, B. (1994) 'Congo: corruption et résistance au changement', *L'Afrique politique 1994. Vue sur la démocratisation à marée basse*, C. d. E. d. A. Noire, Karthala, Paris: 191–8.

Blundo, G. (1994) 'Le conflit dans "l'entente". Coopération et compétition dans les associations paysannes de Koungheul (Sénégal)', in J.-P. Jacob and P. Lavigne Delville (eds), *Les associations paysannes en Afrique. Organisation et dynamiques*, Karthala, Paris: 99–120.

Blundo, G. (1995) 'Les courtiers du développement en milieu rural sénégalais', *Cahiers d'Etudes Africaines* 137: 73–99.

Blundo, G. (1996) 'Gérer les conflits fonciers au Sénégal: le rôle de l'administration locale dans le Sud-Est du bassin arachidier', *Cahiers Africains* 23–4: 101–19.

Blundo, G. (1998) *Elus locaux, associations paysannes et courtiers du développement au Sénégal. Une anthropologie politique de la décentralisation dans le sud-est du bassin arachidier (1974–1995)*, Faculté des Sciences sociales et politiques, Université de Lausanne, Lausanne.

Blundo, G. (ed) (2000) *Monnayer les pouvoirs. Espaces, mécanismes et représentations de la corruption*, *Nouveaux Cahiers de l'IUED*, Genève, no. 9, Presses Universitaires de France, Paris.

Blundo, G. (2001a) 'Négocier l'État au quotidien: intermédiaires, courtiers et rabatteurs dans les interstices de l'administration sénégalaise', *Autrepart* 20: 75–90.

Blundo, G. (2001b) 'La corruption comme mode de gouvernance locale: trois décennies de décentralisation au Sénégal', *Afrique contemporaine* 199, 3e trimestre: 106–18.

Blundo, G. (2001c) '"Dessus-de-table". La corruption quotidienne dans la passation des marchés publics locaux au Sénégal', *Politique Africaine* 83: 79–97.

Blundo, G. (2003) 'Décrire le caché. Autour du cas de la corruption', in G. Blundo and J.-P. Olivier de Sardan (eds), *Pratiques de la description*, Editions de l'EHESS, vol. 3, Paris: 75–111.

Blundo, G. (ed.) (2004) 'La gouvernance au quotidien en Afrique: les services publics et collectifs et leurs usagers', *Bulletin de l'APAD* 23–4, LIT Verlag, Münster.

Blundo, G., and J.-P. Olivier de Sardan (2000) 'La corruption comme terrain. Pour une approche socio-anthropologique', in G. Blundo (ed.), *Monnayer les pouvoirs. Espaces, mécanismes et représentations de la corruption*, *Nouveaux Cahiers de l'IUED*, Genève, no. 9, Presses Universitaires de France, Paris: 21–46.

Blundo, G., and J.-P. Olivier de Sardan (eds) (2001a) *La corruption au quotidien en Afrique de l'Ouest. Approche socio-anthropologique comparative: Bénin, Niger et Sénégal*, Marseille.

Blundo, G., and J.-P. Olivier de Sardan (2001b) 'La corruption quotidienne en Afrique de l'Ouest', *Politique Africaine* 83: 8–37.

Blundo, G., and J.-F. Médard (2002) 'La corruption en Afrique francophone', Transparency International, *Combattre la corruption. Enjeux et perspectives*, Karthala, Paris: 9–36.

Bodian, Y. (2001) *Étude sur les marchés publics*, report, February, Dakar.

Boltanski, L. (1982) *Les cadres. La formation d'un groupe social*, Editions de Minuit, Paris.

Bonnet, D., and Y. Jaffré (eds) (2003) *Les maladies de passage: transmissions, préventions et hygiènes en Afrique de l'Ouest*, Karthala, Paris.

Borghi, M., and P. Meyer-Bisch (eds) (1995) *La corruption: l'envers des droits de l'homme*, Editions Universitaires, Freiburg.

Bouju, J. (2000) 'Clientélisme, corruption et gouvernance locale à Mopti (Mali)', *Autrepart* 14: 143–63.

Bourdieu, P. (1979) *La distinction. Critique sociale du jugement*, Editions de Minuit, Paris.

Bourdieu, P. (1986) 'La force du Droit? Eléments pour une sociologie du champ juridique', *Actes de la Recherche en Sciences Sociales* 64: 3–19.

Bourmaud, D. (1997) *La politique en Afrique*, Montchrestien, Paris.

Brogden, M., and P. Nijhar (1998) 'Corruption and the South African Police', *Crime, Law and Social Change* 30: 89–106.

Brownsberger, W.N. (1983) 'Development and Governmental Corruption – Materialism and Political Fragmentation in Nigeria', *Journal of Modern African Studies*, vol. 21, no. 2: 215–33.

Brunschwig, H. (1983) *Noirs et Blancs dans l'Afrique noire française*, Flammarion, Paris.

Buijtenhuijs, R., and E. Rijnierse (1993) *Démocratisation en Afrique au Sud du Sahara. 1989–1992*, Research Report 52, African Studies Center, Leiden.

Buijtenhuijs, R., and C. Thiriot (1995) *Démocratisation en Afrique au Sud du Sahara. 1992–1995. Un bilan de la littérature*, Centre d'Etudes Africaines – Centre d'Etudes d'Afrique Noire, Leiden and Bordeaux.

Cheickh Dièye (2001) *La corruption dans les transports et la douane au Sénégal*, IUED, Geneva.

Caplan, L. (1971) 'Cash and Kind: Two Media of "Bribery" in Nepal', *Man*, vol. 6, no. 2: 266–78.

Cartier-Bresson, J. (1992) 'Eléments d'analyse pour une économie de la corruption', *Revue Tiers-Monde*, XXXIII, vol. 131, no. 3: 581–609.

Cartier-Bresson, J. (1998) 'Les analyses économiques des causes et conséquences de la corruption: quelques enseignements pour les PED', *Mondes en Développement*, vol. 26, no. 102: 25–40.

Cartier Bresson, J. (2000) 'Les analyses économiques des causes et des conséquences de la corruption: quelques enseignements', OCDE, *Affairisme: la fin du système. Comment combattre la corruption*, Editions de l'OCDE, Paris: 11–31.

Casswell, N. (1984) 'Autopsie de l'ONCAD: la politique arachidière au Sénégal 1966–1980', *Politique Africaine* 14: 39–73.

Chabal, P., and J.-P. Daloz (1999) *L'Afrique est partie ! Du désordre comme instrument politique*, Economica, Paris.

Chaïbou, A. (1997) *Le transfert des concepts du droit processuel français au Niger*, doctoral thesis, Université d'Orléans.

Chauveau, J.-P., M. Le Pape and J.-P. Olivier de Sardan (2001) 'La pluralité des normes et leurs dynamiques en Afrique', in G. Winter (ed.), *Inégalités et politiques publiques en Afrique. Pluralité des normes et jeux d'acteurs*, IRD, Karthala, Paris.

Chibnall, S., and P. Saunders (1977) 'Worlds Apart: Notes on the Social Reality of Corruption', *British Journal of Sociology*, vol. 28, no. 2: 138–54.

Chikulo, B.C. (2000) 'Corruption and Accumulation in Zambia', in K.R. Hope and B.C. Chikulo (eds), *Corruption and Development in Africa. Lessons from Country Case-Studies*, Macmillan, London: 161–82.

CLARION (1994) *The Anatomy of Corruption in Kenya: Legal, Political and Socio-Economic Perspectives*, CLARION Research Monograph no. 7.

Clauzel, J. (ed.) (2003) *La France d'outre-mer (1930–1960): temoignages d'administrateurs et de magistrats*, Karthala, Paris.

Code des marchés publics du Bénin, Ordonnance No. 96–04, 31 January 1996.

Cohen, R. (1980) 'The Blessed Job in Nigeria', in G.M. Britan and R. Cohen (eds), *Hierarchy and Society: Anthropological Perspectives on Bureaucracy*, Institute for the Study of Human Issues, Philadelphia.

Coldham, S. (1995) 'Legal Responses to State Corruption in Commonwealth Africa', *Journal of African Law*, vol. 39, no. 2: 115–26.

Collectif (2003) 'Corruption et valeurs socioculturelles', *Rapport sur le Développement Humain 2003, Corruption et Développement Humain*, PNUD Burkina Faso: 101–20.

Conte, B. (2004) *Côte d'Ivoire: clientélisme, ajustement et conflit*, Centre d'économie du développement, Bordeaux.

Cooksey, B. (1999) *Do Aid Agencies Have a Comparative Advantage in Fighting Corruption in Africa?*, Ninth International Anti-Corruption Conference, Durban, South Africa.

Cooksey, B. (2002) 'Can Aid Agencies Really Help Combat Corruption?', *Forum on Crime and Society*, vol. 2, no. 1: 45–56.

Coolidge, J.G., and S. Rose-Ackerman (2000) 'Kleptocracy and Reform in African Regimes: Theory and Examples', in K.R. Hope and B.C. Chikulo (eds), *Corruption and Development in Africa. Lessons from Country Case-Studies*, Macmillan, London: 57–86.

Copans, J. (2001) 'Afrique noire: un état sans fonctionnaires?', *Autrepart* 20: 11–26.

Copans, J. (2003) 'L'anthropologie politique en France après 1980: une démission programmée?', *Journal des anthropologues* 92–3.

Dahou, T. (2002) 'Déculturaliser la corruption', *Les Temps Modernes* 620–21: 289–311.

Dahou, T. (2003) 'Clientélisme et ONG. Un cas sénégalais', *Journal des anthropologues* 94–5: 145–63.

Daloz, P., and M.H. Heo (1997) 'La corruption en Corée du sud et au Nigeria: quelques pistes de recherche comparatives', *Revue Internationale de Politique Comparée*, vol. 4, no. 2: 361–76.

Daloz, J.P., and P. Quantin (1997) *Les transitions démocratiques africaines*, Karthala, Paris.

Dan Dah, M.L. (2000) *Contribution à un diagnostic du système judiciaire nigérien en vue de sa moralisation*, Ambassade du Canada, Niamey.

Darbon, D. (1985) 'Pour une socio-anthropologie administrative en Afrique', *Revue Française d'Administration Publique* 35: 457–68.

Darbon, D. (1990) 'L'État prédateur', *Politique Africaine* 39: 37–45.

Darbon, D. (2001) 'De l'introuvable à l'innommable: fonctionnaires et professionnels de l'action publique dans les Afriques', *Autrepart* 20: 27–42.

Dartigues, L., and E. de Lescure (2000) 'La corruption, de l'"économie de bazar" au bazar de l'économie', in G. Blundo (ed.), *Monnayer les pouvoirs. Espaces, mécanismes et représentations de la corruption*, Presses Universitaires de France, Paris: 315–44.

Diagne, F.M. (2000) 'Observations sur quelque procédures de désignation des contractants de l'administration', paper in seminar 'La cour des comptes: les marchés publics', 6–9 November, Dakar.

Diamond, L. (1987) 'Class Formation and the Swollen African State', *Journal of Modern African Studies*, vol. 25, no. 4: 567–96.

Dieye, C.T. (2001) *La corruption dans les transports et la douane au Sénégal*, report, February, Geneva.

Diop, M. (2000) 'L'analyse des principaux marchés passés par l'état et ses démembrements et leur impact sur l'économie nationale', seminar paper, 'La Cour des comptes: les marchés publics', 6–9 November, Dakar.

Diop, S. J. (2000) 'Wade veut veiller sur la transparence des marchés', *Walfadjri* 2564, 29 September: 2.

Diouf, M. (1992) 'Fresques murales et écriture de l'histoire. Le Set/Setal à Dakar', *Politique Africaine* 46: 41–54.

Diouf, M. (2002) 'Les poissons ne peuvent pas voter un budget pour l'achat des hameçons. Espace public, corruption et constitution de l'Afrique comme objet scientifique', *Bulletin de l'APAD* 23–24: 23–41.

Doe, L., et al. (2004) *Niger. Evaluation de l'initiative PPTE et du plan d'action*, International Monetary Fund, Department of Public Finances, Washington DC.

Doig, A., and McLvor, S. (1999) 'Corruption and its Control in the Developmental Context: An Analysis and Selective Review of the Literature', *Third World Quarterly*, vol. 20, no. 3: 657–76.

Dozon, J.-P. (2003) 'Les Etats africains contemporains dans l'épistémè africaniste française', *Journal des anthropologues* 92–3: 13–29.

Du Bois de Gaudusson, J. (1990) 'Le statut de la justice dans les Etats d'Afrique Francophone', *Afrique Contemporaine* 156: 6–11.

Dumont, R. (1962) *L'Afrique noire est mal partie*, Seuil, Paris.

Ebin, V. (1992) 'A la recherche de nouveaux "poissons". Stratégies commerciales mourides par temps de crise', *Politique Africaine* 45, March: 86–99.

Eisenstadt, S. (1973) *Traditional Patrimonialism and Modern Neopatrimonialism*, Sage, Beverly Hills CA.

Ekeh, P. (1975) 'Colonialism and the Two Publics in Africa: A Theoretical Statement', *Comparative Studies in Society and History* 17: 91–112.

Eker, V. (1981) 'On the Origins of Corruption: Irregular Incentives in Nigeria', *Journal of Modern African Studies*, vol. 19, no. 1: 173–82.

Ekpo, M.V. (1979) 'Gift-Giving and Bureaucratic Corruption in Nigeria', in M. V. Ekpo, *Bureaucratic Corruption in Sub-Saharan Africa: Toward a Search for Causes and Consequences*, University Press of America, Washington DC: 161–88.

Emizet, K.N.F. (1998) 'Confronting Leaders at the Apex of the State: The Growth of the Unofficial Economy in Congo', *African Studies Review*, vol. 41, no. 1: 99–137.

Escobar, A. (1991) 'Anthropology and the Development Encounter: The Making and Marketing of Development Anthropology', *American Ethnologist*, vol. 18, no. 4: 658–82.

Escobar, A. (1995) *Encountering Development: The Making and Unmaking of the Third World*, Princeton University Press, Princeton NJ.

Escobar, A. (1997) 'Anthropologie et développement', *Revue Internationale des Sciences Sociales* 154: 539–59.

Fall, B.A. (2003) 'Le juge, le justiciable et les pouvoirs publics: pour une appréciation concrète de la place du juge dans les systèmes politiques en Afrique', *Revue Electronique Afrilex* 3: 4–34.

Fatton, R. (1992) *Predatory Rule: State and Civil Society in Africa*, Lynne Rienner, Boulder CO.

Fay, C. (1995) 'La démocratie au Mali, ou le pouvoir en pâture', *Cahiers d'Etudes Africaines*, vol. XXXV-1, no. 137: 19–53.

Ferguson, J. (1990) *The Anti-Politics Machine: Development, Depoliticization and Bureaucratic Power in Lesotho*, Cambridge University Press, Cambridge.

FIDH (2004) *La justice au Bénin: corruption et arbitraire*, International Inquiry, Report no. 384.

Finch, C.D. (1996) 'Role of International Agencies in Fighting Corruption',

Governance and Anti-Corruption, Publications, Working Papers and Articles, World Bank Group, mimeo.

Fjeldstad, O.H. (2001) 'La décentralisation fiscale en Tanzanie: pour le meilleur ou pour le pire?', *Afrique Contemporaine* 199: 128–42.

Fjeldstad, O.H. (2003) 'Fighting Fiscal Corruption: Lessons from the Tanzania Revenue Authority', *Public Administration and Development* 23: 165–75.

Flanary, R., and D. Watt (1999) 'The State of Corruption: A Case Study of Uganda', *Third World Quarterly*, vol. 20, no. 3: 515–36.

Fombad, C.M. (2000) 'Endemic Corruption in Cameroon: Insights on Consequences and Control', in K.R. Hope and B.C. Chikulo (eds), *Corruption and Development in Africa: Lessons from Country Case-Studies*, Macmillan, London and St Martin's Press, New York: 234–60.

FONAC (1998) *Actes du Forum, tome 2: Communications et rapports des ateliers et comptes-rendus des journées des 26 et 27 Mars 1998*, provisional document, Cotonou.

Forum Civil (1999) *Séminaire sur la transparence et la gestion des affaires publiques*, 28–29 April, Dakar.

Geschiere, P. (2000) 'Sorcellerie et modernité: retour sur une étrange complicité', *Politique Africaine* 79: 17–32.

Glaser, B.G., and A.L. Strauss (1973) *The Discovery of Grounded Theory: Strategies for Qualitative Research*, Eldin, Chicago.

Gocking, R. (1996) 'Ghana's Public Tribunals: An Experiment in Revolutionary Justice', *African Affairs*, vol. 95, no. 379: 197–223.

Goldsmith, A.A. (1999) 'Africa's Overgrown State Reconsidered: Bureaucracy and Economic Growth', *World Politics*, vol. 51, no. 4: 520–46.

Good, K. (1992) 'Interpreting the Exceptionality of Botswana', *Journal of Modern African Studies*, vol. 30, no. 1: 69–95.

Good, K. (1994) 'Corruption and Mismanagement in Botswana: A Best-Case Example?', *Journal of Modern African Studies*, vol. 32, no. 3: 499–521.

Goudie, A.W., and D. Stasavage (1997) *Corruption: The Issues*, OCDE Technical Papers, no. 122.

Gould, D.J. (1980) *Bureaucratic Corruption and Underdevelopment in the Third World: The Case of Zaire*, Pergamon Press, New York.

Greenstone, D.J. (1966) 'Corruption and Self-Interest in Kampala and Nairobi: A Comment on Local Politics in East Africa', *Comparative Studies in Society and History*, vol. 8, no. 2: 199–210.

Gueye, M. (1997) 'Justice indigène et assimilation', in B. Charles, M. Saliou and T. Ibrahima (eds), *AOF: réalités et héritages. Sociétés ouest africaines et ordre colonial, 1895–1960*, Direction des Archives du Sénégal, vol. 1, Dakar: 153–69.

Gupta, A. (1995) 'Blurred Boundaries: The Discourse of Corruption, the Culture of Politics, and the Imagined State', *American Ethnologist*, vol. 22, no. 2: 375–402.

Hadjadj, D. (ed.) (2002) *Combattre la corruption. Enjeux et perspectives*, Karthala, Paris.

Hagberg, S. (2002) ''Enough is Enough': An Ethnography of the Struggle against Impunity in Burkina Faso', *Journal of Modern African Studies*, vol. 40, no. 2: 217–46.

Hamer, J.H. (1981) 'Self-Interest and Corruption in Bukusu Cooperatives', *Human Organization*, vol. 40, no. 3: 202–10.

Hanlon, J. (2004) 'Do Donors Promote Corruption? The Case of Mozambique', *Third World Quarterly*, vol. 25, no. 4: 747–63.

Hansen, H.K. (1998) 'Governmental Mismanagment and Symbolic Violence: Discourses on Corruption in the Yucatan of the 1990s', *Bulletin of Latin American Research*, vol. 17, no. 3: 367–86.

Harrison, G. (1999) 'Corruption as "Boundary Politics": The State, Democratisation and Mozambique's Unstable Liberalisation', *Thid World Quarterly*, vol. 20, no. 3: 537–50.

Harsch, E. (1993) 'Acccumulators and Democrats: Challenging State Corruption in Africa', *Journal of Modern African Studies*, vol. 31, no. 1: 31–48.

Hasty, J. (2005) 'The Pleasures of Corruption: Desire and Discipline in Ghanaian Political Culture', *Cultural Anthropology*, vol. 20, no. 2: 271–301.

Heidenheimer, A.J., M. Johnston and V.T. Le Vine (1990) *Political corruption. A handbook*, Transaction, New Brunswick and London.

Heidenheimer, A.J., and M. Johnston (2002) Introduction to Part VII, in A.J. Heidenheimer and M. Johnston (eds), *Political Corruption. Concepts and Contexts*, Transaction, New Brunswick and London: 375–8.

Heidenheimer, A.J. (1990) 'Perspectives on the Perception of Corruption', in A.J. Heidenheimer, M. Johnston and V.T. Le Vine, *Political Corruption. A Handbook*, Transaction, New Brunswick and London: 149–63.

Heidenheimer, A.J. (1996) 'A la recherche de définitions: études dans la perspective comparative', *Revue internationale de sciences sociales* 149: 389–99.

Hertzfeld, M. (1992) *The Social Production of Indifference. Exploring the Symbolic Roots of Western Bureaucracy*, University of Chicago Press, Chicago and London.

Hibou, B. (ed.) (1999) *La privatisation des Etats*, Karthala, Paris.

Hope, K.R. (2000) 'Corruption and Develoment in Africa', in K.R. Hope and B.C. Chikulo (eds), *Corruption and Development in Africa: Lessons from Country Case-Studies*, Macmillan, London: 17–39.

Igué, J.O. (1998) *Le Bénin et la mondialisation de l'économie. Les limites de l'intégrisme du marché*, Karthala, Paris.

Igué, J.O., and O.G. Soulé (1992) *L'État-entrepôt au Bénin. Commerce informel ou solution à la crise?*, Karthala, Paris.

Issa Abdourhamane, B. (1999) 'Alternances militaires au Niger', *Politique africaine* 74: 85–94.

Issa, S. (2004) 'Cadeaux et corruption à la cour des chefs traditionnels au Nord-Caméroun', *Méga-Tchad* 1–2.

Jacob, J.-P. (2001) 'Introduction à la thématique des rapports entre corruption et sociétés anciennes. Les particularités du tiers inclus', in Collectif, *Morale et corruption dans les sociétés anciennes du Burkina (Bobo, Moaga, San et Winyé)*, REN–LAC, Ouagadougou.

Jaffré, Y. (1999) 'Les services de santé "pour de vrai". Politiques sanitaires et interactions quotidiennes dans quelques centres de santé (Bamako, Dakar, Niamey)', *Bulletin de l'APAD* 17: 3–17.

Jaffré, Y., and J.-P. Olivier de Sardan (eds) (2003) *Une médecine inhospitalière. Les difficiles relations entre soignants et soignés dans cinq capitales d'Afrique de l'Ouest*, APAD–Karthala, Paris.

Johnston, M. (1997) 'Frontier Corruption: Point of Vulnerability and Challenges for Reform', *in* UNDP-PACT-OECD, Workshop on Corruption and Integrity Improvement Initiatives in Context of Developing Economies.

Joseph, R. (1987) *Democracy and Prebendal Politics in Nigeria*, Cambridge University Press, Cambridge.

Keesing, R. (1985) 'Conventional Metaphor and Anthropological Metaphysics: The Problematic of Cultural Translation', *Journal of Anthropological Research* 41: 201–17.

Khembo, N.S. (2004) 'The Multiparty Promise Betrayed: The Failure of Neo-Liberalism in Malawi', *Africa Development*, vol. 29, no. 2: 80–105.

Klitgaard, R. (1988) *Fighting Corruption*, University of California Press, Berkeley.

Klopp, J.M. (2000) 'Pilfering the Public: The Problem of Land Grabbing in Contemporary Kenya', *Africa Today*, vol. 47, no. 1: 7–26.

Kondos, A. (1987) 'The Question of "Corruption" in Nepal', *Mankind*, vol. 17, no. 1: 15–29.

Kpundeh, S.J. (1994) 'Limiting Administrative Corruption in Sierra Leone', *Journal of Modern African Studies*, vol. 32, no. 1: 139–57.

Lakoff, G., and M. Johnson (1980) *Metaphors We Live By*, University of Chicago Press, Chicago.

Lalèyè, M. (2001) 'La corruption dans la chaîne des transports au Bénin', research report.

Lambsdorff, J.G. (1998) 'An Empirical Investigation of Bribery in International Trade', *The European Journal of Development Research*, vol. 10, no. 1: 40–59.

Lambsdorff, J.G. (1999) *The Transparency International Corruption Perceptions Index 1999 – Framework Document*, TI, October,http://gwdu19.gwdg.de/~uwvw/1999_CPI_FD.pdf.

Lange, M.-F. (1999) 'Insoumission civile et défaillance étatique: les contradictions du processus démocratique malien', *Autrepart* 10: 117–34.

Langseth, P. (1997) *Good Governance in Africa: A Case Study from Uganda*, Economic Development Institute of the World Bank, Washington DC.

Langseth, P., and B. Michael (1998) 'Are Bribe Payments in Tanzania "Grease" or "Grit"?', *Crime, Law and Social Change* 29: 197–208.

Lascoumes, P. (2000) 'Analyse des corruptions, construction d'un champ de recherche. L'exemple des Etats-Unis (1902–1980)', in G. Blundo (ed.), *Monnayer les pouvoirs. Espaces, mécanismes et représentations de la corruption*, *Nouveaux Cahiers de l'IUED*, no. 9, Presses Universitaires de France, Paris: 47–64.

Laurent, P.-J. (2000) 'Sémantique populaire du détournement dans les associations de développement en pays mossi (Burkina Faso)', in G. Blundo (ed.), *Monnayer les pouvoirs. Espaces, mécanismes et représentations de la corruption*, *Nouveaux Cahiers de l'IUED*, no. 9, Presses Universitaires de France, Paris: 221–48.

Le Roy, E. (2004) *Les Africains et l'institution judiciaire. Entre Mimétismes et métissages*, Dalloz, Paris.

Le Vine, V. (1975a) *Political Corruption: The Ghana Case*, Hoover Institution, Stanford.

Le Vine, V. (1975b) 'Corruption in Ghana', *Transition* 47: 48–50, 52–61.

Le Vine V. (1990) 'Supportive Values of the Culture of Corruption in Ghana', in A. J. Heidenheimer, M. Johnston and V. Le Vine (eds), *Political Corruption: A Handbook*, Transaction, New Brunswick: 363–73.

Lewis, P. (1996) 'From Prebendalism to Predation: The Political Economy of Decline in Nigeria', *Journal of Modern African Studies*, vol. 34, no. 1: 79–103.

Lipsky, M. (1980) *Street-level Bureaucracy*, Russell Sage, New York.

Lodge, T. (1998) 'Political Corruption in South Africa', *African Affairs*, vol. 97, no. 387: 157–87.

Lodge, T. (2002) 'Political Corruption in South Africa: From Apartheid to Multiracial State', in A.J. Heidenheimer and M. Johnston (eds), *Political Corruption: Concepts and Contexts*, Transaction, New Brunswick: 403–24.

Lucchini, R. (1995) 'Universalisme et relativisme dans l'approche de la corruption. Réflexions sociologiques', in M. Borghi and P. Meyer-Bisch (eds), *La corruption: l'envers des droits de l'homme*, Editions Universitaires, Freiburg.

Lund, C. (1998) *Law, Power and Politics in Niger*, LIT Verlag, Hamburg.

Maipose, G.S. (2000) 'Aid Abuse and Mismanagement in Africa: Problems of Accountability, Transparency and Ethical Leadership', in K.R. Hope and B.C. Chikulo (eds), *Corruption and Development in Africa: Lessons from Country Case-Studies*, Macmillan, London: 87–103.

Malaquais, D. (2001) 'Anatomie d'une arnaque: feymen et feymania au Cameroun', *Les études du CERI*, CERI, Paris: 46.

Mamdani, M. (1996) *Citizen and Subject. Contemporary Africa and the Legacy of Late Colonialism*, Princeton University Press, Princeton.

Masquelier, A. (2001) 'Behind the Dispensary's Prosperous Facade: Imagining the State in Rural Niger', *Public Culture*, vol. 13, no. 2: 267–91.

Mathieu, M. (2002) *"Donnant-donnant". Les stratégies d'acteurs villageois face aux conditionnalités des projets de développement au Mali*, doctoral thesis, EHESS, Marseilles.

Mauro, P. (1996) 'The Effects of Corruption on Growth, Investment and Government Expenditure', International Monetary Fund Working Paper no. 96/98, Washington DC.

Mbaku, J.M. (2000a) *Bureaucratic and Political Corruption in Africa. The Public Choice Perspective*, Krieger, Malabar.

Mbaku, J.M. (2000b) 'Controlling Corruption in Africa: A Public Choise Perspective', in K.R. Hope and B.C. Chikulo (eds), *Corruption and Development in Africa: Lessons from Country Case-Studies*, Macmillan, London: 119–36.

Mbembe, A. (2000) *De la postcolonie. Essai sur l'imagination politique dans l'Afrique contemporaine*, Karthala, Paris.

McMullan, M. (1961) 'A Theory of Corruption: Based on a Consideration of Corruption in the Public Services and Governments of British Colonies and Ex-Colonies in West Africa', *Sociological Review*, vol. 9, no. 2: 181–201.

Médard, J.-F. (1982) 'The Underdeveloped State in Tropical Africa: Political Clientelism or Neo-Patrimonialism?', in C. Clapham (ed.), *Private Patronage and Public Power*, Frances Pinter, London: 162–92.

Médard, J.-F. (1986) 'Public Corruption in Africa: A Comparative Perspective', *Corruption and Reform* 1: 115–31.

Médard, J.-F. (1990) 'L'État patrimonialisé', *Politique Africaine* 39: 25–36.

Médard, J.-F. (1997) 'La corruption internationale et l'Afrique sub-saharienne: un essai d'approche comparative', *Revue Internationale de Politique Comparée*, vol. 4, no. 2: 413–40.

Médard, J.-F. (1998) 'La crise de l'État néo-patrimonial et l'évolution de la corruption en Afrique sub-saharienne', *Mondes en Developpement*, vol. 26, no. 102: 55–67.

Médard J.-F. (2001) 'L'évaluation de la corruption: approches et problèmes', in J.F. Baré (ed.), *L'évaluation des politiques de développement. Approches pluridisciplinaires*, L'Harmattan, Paris: 53–90.

Médard, J.-F. (2002) 'Corruption in the Neo-Patrimonial States of Sub-Saharan Africa', in A.J. Heidenheimer and M. Johnston (eds), *Political Corruption: Concepts and Contexts*, Transaction, New Brunswick: 379–402.

Médard, J.-F. (2003) 'Les paradoxes de la corruption institutionnalisée', conference paper, Centre d'Étude d'Afrique Noire, Bordeaux.

Métangmo-Tatou, L. (2000) *Lorsque la cola n'est plus le fruit du colatier. Cryptonimie et évolution diachronique du lexique de la corruption au Cameroun*, La corruption au Cameroun. Intelligence du phénomène et itinéraires d'éradication, Ngaoundéré.

Meyer-Bisch, P. (1995) 'Le principe du tiers exclu', in M. Borghi and P. Meyer-Bisch (eds), *La corruption. L'envers des droits de l'homme*, Editions Universitaires de Fribourg, Fribourg: 285–327.

Michael, B. (2004) 'What Do African Donor-sponsored Anti-corruption Programmes Teach Us about International Development in Africa?', *Social Policy and Administration*, vol. 38, no. 4: 320–45.

Ministère des travaux publics et des transports (1998) *Journée de réflexion sur la corruption et la pratique des faux frais au port de Cotonou: impacts sur la compétitivité de la chaine béninoise des transports*, general report, 31 March, Cotonou.

Monjardet, D. (1996) *Ce que fait la police. Sociologie de la force publique*, La Découverte, Paris.

Monteil, P.-L. (2001) *La corruption en milieu judiciaire sénégalais*, report of inquiry, February, Geneva.

Mopoho, R. (2001) 'Statut de l'interpète dans l'administration coloniale en Afrique francophone', *Meta*, vol. 46, no. 3: 615–26.

Morat Lafia, A. (2001) *La corruption dans la justice au Bénin*, report of inquiry, Parakou.

Morice, A. (1985) 'Commerce parallèle et troc à Luanda', *Politique Africaine* 17: 105–20.

Morice, A. (1987) 'Guinée 1985: État, corruption et trafics', *Les Temps Modernes* 487: 108–36.

Mukenge, T. (1973) 'Les hommes d'affaires zaïrois: du travail salarié à l'entreprise personnelle', *Canadian Journal of African Studies* 3: 455–75.

Mwenda, A.M., and R. Tangri (2005) 'Patronage Politics, Donor Reforms, and Regime Consolidation in Uganda', *African Affairs*, vol. 104, no. 416: 449–67.

Nansounon, C. (2001) *La corruption dans les transports au Bénin*, report of inquiry, Parakou.

N'Diaye, M. (1998) 'L'éthique ceddo et la société d'accaparement (ou les conduites culturelles des Sénégalais d'aujourd'hui)', T2: *Les Moodu Moodu ou l'ethos du développement au Sénégal*, Presses Universitaires de Dakar, Dakar.

Nembot, M. (2000) *Le glas de la fonction publique dans les Etats d'Afrique francophone. Essai sur la signification d'une institution en quête de légitimité*, L'Harmattan, Paris.

Ngimbog, L.R. (2002) 'La justice administrative a l'epreuve du phenomene de la corruption au Cameroun: Le quotidien de la justice en Afrique', *Droit et société* 51–52: 301–23.

Niane, B. (2000) 'L'informel au Sénégal: un nouveau paradigme face à la crise de l'État?', paper for conference, État et acteurs émergents en Afrique, Maison des Sciences de l'Homme, 16–18 November, Paris.

Niger-Thomas, M. (2000) 'Les femmes et l'art de la contrebande', *Bulletin du CODESRIA* 2, 3 and 4.

Njoku, U.J. (2005) 'Colonial Political Re-Engineering and the Genesis of Modern Corruption in African Public Service: The Issue of the Warrant Chiefs of South Eastern Nigeria as a Case in Point', *Nordic Journal of African Studies*, vol. 14, no. 1: 99–116.

Nye, J. (1967) 'Corruption and political development: a cost–benefit analysis', *American Political Science Review* 61–2: 417–27.

Olivier de Sardan, J.-P. (1984) *Les sociétés songhay-zarma (chefs, guerriers, esclaves, paysans...)*, Karthala, Paris.

Olivier de Sardan, J.-P. (1990) 'Populisme développementiste et populisme en sciences sociales: idéologie, action, connaissance', *Cahiers d'Etudes Africaines*, vol. XXX-4, no. 120: 475–92.

Olivier de Sardan, J.-P. (1995) 'La politique du terrain. Sur la production des données en anthropologie', *Enquête* 1: 71–109.

Olivier de Sardan, J.-P. (1996a) 'L'économie morale de la corruption en Afrique', *Politique Africaine* 63: 99–116.

Olivier de Sardan, J.-P. (1996b) 'La violence faite aux données. Autour de quelques figures de la surinterprétation en anthropologie', *Enquête, anthropologie, histoire, sociologie*, 3, *Interpréter, surinterpréter*: 31–59.

Olivier de Sardan, J.-P. (1998) 'Emique', *L'Homme* 147: 151–66.

Olivier de Sardan, J.-P. (1999) 'A Moral Economy of Corruption in Africa', *Journal of Modern African Studies* 37: 25–52.

Olivier de Sardan, J.-P. (2001) 'La sage-femme et le douanier. Cultures professionnelles locales et culture bureaucratique privatisée en Afrique de l'Ouest', *Autrepart* 20: 61–73.

Olivier de Sardan, J.-P. (2004) 'État, bureaucratie et gouvernance en Afrique de l'Ouest francophone. Un diagnostic empirique, une perspective historique', *Politique Africaine* 96: 139–62.

Olivier de Sardan, J.P. (2005) 'Classic Ethnology and the Socio-anthropology of Public Spaces. New Themes and Old Methods in European African Studies', *Afrika Spectrum* 40: 485–97.

Olivier de Sardan, J.-P. and A. Elhadji Dagobi (2000) 'La gestion communautaire sert-elle l'intérêt public? Le cas de l'hydraulique villageoise au Niger', *Politique Africaine* 80: 153–68.

Osei-Hwedie, B.Z. and K. Osei-Hwedie (2000) 'The Political, Economic, and Cultural Bases of Corruption in Africa, in K.R. Hope and B.C. Chikulo (eds), *Corruption and Development in Africa: Lessons from Country Case-Studies*, Macmillan, London.

Ottenberg, S. (1967) 'Local Government and the Law in Southern Nigeria', *Journal of Asian and African Studies*, vol. 2, no. 1–2: 26–43.

Ouattara, F. (1999) 'Savoir-vivre et honte chez les Sénoufo-Nanergé (Burkina-Faso)', doctoral thesis, EHESS, Marseilles.

Ouattara, F. (2002) Gouvernances quotidiennes au cœur des professionnels de santé (exemples pris à Orodara et à Banfora au Burkina Faso), *Bulletin de l'APAD* 23–4: 111–31.

Ouma, S.O.A. (1991) 'Corruption in Public Policy and its Impact on Development:

The Case of Uganda since 1979', *Public Administration and Development*, vol. 11, no. 5: 473–89.

Perret, C. (2002) *Le commerce des véhicules d'occasion au Bénin: problématique régionale et impacts nationaux*, LARES, Cotonou.

Piermay, J.-L. (1986) 'Le détournement d'espace. Corruption et stratégies de détournement dans les pratiques foncières urbaines en Afrique centrale', *Politique Africaine* 21: 22–36.

Pizzorno, A. (1992) 'La corruzione nel sistema politico', in D. Della Porta (ed.), *Lo scambio occulto. Casi di corruzione politica in Italia*, Il Mulino, Bologna: 13–74.

Polzer, T. (2001) *Corruption: Deconstructing the World Bank Discourse*, Working Paper Series 01–18, Development Studies Institute, LSE, London.

Price, R.M. (1975) *Society and Bureaucracy in Contemporary Ghana*, University of California Press, Berkeley and Los Angeles.

Razafindrakoto, M., and F. Roubaud (1996) 'Ce qu'attendent les Tananariviens de la réforme de l'État et de l'économie', *Politique Africaine* 61: 54–72.

Reno, W. (1993) 'Old Brigades, Money Bags, New Breeds, and the Ironies of Reform in Nigeria', *Canadian Journal of African Studies*, vol. 27, no. 1: 66–87.

Reno, W. (1995) *Corruption and State Politics in Sierra Leone*, Cambridge University Press, Cambridge and New York.

Robinson, M. (1997) Workshop on Corruption and Development, Institute of Development Studies, University of Sussex.

Robinson, M. (1998) 'Corruption and Development: An Introduction', *European Journal of Development Research*, vol. 10, no. 1: 1–14.

Rocca, J.-L. (1993) *La corruption*, Syros, Paris.

Rose-Ackerman, S. (1978) *Corruption. A Study in Political Corruption*, Academy Press, New York.

Sampson, S.L. (1983) 'Bureaucracy and Corruption as Anthropological Problems: A Case Study from Romania', *Folk* 25: 63–96.

Sanou, A. (2001) 'La corruption dans la société traditionnelle Bobo', in *Morale et corruption dans les sociétés anciennes du Burkina (Bobo, Moaga, San et Winyé)*, REN-LAC, Ouagadougou: 27–36.

Sarassoro, H. (1979) *La corruption des fonctionnaires en Afrique. Étude de droit pénal comparé*, Economica, Paris.

Sarassoro, H. (1990) 'La corruption et l'enrichissement sans cause en Afrique aujourd'hui', *Afrique Contemporaine*, vol. 4, no. 156: 195–206.

Sariki, R. (2001) *La corruption dans les marchés publics au Bénin*, report of inquiry, Parakou.

Schwarz, A. (1974) 'Mythe et realite des bureaucraties africaines', *Canadian Journal of African Studies*, vol. 8, no. 2: 255–84.

Scott, J. (1969) 'The Analysis of Corruption in Developing Nations', *Comparative Studies in Society and History* 11: 315–41.

Shore, C., and D. Haller (2005) 'Sharp Practice: Anthropology and the Study of Corruption', in C. Shore and D. Haller, *Corruption: Anthropological Perspectives*, Pluto Press, London: 1–26.

Sibeud, E. (2002) 'L'administration coloniale', in V. Duclert and C. Prochasson (eds), *Dictionnaire critique de la République*, Flammarion, Paris: 622–7.

Sidibé Soumana, D. (1998) 'Le juge et la construction de l'État de droit au Niger, mission impossible?', *Revue Saman* 1: 20–21

Sindzingre, A. (1994) *État, développement et rationalité en Afrique: contribution à une analyse de la corruption*, Institut d'Etudes Politiques, Universite de Bordeaux I, Centre d'étude d'Afrique noire, Talence.

Sindzingre, A. (1997) 'Corruptions africaines: éléments d'analyse comparative avec l'Asie de l'Est', *Revue Internationale de Politique Comparée*, vol. 4, no. 2: 377–412.

Smith, D.J. (2001) 'Kinship and Corruption in Contemporary Nigeria', *Ethnos*, vol. 66, no. 3: 344–64.

Smith, D.J. (2003) 'Patronage, per diems and the "Workshop Mentality": The Practice of Family Planning Programs in Southeastern Nigeria', *World Development*, vol. 31, no. 4: 703–15.

Smith, D.J. (2005) 'Oil, Blood and Money: Culture and Power in Nigeria', *Anthropological Quarterly*, vol. 78, no. 3: 725–40.

Smith, M.G. (1964) 'Historical and Cultural Conditions of Political Corruption among the Hausa', *Comparative Studies in Society and History*, vol. 6, no. 2: 164–94.

Socpa, A. (2000) 'Les dons dans le jeu électoral au Cameroun', *Cahiers d'études africaines*, vol. 40, no. 1: 91–108.

Soulier. G. (1985) 'Les institutions judiciaires et répressives', *in* M. Grawitz and J. Leca (eds), *Traité de science politique*, Volume 2: *Les régimes politiques contemporains*, Presses Universitaires de France, Paris: 510–52.

Sow, M.A. (2000) 'Présentation du projet de réforme de la réglementation sur les marchés publics', communication présentée à la Journée d'études 'La Cour des comptes: les marchés publics', 6–9 November, Dakar.

Sow, M.K. (2000) 'Analyse critique des procédures: atouts et faiblesses', communication présentée à la Journée d'études, 'La Cour des comptes: les marchés publics', 6–9 November, Dakar.

Stasavage, D., and Daubrée, C. (1997) 'Determinant of Customs Fraud: Evidence from two African Countries', Workshop on Corruption and Integrity Improvement Initiatives in Context of Developing Economies, UNDP–PACT–OECD.

Szeftel, M. (1982) 'Political Graft and the Spoils System in Zambia – the State as a Resource in Itself', *Review of African Political Economy*, vol. 24., no. ?.

Szeftel, M. (1998) 'Misunderstanding African Politics: Corruption and the Governance Agenda', *Review of African Political Economy*, vol. 25, no. 76: 221–40.

Tangie, F. (2005) *The State and Development in Africa*, Rethinking African Development: Beyond Impasse, Towards Alternatives, Maputo.

Tangri, R. (1982) 'Servir ou se servir? A propos du Sierra Leone', *Politique Africaine* 6: 5–18.

Tanzania, T.U.R.O. (1996) *Presidential Commission of Inquiry on the Causes of Corruption in the Country: Report on the Commission on Corruption*, Dar es Salaam.

Terray, E. (1987) Introduction, in E. Terray, *L'État contemporain en Afrique*, L'Harmattan, Paris: 9–19.

Thalès, DGD (2002) *Mission d'analyse et de formulation du cadre général du processus de réformes et du programme d'appui aux réformes judiciaires au Niger (PARJ)*, final report.

Theobald, R., and R. Williams (1999) 'Combatting Corruption in Botswana: Regional Role Model or Deviant Case?', *Commonwealth and Comparative*

Politics, vol. 37, no. 3.

Thompson, B., and G. Potter (1997) 'Governmental Corruption in Africa: Sierra Leone as a Case Study – A Criminal Justice Perspective', *Crime Law and Social Change*, vol. 28, no. 2: 137–54.

Tidjani Alou, M. (2000) 'Courtiers malgré eux. Trajectoires de reconversion dans l'association Timidria au Niger', in T. Bierschenk, J.-P. Chauveau and J.-P. Olivier de Sardan (eds), *Courtiers en développement. Les villages africains en quête de projets*, Karthala, Paris.

Tidjani Alou, M. (2002a) *La petite corruption au Niger*, Études et Travaux du LASDEL, no. 3.

Tidjani Alou, M. (2002b) 'L'avenir du processus de démocratisation en Afrique: les avatars de la consolidation démocratique', *Bulletin du CODESRIA* 3–4: 31–8.

Tignor, R.L. (1971) 'Colonial Chiefs in Chiefless Societies', *Journal of Modern African Studies*, vol. 9, no. 3: 339–59.

Tignor, R.L. (1993) 'Political Corruption in Nigeria before Independence', *Journal of Modern African Studies*, vol. 31, no. 2: 175–202.

Treves R., 1995, *La sociologie du droit*, Presses Universitaires de France, Paris.

Usinier, J.-C. and G. Verna (1994) La grande triche: éthique, corruption et affaires internationales, La Découverte, Paris.

Van der Geest, S. (1984) 'Anthropology and Pharmaceuticals in Developing Countries – II', *Medical Anthropology Quarterly*, vol. 15, no. 4: 87–90.

Van Walvaren, K., and C. Thiriot (2002) *Démocratisation en Afrique au Sud du Sahara. Transitions et virages. Un bilan de la littérature (1995–1996)*, Research Report No. 66, African Studies Centre, Leiden.

Vaughan, M. (1987) *The Story of an African Famine: Gender and Famine in Twentieth Century Malawi*, Cambridge University Press, Cambridge.

Verschave, F.-X. (1998) *La Françafrique*, Stock, Paris.

Veyne, P. (1976) *Le pain et le cirque. Sociologie historique d'un pluralisme politique*, Seuil, Paris.

Werlin, H.H. (1972) 'The Roots of Corruption: The Ghanaian Enquiry', *Journal of Modern African Studies*, vol. 10, no. 2: 247–66.

Werner, C. (2000) 'Gifts, Bribes, and Development in post-Soviet Kazakhstan', *Human Organization* 59: 11–22.

Williams, R. (1987) *Political Corruption in Africa*, Gower, Aldershot and Brookfield VT.

Williams, R. (1999) 'New Concepts for Old?', *Third World Quarterly*, vol. 20, no. 3: 503–13.

World Bank (1993) *Rapport d'évaluation des procédures de passation des marchés au Sénégal*, World Bank, Dakar.

World Bank (1996) *Programme d'investissement dans le secteur des transports au Bénin*, report, World Bank, Washington DC.

Wraith, R., and E. Simpkins (1970) 'Nepotism and Bribery in West Africa', in A.J. Heidenheimer (ed.), *Readings in Comparative Analysis on Political Corruption*, Holt, Rinehart & Winston, New York: 331–40.

Znoj, H. (forthcoming) 'The Dynamic between Critical and Legitimizing Discourses about Corruption in Indonesia', in G. Anders and M. Nuijten (eds), *Corruption and States of Illegality*, Glasshouse/Routledge.

Index